MADAM
PRIME
MINISTER

Madam *Prime* *Minister*

Margaret Thatcher

and her rise to power

ALLAN J. MAYER

Newsweek Books, New York

Library of Congress Cataloging in Publication Data

Mayer, Allan J.
Madam prime minister: Margaret Thatcher and her rise to power.
  1. Thatcher, Margaret.   2. Great Britain—Politics
and government—1964-   3. Prime ministers—Great
Britain—Biography. I. Title.
DA591.T47M39   941.085'7'0924 [B] 79-3025
ISBN 0-88225—285-2

BOOK DESIGN: MARY ANN JOULWAN

CONTENTS

Acknowledgments

MORE SO THAN MOST PEOPLE, journalists are dependent in their work on the kindnesses of others. This book was no exception. Dozens of people who have known and worked with Margaret Thatcher patiently and generously shared their reminiscences and impressions of her, and to them I am enormously grateful. In addition, the book would not have been possible without the valuable assistance of James LeMoyne, who provided much of the research and legwork. However, the responsibility for any errors or misinterpretations belongs solely to the author.

A number of other people also helped in various ways, among them Eve Arnold, Peter Davies, Bija Bociek, and Michael Conroy. I am particularly indebted to Anthony Sampson, who generously allowed me to quote from his classic study of British institutions, *The New Anatomy of Britain*; and to my fellow correspondents in the London bureau of *Newsweek* magazine, Tony Collings and Tony Clifton, who good-naturedly put up with my temporary Thatcher obsession. Finally, I could not have gotten through the project without the advice, encouragement, support, and typing of Lïse Hilboldt.

ALLAN J. MAYER
London, July 1979

To Lïse

Whilst timorous knowledge stands considering,
Audacious ignorance hath done the deed.
SAMUEL DANIEL

1
No. 10

"I wasn't lucky. I deserved it."

IT IS SEVEN A.M., and the great Georgian house in Downing Street is shrouded in a museum-like quiet. Downstairs, sleepy-eyed secretaries and personal assistants are beginning to drift in through the famous black front door, nodding to the uniformed policeman who has been on duty all night. Soon he will be relieved by a frock-coated doorkeeper, who will take his station in the dark-green leather hooded porter's chair, a splendid old relic dating from Gladstone's time that sits just inside and to the left of the entrance. But at this hour there is no need for ceremony; the tired bobby merely sips at his mug of tea and gazes idly at the early risers padding silently across the entrance hall's checkered marble floor and disappearing into the warren of offices beyond.

Upstairs, in the private quarters overlooking the garden at the back, the lady of the house is awake. Although she didn't get to bed until well past one the previous night, there is no hesitation as she rises and steps briskly into her dressing room to prepare for her morning bath. She is a handsome woman approaching her mid-fifties in robust health, with icy blue eyes and one of those flawless complexions the English insist on comparing to a rose. Her full-bodied hair, swept back in a series of flowing waves, is actually dark brown and going gray at the sides. But regular visits by her hairdresser keep it a respectable and distinctive blond. She has long—and, for the most part, successfully—fought a tendency to weight; at 5'5" and 133 pounds, she presents a reasonably trim figure, erect and firm of jaw, though clearly the battle against the jowls of middle age has already begun.

As she dresses, listening to the morning BBC radio news, she can hear her husband stirring, and soon he joins her in the kitchen, where she is preparing eggs and bacon for him, half a grapefruit and light coffee for herself. They read the morning papers and drink their coffee, discussing the news in those cryptic half-sentences that speak volumes between long-married couples. By nine A.M., breakfast is finished and it is time to get on with the day. The dishes are left in the sink. She may still insist on cooking breakfast for herself and her husband, but no longer can she manage the washing up; that will be left to a housekeeper. The Right Honorable Margaret Hilda Thatcher, MP, Prime Minister, and First Lord of the Treasury of Her Majesty's Government, has more pressing claims on her time.

Margaret Thatcher is the fiftieth person, in a line stretching back more than two and a half centuries to Sir Robert Walpole, to serve as prime minister of Great Britain. She is also the first woman prime minister—not only of Britain, but of any major Western nation. As such, her electoral triumph in May 1979 inspired an international interest and curiosity quite out of proportion to Britain's sadly diminished role in the world today. And she has become, inevitably, something of a symbol—not so much to feminists, who for the most part despise her politics, but to less ideological women, who see in her an exciting role-model: someone who has managed to have a superlatively successful career as well as a husband and family.

She comes to power at a time when Britain is a deeply demoralized country, wracked by doubts about itself and its role in a world it no longer recognizes. The memory of empire sticks in its collective consciousness like an angry thorn, reminding some of how much they have lost, others of an imperialist heritage they would rather not carry in these egalitarian times. Having built themselves a sprawling socialist welfare state, the British find themselves wondering if that's really what they want—and worrying that they may no longer have any choice in the matter. The promise and excitement of the sixties, when the Beatles sang of a cultural revolution and Harold Wilson promised a technological one, are gone. The long-sought membership in the Common Market, heralded as the gateway to a new economic future, has turned out to be a questionable prize, costing Britain more than it has gained and, in the minds of some, threatening their nation's very sovereignty. Waves of immigration—now subsiding—from what is euphemistically called "the New Commonwealth" (that is, the Caribbean, black Africa, and the Indian subcontinent) have dappled its once-homogeneous complexion and badly strained its traditional, though until now largely untested, tolerance. Drained by thirty years of stagflation, labor unrest, and industrial decay, and succored now only by the reassuring, if temporary, drip-drip of North Sea oil, the British have been searching anxiously for something—a faith, or philosophy to put their world right again.

A prime minister, of course, is not the embodiment of the British nation in the way that, say, a president can come to personify the United States. In the United Kingdom, that role belongs to the monarch. Officially, the prime minister is no more than the *primus inter pares* among the Queen's ministers—the chairman of a collective government, a manager more than a ruler. Nonetheless, the prime ministership is becoming an increasingly presidential office. The enormous patronage a prime minister can dispense—ranging from well-paid sinecures on "blue-ribbon" commissions (known as quasi-autonomous governmental organizations, or Quangos) to life peerages in the House of Lords—plus the huge personal prestige conferred by television and the growing personalization of international relations, have helped extend the position far beyond its traditional bounds. As journalist and political analyst Anthony Sampson has noted: "A Prime Minister . . . sets the scenery and style for the whole government, and however oversimplified, the conception of the Age of Macmillan or the Era of Wilson has the same kind of validity as the Age of Queen Anne or of Charles II."

So just who is the eponymous prime minister now taking Britain into the Thatcher era? She is clearly no great wit or brilliant stylist. She is a pedestrian orator and her tastes are, for the most part, relentlessly conventional. She dresses, as she puts it, "to look well turned out" and no more, rarely appearing in other than Tory blue. Nor is she a particularly brilliant or creative political thinker. Her ideology is empirical and instinctive, not the product of great study or reflection, and it amounts to a rather simple (though not unsophisticated) radical libertarianism. And she is hardly a mother-figure for the nation. Though she is far more caring and considerate with close associates than most political leaders, she does not project warmth. "Perhaps it is because I do not believe in losing my temper," she once suggested. "Because I stay cool on television [people] seem to confuse calmness with coldness." In any case, to the public she seems far more a nanny—and a rather strict one at that—than a mommy.

POLITICIAN OF CONVICTION

Margaret Thatcher's appeal lies in her image as a true and passionate believer—a mixture of faith and energy that harks back to an almost forgotten national heritage as pious as it was practical. "I am not a consensus politician or a pragmatic politician," she declared in an interview three months before she was swept into office. "I'm a *conviction* politician." By that she meant to distinguish herself from the styles of her three predecessors: the technocratic flash of Harold Wilson, the managerial aura of Edward Heath, and the shrewd manipulations of James Callaghan. *Her* politics proceeded, not from analytic calculations or abstract theorizing, but from an almost religious belief in the existence of moral certainties. As she told a rally in Cardiff two weeks before her electoral triumph: "The Old Testament prophets didn't say, 'Brothers, I want consensus.' They said, 'This is my faith and my vision. This is what I passionately believe.' "

And she does passionately believe—in the virtue of hard work, the value of self-reliance, the necessity for incentive, and, above all, the importance of individual enterprise and freedom. To her, these are all axioms, beyond question. "Certainly," she once said, "I never have doubts about my fundamental convictions."

Out of this certainty flows her determination (which some might compare to Canute's) to roll back the tide—in her case, the post-war tide of socialism that has transformed Britain over the last thirty years. The last prime minister to attempt such an audacious undertaking with any success was her political idol, Winston Churchill. And Mrs. Thatcher is quick to cite his 1951–55 government as proof that Britain's leftward drift not only can be checked, but actually reversed.

Whether there is any validity to such an argument is questionable; Churchill's post-war government made precious little headway towards dismantling the burgeoning welfare state and growing government involvement in industry that, in fact, began under previous Tory governments and was extended by Churchill's own wartime coalition. But she is determined to try—and it is this radical ambition that makes Margaret Thatcher's rise to power especially significant.

As she herself admits, it will be at least a decade before her antisocialist revolution begins to bear any real fruit. But like Churchill's, her Old Testament fervor is coupled with an awesome stamina and a tenacious spirit. She is tough-minded ("talking to her is like playing a hard game of tennis," says a friend), combative ("this animal, if attacked, naturally defends itself," she recently warned an interviewer), and monumentally hardworking. "She is not a genius, she is not staggeringly brilliant, but I have never known anybody with a better capacity for devoting themselves single-mindedly to mastering something," says Brian Walden, a former Labor MP who is now one of British television's leading political journalists. "Anything that can be done by effort, Margaret can do." She is also overwhelmingly ambitious—so much so that she even put off Indian Prime Minister Indira Gandhi, herself no shrinking violet. "Thatcher—quite a different personality," Mrs. Gandhi told a visitor in 1978 after the two had met for the first time. "She is so desperate to become Prime Minister. I felt like telling her, 'If you want to be Prime Minister so much, you'll never make it'."

Indeed, by her own admission, she simply does not know what it is to relax. After working for a solid month, seven days a week, her secretaries finally had to conspire to force her to take a weekend off following her election as leader of the Conservative party in 1974. And what did she do with the time? She wallpapered the bathroom of her country cottage. "I would find it acutely difficult if all of a sudden I had ten days off without something specific to do," she has admitted. "I should be at a loss because I've always had to do things with an object in view." More than once the Thatchers have cut short a vacation because Margaret was itching to get back to the office. It is these qualities that brought her to power.

A WOMAN IN A MAN'S WORLD

In Margaret Thatcher's view, her sex is an irrelevancy, and she is annoyed by people who make too much of a fuss over it. "It doesn't matter whether you are a man or a woman," she insisted a few years ago. "What matters is your grasp of the problems and the need for action." Still, she is enough of a realist to recognize that, for all the hard-won accomplishments of twentieth-century feminism (a movement for which she has remarkably little sympathy), women leaders in any field, no less the hidebound arena of politics and statecraft, are still so rare as to make them freaks of a sort. Indeed, she is enough of a pragmatist (a characterization she herself rejects, on the somewhat ingenuous grounds that "it implies there are no values worth fighting for") to have used her sex, and the reactions it has provoked, to her advantage. Not that she is duplicitous or particularly cunning—though as a former secretary of hers notes: "She has more guile than any of them." Rather, she has simply never made any bones about the fact that she *is* a woman in what, until quite recently, has been overwhelmingly a man's world. Instead of trying to suppress her femininity, as did many would-be career women of her generation and previous ones, she has triumphantly made a virtue of it. "She is just soft, feminine, and sweet," says the secretary. "It throws off the men, but she knows just what she is doing."

Rather than trying to transcend her sex, she has managed to transform it from a liability into a major political asset. Here she was, a university graduate in a country where most people never finish secondary school, a committed career woman in a society that still tends to look with suspicion at women who work for any other reason than sheer economic necessity, and a professional politician of more than two decades standing. Yet, throughout her public life, she has constantly invoked and attempted to identify with the image of the ordinary housewife. That may seem a trifle bizarre, if not downright dishonest. But the fact is, it has worked. Because she is a woman, a wife, and a mother, and because she has always taken pains to stress that fact, people have come to believe that she is somehow more in touch with the realities of daily life than any male politician—even those who happen also to be husbands and fathers.

In part, she has been successful in using her sex this way because, in a very real sense, she has not been "using' it at all. She has simply been presenting herself as she firmly believes herself to be. To her own mind, she is, as she once put it, "a plain, straightforward provincial" who is distinguished from the mass of her countrymen only by the depth of her convictions and her prodigious appetitie for hard work. She is middle-class to her bones—"she is with and of the *petite bourgeoise*," says a long-time colleague—and she is refreshingly proud of it. "The charm of Britain," she said in 1974, "has always been the ease with which one can move into the middle classes. It has never been simply a matter of income, but a whole attitude to life, a will to take responsibility for oneself."

She has a deep-seated conviction, which in many ways is far more American than British, that hard work inevitably pays off. There is an often retold anecdote about the time when, as a nine-year-old schoolgirl, she won first prize in a poetry-reciting competition. Her schoolmistress incautiously suggested that she had been lucky to win. "I wasn't lucky," the young Margaret bristled. "I deserved it." Forty years later, just after she ousted Edward Heath as Tory leader, she showed a similar face at a post-victory press conference. How did she account for her unexpected success? asked a reporter. "Merit," came the one-word reply.

10 DOWNING ST.

This prickly sense of personal pride and self-worth has alienated many who like their leaders softer and more easygoing. But it has enabled Mrs. Thatcher to move into 10 Downing Street, the official prime minister's residence, with an assurance and self-confidence (at least in public) that many of her predecessors would have envied. As far as she is concerned, she has truly earned her place there.

To be sure, No. 10 (as it is usually referred to) is not the most congenial of homes. "I do not think I should ever recommend it as a house for a family," was the 1976 pronouncement of Lady Falkender, who, as Marcia Williams, worked there for eight years as Harold Wilson's political secretary. Like the White House, it is a warren of offices, state rooms, and private apartments that have accreted over the centuries. Unlike the White House, it is relatively small and hemmed in on all sides by government buildings.

Of course, Mrs. Thatcher is not unused to living above the shop. She grew up in a small flat over her father's grocery store in the provincial Lincolnshire town of Grantham. But No. 10 is something else again. Not only is it a fishbowl perpetually in the public eye; it is a sprawling office complex she and her family must share during the day with 150 or so civil servants, clerks, and secretaries. Complete privacy is available only in the rather gloomy four-bedroom apartment on the top floor. Even the spacious and lovely garden in the back offers no escape, overlooked as it is by offices on two sides.

The house sits in the heart of London, on a small street (now blocked off by a police barrier) just off Whitehall, a wide imperial boulevard lined with most of the government's ministries, just a two-minute walk from Big Ben and the Houses of Parliament. It is, in fact, three houses joined together in a sort of T-shape—which accounts for its somewhat chaotic layout.

The original 10 Downing Street was the work of a seventeenth-century property speculator named George Downing. He was a singularly unattractive character, described by diarist Samuel Pepys as a "doubly perjured traitor" and, three centuries later, by Winston Churchill as "a racketeering contractor." As a young man, Downing had emigrated to America, where he was educated at Harvard. But he returned to England to go to work as a spy for Oliver Cromwell, the Puritan revolutionary who overthrew Charles I in 1649. When the days of the antimonarchists looked numbered, the wily Downing switched sides; he transferred his loyalties to the forces of Charles II and proceeded to betray most of his previous colleagues.

The monarchy was restored in 1660, and Downing prospered under it. Between 1682 and 1684, he built fifteen houses in what he called Downing Street. Number 10 stood in front of a much grander house that was owned by the Crown. It was this house, which overlooked Horse Guard Parade and St. James's Park, that George I turned over to his—and Britain's—first prime minister, Sir Robert Walpole, as an official residence. Later on it was joined to No. 10, and eventually a third house, a cottage on the Whitehall side, was also attached.

Through the eighteenth-century, Downing Street was a residential block, even boasting its own pub on the corner. In 1828 the pub was torn down to make way for new government offices. And over the following fifty years, most of the rest of Downing Street suffered the same fate. Today, only three of Downing's original houses remain: No. 10, No. 11 (which is now the official residence of the chancellor of the exchequer, Britain's chief economic minister), and No. 12 (which houses the offices of the government's parliamentary whips, whose job it is to instruct the governing party's members of Parliament how to vote on legislation in the House of Commons.)

Though No. 10 has been refurbished many times over the years, the house still bears some scars of its relatively primitive construction. Downing built the street that bears his name long before anyone had thought of setting official standards for things like foundation-depths, footings, and so on. He also paid precious little attention to the fact that he was building quite close to the Thames, and that the subsoil was extremely wet. As a result, No. 10 had been sinking for centuries until a major reconstruction under Harold Macmillan inserted great steel girders to underpin the building. Still, there remains a limit on the number of people that can be safely entertained in the state rooms on the first floor. When astronauts Neil Armstrong and Buzz Aldrin came to visit shortly after their historic flight to the moon, the crowd that accompanied them to No. 10 was so great that engineers feared the reception rooms might give way. Fortunately, they stood the strain.

The house may also have a ghost. In 1976, Lady Falkender told the story of a cleaning-lady who came rushing out of the prime minister's apartment in a great panic. She said she had seen a pink shape in the corridor, and when she ran into the bathroom she found it icy cold even though the heat was on. Harold Wilson heard of the commotion, and according to Lady Falkender, before anyone had told him the facts, he offered the information that one morning he had awoken to find a lady in pink looking at him.

It is in these somewhat eerie precincts that Mrs. Thatcher has set up home and office. She and her husband Denis have a more comfortable home of their own just twenty minutes away in fashionable Chelsea. And for the first month of her prime ministership, they continued to live there. It was not an unusual arrangement; many prime ministers, most recently James Callaghan, have been loath to take up residence at No. 10. But Mrs. Thatcher very much intended to move into the official residence as soon as she could. It was just that the first few weeks of her prime ministership were so busy that she simply wasn't able to find the time. (Still, she had no plans to give up—or even rent out—her comfortable, four-story terrace house in Chelsea. "If you get in by a democratic system," she once noted realistically, "a day may come when you will be turned out by it"—and she was, as she put it, "determined never, never to put myself in a position of being turned out . . . without a toehold of one's own to which one could retreat.")

"THE BOSS"

Living above the shop is not without its advantages. Instead of fighting the rush-hour traffic in her official limousine, all Mrs. Thatcher has to do after finishing breakfast is descend a flight of stairs to her private office. It is an elongated room, its walls covered with light wallpaper and pastoral oil paintings on loan from the government's huge collection. At one end in front of a low bookcase sits her dark-wood desk, a leather-framed photograph of her twins propped to one side. In the middle of the room is an oak pedestal table with Chippendale chairs, and at the other end is a conversation area, with sofa, coffee table, and armchairs. There, every weekday morning at nine she starts her working day with a staff meeting—an informal get-together attended by six to eight of her personal assistants. Some of them, such as Richard Ryder, the earnest young Tory politician who ran her office when she was opposition leader and now serves as her political secretary, and Carolyn Stephens, her discreet and efficient appointments secretary, have been with her for years. Others are civil servants attached to No. 10 who met her for the first time when she was voted into office.

The main purpose of the meeting is to apprise the prime minister of any important developments that took place overnight, to discuss what's in the morning's newspapers, and to brief her on what to expect during the coming day. The atmosphere is chatty but restrained. Though among themselves the staff refer to Mrs. Thatcher as "the Boss," "Mrs. T.," and even "Margaret," to her face she is always addressed as "Prime Minister." Unlike some of her predecessors—and some American presidents—who always insisted on having a written memo before they would listen to a verbal presentation, Mrs. Thatcher is content to hear her staff's news and views fresh from their mouths. But such reports must always be backed up by a memo citing sources and statistics, and if she is interested in going more deeply into the subject, which is often, a more detailed memo must be prepared for her perusal. "If, for example, I'm telling her about what some MP said in the House of Commons, she'll listen to me but she'll also want a piece of paper quoting exactly what he said," reports one aide. "And if it's important, she may also ask to see Hansard's [the official record of procedings in the House] so she can see what was said before and after the point in question. The context of things is very important to her." Or as she once put it herself: "I never rely only on my briefs. I like to go deeper into the subject for myself."

The morning staff meeting lasts between fifteen minutes and a half-hour. When it's done, the prime minister begins her daily round of official meetings. Sometimes they are with visiting dignitaries, such as the prime minister of a Commonwealth nation who happens to be in town for a state visit; sometimes they are with local nabobs: other politicians, top businessmen or, very occasionally, union leaders. These get-togethers usually take place in one of the three state drawing rooms at No. 10—though more than one participant has come away feeling that he has been in a classroom. Mrs. Thatcher is known to prefer to lecture her guests rather than to listen to them, and it takes particular persistence—not to mention fortitude—to break into her monologues. "It's not simply that you find it difficult to get a word in edgewise," reports one veteran of several such meetings, "she gives the impression that it is inadvisable as well."

On Tuesday and Thursday mornings, there are usually cabinet meetings or meetings of one of the half-dozen or so cabinet committees that the prime minister chairs. These take place in the ground-floor cabinet room, a grand white-pillared room with a marble fireplace over which hangs a portrait of Walpole. The room originally was Walpole's study but was enlarged by the Duke of Portland when he was prime minister in 1807. Portland lengthened the room, adding four splendid Corinthian columns to provide extra support. The ministers sit around a long coffin-shaped table brought in by Harold Macmillan, who claimed that from his chair in the center he couldn't see all his colleagues around the old oblong table. It is covered in fawn and has brown leather blotters and writing sets. These meetings are usually governed by a strict agenda, and Mrs. Thatcher dominates them completely. The last Conservative prime minister, Ted Heath, was known for letting his ministers go on at length in cabinet, while he sat quietly and enigmatically taking it all in. He rarely expressed his own opinions until days or weeks after an issue was first broached in cabinet. So inscrutable was Heath that many an official in his government left a cabinet meeting convinced that the prime minister was totally opposed to whatever it was that he had been arguing—only to find later that Heath was actually on his side all along. Mrs. Thatcher, on the other hand, is scrutable to a fault. Though with great and sustained effort she can be persuaded to change her mind, such is often impossible. She tends to cut off ministers with whom she disagrees, thereby preventing really freewheeling cabinet debates. "Occasionally," says one of her ministers, "we're told the conclusions before the opening remarks."

Still, the atmosphere at her cabinet meetings is usually low key. Most of the 22 members of her cabinet have known and worked with each other for years; they are all on a first-name basis, though as with her personal staff, in cabinet Mrs. Thatcher is addressed by her title.

If she doesn't have an official banquet scheduled, Mrs. Thatcher usually will eat lunch at her desk. Given her tendency to put on weight, she generally restricts herself to a salad and cheese. She rarely eats sandwiches; "not too keen on bread," explains an aide. About once every two weeks, she'll take lunch in the House of Commons dining room. The cuisine there is not among the finest. "Her tolerance for seedy House of Commons salads, a yoghurt and a tomato is remarkable," one long-time acquaintance has written. But it is a good way to keep in touch with the backbench MPs whose support was instrumental in her rise to power.

Her afternoons are much like her mornings, though on Tuesdays and

Thursdays she must appear in the House of Commons for that unruly though vitally important ritual known as "Question Time." During these sessions, any MP, no matter what his party or his station in the House, can (if he is lucky enough to be called on by the speaker) ask the prime minister or any of her cabinet questions about any aspect of government policy. In some ways, Question Time is a bit of a sham: the British tradition of governmental secrecy and the tough legislation that has grown up around it make it quite easy for the prime minister to refuse point-blank to answer a startling variety of questions on the grounds of national security. Alternately, ministers can avoid answering questions on the spot by promising to provide a written answer at a later date. These written answers always come eventually, though sometimes they don't arrive until long after whatever controversy inspired them has died down—and even then they are so cloaked in jargon and so drenched in bureaucratic minutiae that it's often difficult to recall just what the question was that inspired them in the first place. Still, these sessions force the prime minister to stay on his or her toes; especially now that Question Time can be broadcast live on the radio, a prime minister must take care not to seem overly obfuscatory.

A TOLERANCE FOR TEDIUM

Generally, Mrs. Thatcher will be driven in her official red Daimler limousine back to No. 10 immediately after Question Time; however, if a major debate is scheduled, or there is a speech she particularly wants to hear, she will remain in the House—to observe as well as take part. Though it doesn't always show, she devotes enormous effort to her speeches, both in and out of the Commons. Recognizing that she is not a very stirring speaker, she has always tried to compensate for her lack of histrionic talent by researching her efforts thoroughly. In preparing for the 1966 debate on the finance bill, for example, she hid herself away in the House of Commons library and read every budget speech by every chancellor of the exchequer for the previous twenty years—a feat that later led Germain Greer, the feminist writer and no great fan of Mrs. Thatcher's, to marvel at her "superhuman tolerance of tedium."

Mrs. Thatcher used to write all her speeches herself, often between 11 P.M. and 4:30 A.M. the night before they were to be given. She favored such unorthodox hours, she once explained, because that's "when everybody has gone to bed and I can be quiet and the telephone isn't going . . . It is during that time that the ideas that have been gradually forming in my mind suddenly begin to crystalize and the words flow." She no longer has the time for such efforts, but neither does she simply accept whatever her speech-writers hand her. An aide contrasts her approach with that of the last Tory prime minister: "Ted Heath used to discuss a speech with his speech-writer. The guy would write it. Ted would read it. Right. Fine. That was it. For Margaret, there are endless drafts and redrafts and revisions of the redrafts, all of which adds up to an awful lot of typing." Her attention to (some would say her obsession with) detail is legendary. On a 1978 trip to Northern Ireland, for example, she threw away an entire speech that had taken days to write because she found it contained one set of incorrect figures. "I can't trust anyone anymore," she stormed at the hapless writer.

She is similarly demanding of the civil servants who actually make the government function. When memos are not up to her standards, she communicates her displeasure with caustic, hand-written comments such as "wooly," "waffly," and "slipshod thinking". Her hard-driving attitude has both terrorized and impressed the career bureaucrats upon whom she must depend. "She gives the civil servants hell," says an aide. "Yet in a funny way they admire her. She really does do her homework, and they're amazed at the way she has picked up the ball and run with it."

But though she demands an enormous amount from the people who work for her, she is not regarded as a hard and unfeeling taskmaster. For all her public coldness, her consideration towards the people who work for her is well known. "She may be able to get by on hardly any sleep," says a secretary, "but she realizes that the rest of us can't. And she is always deeply apologetic when we have to work late or over the weekend." An apology may not get a secretary home any earlier, but it is more than most politicians, a notoriously self-absorbed group, are usually willing to give. Mrs. Thatcher is also known for always remembering staffers' birthdays, and for coming up with gifts, that, as one former employee puts it, "were always exactly right—showing she had really thought about the person and the gift."

Indeed, if Mrs. Thatcher is guilty of anything with regard to her staff, it is in being too devoted to them. Like many politicians, she finds it extremely hard to fire people, and her personal staff includes a few who may have been adequate while she was just another Tory MP, but who are now way over their heads in the lofty precincts of 10 Downing Street.

More than once, the prime minister has been embarrassed by tales of assistants forgetting to show up for appointments or neglecting to return telephone calls. But she staunchly defends her small personal staff—"if things go wrong," she maintains, "their presence seems to come around me like a sort of nice warm blanket"—and she has steadfastly refused to heed the advice of colleagues who have urged her to dispense with the services of one or two aides whose main asset seems to be little more than a limitless store of loyalty.

Although as prime minister Mrs. Thatcher is the head of the British government, she is not Britain's head of state. That distinction belongs to the Queen. And though the Queen is bound by Britain's unwritten constitution to take her prime minister's advice, she is still nominally the prime minister's superior. Thus, every Tuesday evening when both are in London, the prime minister is expected to turn up at Buckingham Palace to brief the Queen on what Her Majesty's Government has been up to. These meetings are a combination of ritual and relaxation, but they are more than merely a reassuring historical charade—as an embarrassed Harold Wilson found out when, at his first prime ministerial audience with the Queen, the monarch appeared to be considerably more in touch with what was going on than he did. Not only does the monarch have the advantage of having met far more world leaders and former British prime ministers than any single inhabitant of No. 10 (Mrs. Thatcher is, after all, the eighth prime minister of Elizabeth II's reign), she also has been privy to the secrets of previous governments—something that, by strict tradition, a new prime minister is not.

Mrs. Thatcher appears at the palace for her weekly audience just before six thirty P.M. She is greeted by the Queen's urbane private secretary, Sir Philip Moore, who takes her up the red-carpeted stairs to a large and somewhat intimidating anteroom in the north wing, which houses the private royal apartments. He knocks firmly on the well-polished double doors at the end of the room, opens them, and announces: "Your Majesty, the prime minister . . ." He then shows Mrs. Thatcher in, bows to the Queen and retires, leaving the two most powerful women in Britain alone in the spacious and elegant sitting room that overlooks the vast private gardens behind the palace. Mrs. Thatcher, hatless but wearing gloves, curtseys and then shakes hands with the Queen.

According to the strict protocol that governs such occasions, the Queen sits down first, usually in an upholstered easy chair. Mrs. Thatcher follows suit, removing her gloves and placing her handbag on the floor beside her. There are no cigarettes, no drinks, and virtually no small talk. This is a business meeting first and foremost, and wasting time is frowned upon. The Queen, who always begins the conversation, refers to Mrs. Thatcher solely as "Prime Minister." In turn, after her opening "Good evening, Your Majesty," Mrs. Thatcher addresses the Queen always as "Ma'am." (The same holds true even during the more informal weekend visits at Windsor Castle in April and Balmoral in Scotland in September to which the prime minister is traditionally invited.)

Under the unwritten constitution, British monarchs have three basic rights in dealing with their government: the right to be consulted, the right to encourage, and the right to warn. To this end, the Queen is kept fully informed as to every activity of the government—no matter how top-secret it may be. Every day she receives a huge stack of briefing papers, reports, and documents from Whitehall and No. 10. She reads them all, and on the basis of what she has read, she will often pepper the prime minister with sharp questions and shrewd suggestions on the implications of this or that government initiative.

For her part, Mrs. Thatcher is obligated to brief the Queen fully not only on what is going on, but also on what is likely to be going on in the near future. Some of her predecessors used notes, but Mrs. Thatcher can rattle off her presentation from memory, interrupted only by an occasional royal query. After a half-hour or so, the Queen will rise and announce: "Well, Prime Minister, it has all been very interesting." She walks Mrs. Thatcher to the door, and the audience is over.

On evenings when formal engagements don't demand her presence elsewhere, Mrs. Thatcher often has dinner at the House of Commons, usually inviting five or six Tory MPs to dine with her. She pays the bill out of her own purse, considering it a prudent investment. "She has no intention of becoming a remote figure like Ted Heath," an aide explains. "People used to complain that the only time they saw Heath was when there was a crisis on. That's not Mrs. Thatcher's style."

Blessed as she is with a constitution that enables her to cope nicely on just four or five hours of sleep a night, she often works well into the early hours of the morning, long after most of her assistants have gone to bed, going over what are called "the boxes"—the red official dispatch cases containing briefings, memoranda, and government reports. Her day rarely ends before one A.M., usually with a scotch-and-soda nightcap and a vigorous washing-up for the sake of her complexion. "From my teens I've looked after my skin," she once told an inquiring women's-page reporter. "I never use soap and water on it, although I come from a soap-and-water family. However late and however tired, I use cleanser to get the makeup off and then a good moisturiser."

One thing she doesn't have to worry about anymore is her wardrobe.

The buying and maintenance of her clothing is taken care of by Maureen Baker, who designed Princess Anne's wedding dress. "Her tastes are easy to define," says Ms. Baker. "She prefers soft fabrics and is particularly fond of naturals like pure wool and silk. Colors, too, are gentle. Her daywear is smart, concentrating on pleated skirts, silk blouses, and jackets." Mrs. Thatcher no longer wears hats with every outfit, as she used to, and she has learned to avoid ordering clothes for a particular occasion. "They must suit several events," says a spokesman for Mansfields, one of several London fashion houses the Prime Minister patronizes. "She favors the 'English Rose' look and does not buy foreign clothes." That last restriction is as much a matter of political necessity as personal taste. As the Mansfields' spokesman notes: "This is a great advertisement for British clothing, showing it has the style and resilience to stand up to a working woman's life."

Though she likes to present herself as such, Margaret Thatcher is not a simple person. Like most people, she is a mixture of conflicting beliefs, attitudes, and temperaments—though unlike many, most of her convictions run quite deep. She can say in the course of a single interview (as she did with Ronald Butt of *The Times of London* in March 1977) that "you can't find an absolute answer to everything" but that, at the same time, she never doubts her most basic beliefs. She can concede, as she did in another interview, the self-evident truth that "politics is about compromise" but in the next sentence insist that "there comes a point at which the compromising has to stop." By way of explanation, John Biffen, a long-time colleague who as the new chief secretary to the treasury is now a member of her cabinet, once noted that "her ideas often flow from her sympathies, and that introduces some inconsistencies."

Another way of putting it is to say that she is philosophically radical but politically cautious. As another member of her cabinet has suggested, perhaps that is "because she is surer of where she wants to go than how to get there." More than most politicians, her politics have been forged by the facts of her life; they are untainted, as it were, by passive theorizing. She is no stranger to the subject of political philosophy, but she has read selectively—for the most part, right-wing philosophers and economists such as F. A. Hayek and Milton Friedman whom she was told in advance she would find congenial to her already well-formed attitudes. Perhaps her reliance on personal experience *has* put her more in touch with the daily realities than most leaders of her station can claim to be. But it also opens her to the charge, as one not so admiring Tory colleague phrases it, of being a "woman of sharp focus and narrow vision." For her, as for most people, the measure of the world is defined by the measure of her own life. Propelled by little more than an awesome doggedness and a keen though unfocussed ambition to better herself, she managed to break out of her provincial beginnings and attain the highest rank her nation can offer. Is it, then, in any way surprising that, having done it all herself, she has come to believe with unquenchable passion that, given sufficient energy and enterprise, there isn't anything an individual can't do?

2

Grantham Schoolgirl

*"Well, of course, I just owe almost everything to
my own father [and] the things which I learned in
a small town, in a very modest home . . . "*

TUCKED AMID the rolling limestone hills of agricultural south
Lincolnshire, 105 miles almost due north of London,
Grantham is a typically undistinguished provincial market
town. It can—and its people often do—boast of a long and
important history, cluttered with royal associations. But
then, so can most English towns.

Grantham first took shape about the third century B.C., under the
reign of Gorbananus, one of the early barbarian kings of Britain; at one
time, it may have been a Roman outpost. The Domesday Book of the
early thirteenth century describes it at length, and King John held court
there shortly before he signed the Magna Carta in 1215. John was the
first of a series of royal visitors. In 1290, the pious Edward I stopped in
Grantham on the first night of his journey from Nottinghamshire to
London with the body of his dead queen, Eleanor. And in 1483, the vil-
lainous Richard III signed the Duke of Buckingham's death warrant at
Grantham's Angel Hotel, which in later centuries also played host to
Charles I and, while he was still Prince of Wales, to the future Edward
VII. (History fails to record what they were doing in Grantham; most
likely, as with the majority of visitors, they were on their way to some-
where else.)

Isaac Newton, who was born in 1643 in the nearby village of Wools-
thorpe, attended the Grantham Grammar School before going to Cambridge. And in 1643, an obscure regimental commander named Oliver

Cromwell began his climb to power by recapturing Grantham from the Royalists.

Through the eighteenth century, Grantham sat astride the Great North Road from London to Scotland, and splendid coaching inns grew up in the center of town to handle the traffic. But the invention of the steam engine and the coming of the railways killed off the coaching trade. Grantham's importance began to wane and in this century, when new roads bypassed the town entirely, it slipped back into obscurity.

Grantham's medieval parish church of St. Wulfram, whose 272-foot spire dominates the town and the surrounding countryside, is still regarded as one of the finest in England. The superb pre-Reformation Angel Hotel, now known as the Angel and Royal, continues in business after 750 years—and, carrying on the legacy of a former owner of the Angel who died in 1706, a sermon on the evils of drunkeness is still preached in Grantham each year on Michaelmas Day. But little else of note has survived from what passed for the town's glory days. Today, Grantham is a quiet farming center, the administrative headquarters of the Lincolnshire district of South Kesteven. With few attractions for the young and, consequently, a static population (currently just under 30 thousand), it earns its living mainly from agricultural and mechanical engineering, and by entertaining airmen from the nearby RAF base at Cranwell.

SHOPKEEPER'S DAUGHTER

Things haven't changed all that much in Grantham since 1925, when on the morning of October 13, Beatrice Ethel Roberts gave birth to her second daughter, Margaret Hilda, in the flat above her husband Alfred's grocery shop on the town's North Parade. The Roberts were a working-class couple with an exceedingly humble background. Beatrice's family was Irish, though she had been born in Lincolnshire. Her mother, a severe Victorian woman who still lived with her, had been a railway cloak-room attendant, and her father had worked as a factory machinist. She herself had trained to be a dressmaker—a trade that was to stand her in good stead when it came time to clothe a family of her own on a frugal budget.

Alfred Roberts, known as "Sugar" to some of his customers (in part because of his business, and possibly also because of his impressive shock of white hair), was a tall, charming, and determined man who came from a long line of Northamptonshire shoemakers. The eldest of seven children, he had been forced to leave school in 1905 at the age of twelve to help support his family. Though his father, grandfather, and great-grandfather all had been cobblers, Alfred had no intention of continuing that tradition. He had other ideas—most of them centering around a fierce desire to better himself. He felt strongly that had he been able to continue his education, he could have been a schoolmaster. Since that was not possible, he turned his attention to commerce, apprenticing himself as a grocer's assistant.

He had come to Grantham during the First World War. There, he met and married Beatrice Stevenson. The young couple worked hard and saved money with a passion. Before long Alfred was able to open his own grocery shop; eventually he came to own two. In 1921 the couple's first child, a daughter called Muriel, was born. When Margaret arrived four years later, the family was complete.

Their flat above the grocery story was a Spartan place. It had no running hot water, no bath, and an outside toilet. Each bedroom had its own washstand, consisting of a large jug and basin. There was no garden, and the small kitchen was more of a lean-to than a proper room. The furniture was heavy, dark red Victorian mahogany, all of it secondhand. But the flat was not gloomy. Years later, Margaret recalled it as being "as bright as a new pin." Beatrice and her daughters kept it spotless, painting and repainting the walls, scrubbing the floors, and polishing the furniture.

The Robertses' lives centered around work, study, and religion. Though now a family man, Alfred Roberts had lost none of his youthful ambition. He was intent on establishing himself in the community and was determined that his children would go on to greater success than he had enjoyed. "My sister and I were brought up in the atmosphere that you work hard to get on," the future prime minister told Brian Connell of *The Times* in a 1975 interview. The shop was open six days a week, ten to twelve hours a day, and though Mr. Roberts eventually came to employ five assistants, the entire family helped run it. To the young Margaret, as she later told Connell, "it was quite a big shop. It had a grocery section and provision section, with all the mahogany fitments that I now see in antique shops, and beautiful canisters of different sorts of tea, coffee, and spices. There was a post office section, confectionary section and cigarettes. A lot of people came in . . . and knowing we were all interested in what was going on in the world, we would talk quite late."

Despite his long hours in the shop, Alfred Roberts somehow managed to find the time to become phenomenally active in community affairs. He was a cofounder of the Grantham Rotary Club, president of the town Grocers' Association, head of the local National Savings movement, and a member of the board of both the local boys' and girls' schools. He also enjoyed some small success as a politician. Though he had once been a member of the Liberal party, he won a place on the local town council as an independent—in effect, a Conservative. He served on the council for twenty-five years, and he later went on to become chairman of its finance committee. In the 1940s came what must have been an especially sweet achievement for this ambitious shoemaker's son: he was selected for the largely honorary but still prestigious post of Mayor of Grantham. And for nine years, he served as town alderman.

All this activity made a normal family life somewhat difficult, if not impossible. The Robertses rarely sat down to meals together; they even vacationed separately. Once a year, Beatrice would take the girls to a boardinghouse (where they would cook their own meals) in the modest seaside town of Skegness. A few months later, Alfred would take his own one-week vacation there by himself.

Nonetheless, they were a close-knit family, bound together by Alfred Roberts's determination to see them all improve their lot. He would take his wife and daughters to weekly university extension lectures, monthly music club recitals—anything that smacked of the culture and education he so hungrily sought. The local librarian, Peter Willard, recalls him as "the best-read man in Grantham." The young Margaret, he says, used to appear at the library to collect "armfuls of books for him every week." Those books, mostly biographies and studies of current affairs, were thoroughly discussed at home. Roberts fancied himself a keen student of world events, and he insisted that his daughters share his interest. They did, particularly Margaret. Madeline Hellaby, a schoolmate of young Margaret's during World War II, tells the story of how, during a classroom "discussion of an RAF bombing raid in Europe, she knew where the place of the raid was and no one else did. The mistress asked how, and she said, 'Any time a bombing raid is mentioned on the wireless, we get the atlas out and put a pin in to mark the location.'"

Alfred Roberts did more than just discuss events with his daughters. He had keenly-held political beliefs, and he discussed those too. As one might expect of a self-made man blessed with considerable personal initiative and individual enterprise, he had absolutely no sympathy for the growing trade union movement in prewar Britain. "He was antisocialist," recalls Grantham newspaper editor F. W. Goodliff, "and Margaret absorbed a lot of his politics at the dinner table."

Above all, however, Alfred Roberts was a deeply religious man and a stern moralist. "We were Methodist and Methodist means method," his admiring younger daughter explained years later. "We were taught what was right and wrong in considerable detail. There were certain things you just didn't do and that was that. Duty was very, very strongly ingrained into us."

Indeed, there was little place for frivolity—or even the normal high-spiritedness of youth—in the Roberts household; by her own later description, young Margaret's upbringing was "rather Puritan." Though they stocked sherry and brandy for the benefit of guests, the Robertses were themselves teetotalers. Games were not allowed in the house, and dancing was absolutely forbidden. The austere Finkin Street Methodist Church, which the family attended regularly, was the hub of the family's social life, providing them with an apparently endless round of church socials, singalongs, suppers, and spelling bees. On Wednesday evenings, Beatrice Roberts would go off to the church sewing circle, and on Fridays there was the church youth club for the girls.

Alfred Roberts approved of these social aspects of religious life, but as far as he was concerned they were clearly secondary. To him, religion was something to be taken with the utmost seriousness. He was a highly popular lay preacher himself, serving as a trustee of no less than ten Lincolnshire churches, and he took the Biblical injunction "to honor the Sabbath and keep it holy" so much to heart that for years he kept the town council from opening the municipal parks, swimming pools, and tennis courts on Sunday. He relented only during World War II, when he was persuaded that local servicemen were entitled to more Sunday diversions than he was willing to permit himself or his family.

For the Robertses, Sunday was a day of prayer and study—and nothing else. The shop was closed and going to the movies was out of the question; even Sunday newspapers were barred from the household. The family was up for breakfast at eight A.M. and at ten the girls were sent off to Sunday school. They would join their parents for the morning service at eleven, return to Sunday school in the afternoon, and then attend another church service at six in the evening. The young Margaret was a willing participant in this strict and unswerving regimen, though she admitted years later with a hint of regret that it did cut her off from many of her girlhood friends, whose own families were not quite so pious as the Robertses.

MODEL STUDENT

Margaret—she was never called Maggie, Peggie, or anything but her proper name—was a serious-minded though not solemn child who adored her demanding father. "She was bright, studious, serious even as a five-year-old," says John Foster, a Grantham shop owner and local Tory politican who went to school with her. Above all, he notes, "she wanted to please her father." That she did, for Alfred Roberts appears to have realized early on that Margaret was by far the more promising of his two daughters. "He did a good deal to push her on in school and her career," recalls John Guile, a long-time family friend, "and she was quite willing to be pushed." ("He did try to realize his ambitions in me," she was later to tell biographer Tricia Murray without a hint of resentment.)

Her sister Muriel, now the wife of a wealthy Essex landowner, says Margaret was a neat and thrifty youngster. "I never remember Margaret scruffy," she notes, adding that "Margaret was the sort of child who would make a pound worth one pound and sixpence. She always used to keep a good watch on her pocket money and seemed to make it last longer."

At the age of five, she was started on piano lessons. She practiced religiously, and within a few years was good enough to be drafted as accompanist at the Methodist church on Sundays.

She began her formal education at the state-run Huntingtower Road elementary school. Huntingtower Road was a mile's walk from the Roberts home, but since the school was new and highly regarded Margaret, like her older sister, was enrolled there. "She was sociable and fun, but not what you would call a good-timer," says John Fraser, who was a classmate of hers there and is now leader of the Conservatives on the Kesteven District Council.

It was a few years after she started school that she had her first direct experience with politics. Her father's community activities had made politics a part of the Roberts household for as long as she could remember, and his dinnertable lectures—plus the long conversations with customers in his shop—had always fascinated Margaret. By the time she was ten, she later told Connell, "politics was in my bloodstream—an interest much as theatre is, or music." She never really thought about it much; as she put it, "it isn't that you consciously say you will be a musician, you are naturally interested in music." In any case, in 1935 Alfred Roberts drafted his entire family to help out in a local candidate's campaign—and on election day, the ten-year-old Margaret, to her evident delight,

FINANCIAL TIMES

In what may be the earliest photo ever taken of Britain's first woman prime minister, four-year-old Margaret Roberts shyly poses with her eight-year-old sister, Muriel. Although Margaret quickly outshone her older sister, the two girls remained close.

From humble beginnings, the Roberts family became a formidable force in the small Lincolnshire town of Grantham. Right, a rare formal portrait of the family, taken in 1945. Alderman Alfred Roberts and his wife are wearing their ceremonial robes of office; Margaret (then twenty) is at the far right. Below, the Roberts grocery store in Grantham. Margaret was born in the spartan flat above the store and lived there until she went off to Oxford. Below right, Margaret's fifth-form grammar school class (she's in the back row at the far left). Outwardly, she was indistinguishable from her fellow-fifteen-year-olds, but she dominated the class.

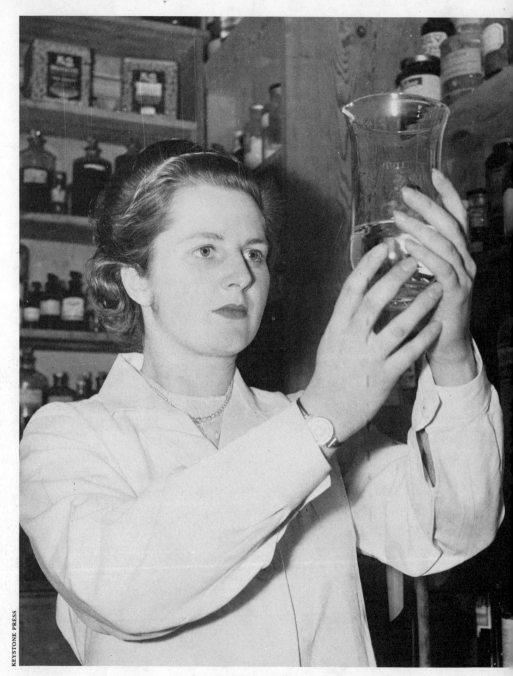

Shortly after she was graduated from Oxford University, Margaret Roberts took a job as a research chemist. She lived in spartan digs in Colchester, a drab industrial town, and commuted about ten miles daily. One of her colleagues said she was always ready for a political debate.

In 1950, Margaret was a 24-year-old candidate campaigning, in her first Parlimentary race, in Dartford, a Socialist stronghold. She lost the election, but her performance impressed the Tory leaders. She urged her generally unsympathetic audiences to "vote right to keep what's left."

In a blue velvet gown and sporting a jaunty plumed hat, Margaret cut a fetching figure at her 1951 wedding to Denis Thatcher. Right, two years later, she gave birth to twins, Carol and Mark, and temporarily retired from active politics. Below right, when her children reached the age of six, she decided to return to the fray, waging her first successful Parliamentary campaign in 1959.

Sharing a word with a policeman outside the House of Commons, Mrs. Thatcher prepares to enter Parliament for the first time as the Member for Finchley. She quickly earned herself a reputation as a dogged and awesomely well-prepared debater, and within two years after her 1959 debut in the House she was invited in Harold Macmillan's Government as a junior minister.

was dispatched to run back and forth between the candidate's headquarters and the polling station carrying lists of those who had voted so their names could be checked off by the campaign staff.

Though her serious nature may have put off some of her classmates in elementary school, it began to pay off for Margaret quite early. At the age of ten, a year younger than normal, she won a scholarship to the Kesteven and Grantham Girls' School, one of the town's two grammar schools. In Britain, a grammar school is a secondary school, similar to an American junior high and high school combined. It is supported partly by government money and partly by relatively modest tuition fees. Unlike state-supported schools in America, however, students are admitted to a grammar school not on the basis of where they live (though one must usually be a local resident to be eligible), but through a fiercely competitive examination. Grammar schools were—and, in many cases, still are—one of the only routes to a white-collar or professional career for the vast majority of British children who have not been fortunate enough to have been born into the upper classes.

Though the Robertses didn't own a radio until 1935—and didn't buy their first automobile, a used Ford, until after World War II—they were not a poor family. Kesteven's tuition of thirteen pounds a year (roughly 65 dollars in the currency of the time), plus the cost of books and supplies, was within Alfred Roberts's means. But practical man that he was, he insisted his daughter take the scholarship exam anyway, so that her education would be provided for in case he happened to die unexpectedly. As it turned out, he wound up living for another forty-two years—until 1970, when he died at the ripe old age of seventy-seven—and, in the process, paying for Margaret's education at Kesteven himself.

It was at Kesteven that the young Margaret Roberts really began to shine. "It was clear to everyone at school that Margaret was quite exceptional," says Madeline Hellaby, who as Madeline Edwards was one of her closest friends there. "She was brilliant academically. She sat up straight at her desk and was a model pupil. She could be relied on to ask penetrating questions on current events." Even at that early age she had something of a parliamentry style about her. Classmates recall that, after visiting lecturers would throw open the floor to questions, she would often jump to her feet and pose her query in a curiously formal way: "Does the speaker think . . . ," she would invariably begin.

Dorothy Gillies, Kesteven's headmistress at the time, remembers Margaret Roberts as having "the power of sustained effort and the ability to think clearly, tackling one thing at a time." Indeed, in her school reports, the phrases "she is a very logical thinker" and "she has a very clear mind" recur again and again. She also had the gift of intense concentration. Once, after finishing an exam, a classmate of hers commented on the terrible thunderstorm that had broken out while everyone was taking the test. Margaret was stunned; she had been so engrossed in the exam she hadn't realized there had even been a storm, much less one with violent thunder and lightning. Such academic gifts led her to finish first in her class every year at Kesteven except one—when she came in second.

But Margaret wasn't simply a grind. "People sometimes get the wrong idea about Margaret," says Madeline Edwards Hellaby. "They think she was so brainy that she must have been a bluestocking. But she was also good at games, pretty and popular." A fearsome competitor, Margaret was the youngest girl to make the school hockey team (of which she eventually became vice-captain). An all-round athlete, she was in her later years at Kesteven selected Captain of Games, which meant that she was Kesteven's chief representative at interschool athletic competitions.

Margaret was also a member of the debating team, and on her own she took elocution lessons. ("One has simply got to speak properly," she told her father when she asked him for the money to pay for them.) She was also something of a budding actress, appearing in many of her school's amateur theatricals. At one point, she dreamed idly of actually pursuing a career in the theater, but quickly dismissed it as an impractical fantasy. (Her life at the time, she said much later, was so lacking in glamor that even her level head was capable of being turned, at least briefly, by the romance of show business.)

In short, she was a formidably versatile student. "Mothers would say to their daughters: 'Why can't you be more like Margaret Roberts?'," reports a former classmate. It was not the sort of thing to endear a teenage girl to her peers, some of whom recall her as being bossy and overbearing—especially to those she felt superior to. But she coped well enough.

THE WORLD BEYOND GRANTHAM

Margaret was thirteen when Britain entered the war in Europe. Her sister Muriel had already left home for Birmingham, where she was studying physiotherapy, and though the buildup at several nearby military bases flooded her sleepy town with dashing young servicemen, there simply wasn't much in Grantham to occupy an energetic young teenager, even one as practical and hardworking as Margaret. Girls her age simply didn't go out with boys; weekly expeditions to Catlin's Cafe for an ice cream sundae with her friends were a special treat, and the occasional trip to Nottingham twenty-four miles away for a Fred Astaire-Ginger Rogers movie was a major event in her life. "In wartime, there were just no dances to go to," recalls Margaret Wickstead, who as Margaret Goodrich struck up what was to become a lifelong friendship with her younger namesake in 1938. "We explored the countryside, picked wildflowers, rode bicycles, and helped the farmers to harvest. Once, we girls at school spent two days picking rose hips to make syrup, and we gathered sheep's wool off hedges to make jumpers as part of the war effort."

Against such a backdrop, her first trip to London, which she made as a teenager, remains vividly imprinted on her mind. Her parents had friends in the metropolis, and when they invited her to come down, she jumped at the chance. "I stayed for a whole week and was given a life of enjoyment and entertainment that I had never seen," she told Tricia Murray years later, her excitement evidently undimmed by the passage of decades. She was taken to see the changing of the guard at Buckingham Palace, the Tower of London, and even to a West End musical imported from the U.S., called "The Desert Song." The lights and the crowds thrilled the provincial teenager, and no doubt reinforced her determination to make a place for herself in the wider world beyond Grantham.

The closest thing she had to personal experience of the war came through a pen pal of her sister's, a Jewish girl called Edith who lived in Vienna. When Hitler's forces marched into Austria, Edith's parents wrote to the Robertses asking if they would take the girl in if they could get her out of the country. The family agreed immediately, and soon Edith came to live with them. Her firsthand account of life under the Third Reich fascinated and appalled Margaret, who would listen to her for hours trying to form a picture of events that must have seemed light-years away.

It was about this time, when she was fifteen, that Margaret had to start thinking seriously about what she wanted to do with her life. The British education system required youngsters of that age to choose between two totally separate curriculums which they would follow for the remainder of their secondary school career. One was an arts and humanities course, the other was science. Margaret had little trouble making up her mind. Though she had always been interested in politics, the idea of a political career seemed out of the question. Members of Parliament were paid only 600 pounds a year at the time and were given no allowances for secretarial or office expenses. That quite deliberately limited professional politics mainly to successful businessmen, lawyers, and the rich. At the same time, science seemed to be the coming thing; research was booming, and a science degree appeared to provide a passport to assured employment. So, influenced by an enthusiastic chemistry teacher at Kesteven, and following the example set by her sister, who had decided to study physiotherapy because it was something from which she could confidently expect to earn a living, Margaret chose science—specifically, chemistry.

But shortly thereafter she began to regret her choice. Her father by this time was serving as a part-time justice of the peace, and on school holidays he would take his daughter with him to the local court. The procedure and arguments fascinated her. One day, at lunch with her father and the town recorder, a lawyer named Norman Winning who presided over the informal court, she blurted out how angry she was with herself for having concentrated on chemistry. What she really wanted to do, she said, was to become a lawyer. But her grammar school curriculum would not equip her to study anything at university but science. What was she to do, she asked; she was just sixteen, and already it seemed too late for her to switch horses.

Winning was the perfect man to advise her. He himself had a degree in physics, and he assured her that a background in science was no handicap to a successful legal career. What she should do, he suggested, was go ahead and get her degree in chemistry at the university. Afterwards, she could study law in her spare time. Not only would she be well-educated in two disciplines; the combination would also qualify her for the lucrative practice of patent law.

Margaret now began to prepare in earnest for her advanced education. University had always been her goal, but she had no specific school in mind. Now, characteristically, she set her sights at the top: Oxford University, the oldest and (along with Cambridge) the most distinguished institution of higher education in Britain, if not the world. It was an awesome, even foolhardy target for a young girl from a provincial grammar school. Few Grantham girls had ever scaled such heights. (One who did was her older friend Margaret Goodrich; she went up to Oxford in 1942, and Margaret Roberts was determined to follow her there.)

In any case, there were more than a few obstacles to be overcome. For one thing, Kesteven did not even offer Latin, which Oxford demanded as one of its entrance requirements. For another, Miss Gillies, the headmistress at Kesteven, thought Margaret was overreaching herself. Whether she was motivated by a mixture of envy and regret at the prospect of losing her best pupil, or by honest concern for the girl's well-being, Miss Gillies did not approve of Margaret's choice. She urged her to reconsider; at the very least, she should put off her ambitions for another year or two.

But the determined young student wanted no part of such faintheartedness. "She's trying to thwart my ambition," Margaret stormed, and on her own found a tutor with whom she proceeded to devour a five-year Latin course in a single year.

Thus prepared, at the age of seventeen, a year younger than most candidates, she sat for the grueling round of examinations one had to pass to gain admittance to Oxford. To her delight, she scored top marks on the Latin test. (She continued to hold a grudge against the timorous Miss Gillies, however, and years later she took her revenge: invited back to Kesteven to give a speech, she was preceded on the podium by her old, now-retired headmistress. A bit nervous perhaps, Miss Gillies misquoted a Latin phrase—whereupon, when she got up to speak, Margaret Thatcher loudly and somewhat cruelly corrected the old lady.)

But however well she did on her exams, Margaret Roberts did not do well enough to win herself an immediate place at Oxford. Instead, she was put on the waiting list of Somerville College, one of the two oldest women's colleges at Oxford. It was a bitter blow, but it did not weaken Margaret's resolve. "She was very ambitious and wanted to go to university as fast as she could," recalls Margaret Goodrich Wickstead. If she did not get into Oxford, there were other universities. With the help of Margaret Goodrich's father, who was a vicar, she won a place at Nottingham, a state university.

Come the next fall, however, she did not go to Nottingham. She remained in Grantham and started what she hoped would be her last year at Kesteven. Her disappointment at remaining there was eased a bit when, along with her friend Madeline Edwards, she was made co-head girl of the school, the highest honor any grammar school student can achieve. She didn't have much time to enjoy it, however, for two weeks later a telegram arrived from Oxford: there was a place for her at Somerville, it said, if she still wanted it.

Being admitted to Somerville and actually going there, however, were two different things. Margaret had tied for first in the competitive exam given to award the one scholarship the college had to offer. But Somerville officials decided to give the scholarship to the other top-scoring candidate, an older girl who had been waiting a year longer than Margaret to get into Oxford. All Margaret got was what was called a bursary, a far more modest stipend that wouldn't cover a fraction of her costs at Somerville.

Having seen his daughter get so far so quickly, Alfred Roberts was not about to let the lack of a scholarship permit the greatest opportunity of her young life to slip through her fingers. He scraped together the money she needed, and in October of 1943, Margaret Roberts moved out of the flat above the grocery store and went off to university.

3

Young Tory

"Yes, I ought *to be an MP."*

FOR SEVEN HUNDRED YEARS, Oxford and Cambridge universities (collectively known as Oxbridge) have educated the British ruling class. To this day, their graduates dominate politics, law, journalism, theology, science, and the arts in the UK in a vast, insular, and occasionally fratricidal old-boy network whose well-fortified walls are only beginning to be breached. Of the two universities, Oxford is the older (its University College dates back to 1249), more classical, and more conservative. Its influence on the course of British history and government is incalculable. From its Gothic quadrangles and ancient cloisters have emerged literally thousands of members of Parliament, hundreds of Cabinet ministers (nearly two hundred in this century alone), and no less than nine out of the last eighteen prime ministers.

For eighteen-year-old Margaret Roberts in 1943, Oxford seemed a far cry from anything she had known before. With its shops, theaters, and concert halls, the town, even under the strain of war-time rationing, presented a sharp and cosmopolitan contrast to sleepy Grantham. And the sprawling campus, with its thirty or so separate colleges, each with its own history, tradition, and social distinction, each competing for reputation, attention, and acclaim like so many medieval fiefdoms, each concealing behind its stony battlements outrageous extremes of high seriousness and infantile silliness—how overwhelming and alien all of it was to an inexperienced and unsophisticated provincial girl.

Oxford was a far cry, too, from what it itself had been just a few years earlier. No longer was it an insulated preserve of the rich and aristocratic. The war had, to a certain extent, democratized the place and hardened its once carefree attitudes. Most of its young men, having volunteered or been called up, were gone off to battle. The undergraduate body was thus smaller and, on average, older than usual; it also included more than a few veterans of combat who had been matured and subdued by their firsthand experience of war, and who worked harder than most of their fellows because they hadn't much time to finish their studies.

Most undergraduates were expected to do war work. Like many, Margaret Roberts found herself tending potato patches in what had once been the university's hockey fields. She also was assigned as a fire-watcher, which meant spending an occasional night on a roof on the lookout for incendiary bombs.

At the beginning of her time at Oxford, Margaret, who had never before been away from home and family for more than a week, was desperately homesick. She was painfully shy in her strange new environment, and for the first few weeks spoke to virtually no one except those few people at the university she already knew. She would turn up regularly at the room of her Grantham friend Margaret Goodrich for tea and sympathy.

But she quickly found herself too busy to tolerate such an emotional handicap. Somerville College was a demanding place. Though the college had been founded in 1879, it wasn't until 1920 that its women were recognized as full members of the university, entitled to Oxford degrees. Thus, in a very real sense, it had something to prove. Its faculty was formidably up to the task. Somerville's principal at the time was Dame Janet Vaughn, a distinguished researcher on the effects of radiation on bone and blood pathology. Margaret's own tutor, who supervised her work throughout her university career, was Dorothy Hodgkin, a brilliant scientist who later went on to win the Nobel Prize for chemistry in 1964 and became the first British woman since Florence Nightingale to be admitted to the Order of Merit, a prestigious and exclusive royal honor limited to twenty-four holders at any one time.

Margaret's dogged and energetic temperament was well-tested by the challenges of Oxford academic life. Her day would begin at six thirty A.M.; as a chemistry student, she would spend all morning and all afternoon in the laboratory. From five to seven in the evening, she attended lectures, and in spare moments there was a formidable reading list to get through. "Margaret was bright and promising," says the now-retired Professor Hodgkin. "I remember her doing nice, clear work while she was with me. She obviously liked chemistry, but I don't believe she had a particularly profound interest in the subject."

Indeed, like her father, who involved himself fully in community affairs while running two shops, Margaret carried a full academic load and still insisted on plunging into a diverse round of extracurricular activities that seemed to define her real interests. Her love for music propelled her into the Oxford Repertory Company, the Somerville-Balliol Choir (Balliol being the men's college at Oxford with perhaps the most impressive academic reputation), and the university-wide Bach Choir. Every Friday evening there were meetings of the Scientific Society, and she also joined a student Methodist group—though as she began to read more widely about theology (specifically the works of C. S. Lewis), she began to move away from the religion of her childhood. Her fundamentalist upbringing slowly yielded to a more Anglican sophistication.

A BUDDING CONSERVATIVE

Certainly, Margaret's life at Oxford was more secular than it had been in Grantham. Her social life no longer revolved around the church, but around the university's lively political world. To a great extent, that world centered around the famed Oxford Union, which along with its counterpart at Cambridge has provided an early forum for innumerable British politicians. As Anthony Sampson notes in his classic study of British institutions, *The New Anatomy of Britain*: "In other universities a union is simply a student center, with its own premises, restaurant, bars and offices. But in Oxford and Cambridge the union has been a quite expensive club, revolving around a debating society with its own rituals and values, which have come to be regarded as an anteroom to parliament." The Oxford Union, founded in 1823, was a particularly lively place. In 1933, it shocked the nation by adopting, after a bitterly fought debate, the pacifist—and, what seemed to many at the time, faintly treasonous—motion: "That this House will in no circumstances fight for its King and Country." Among the Union's former members are an impressive number of prime ministers, including Gladstone, Asquith, Salisbury, Macmillan, Heath, and Wilson.

In Margaret Roberts's time, the Oxford Union didn't admit women as members. For someone with her passion for politics, it must have been keenly frustrating, though she professed not to care. The political organization she wanted to join was the Oxford University Conservative Association (OUCA), and it was open, then as now, to any Oxford undergraduate, male as well as female.

Her membership in the OUCA marked her first formal association with the Conservative party. The Tories, as Conservatives are popularly known, trace their history back to 1782. Modern Toryism, however, began with Benjamin Disraeli, the "brilliant and dandified Jew" (as Macmillan called him) who became prime minister in 1871. One of the giants of British political history, Disraeli based his policies on imperialism abroad and controlled social reform at home, and it was he who developed the idea of the Tories as the party of "One Nation"—not tied to any particular class or ideology, but a patriotic party appealing to all of British society.

Although in this century the Conservative party has become inextricably identified with the political right, the fact is it is extremely difficult to pin down just what Toryism stands for. A particularly cogent and intelligent attempt to define the party's doctrine was made recently by Sir Ian Gilmour, a leading Tory moderate and a member of Mrs. Thatcher's current cabinet. In his book *Inside Right*, Gilmour argues that Tories by definition resist rigid ideologies; instead of being tied to abstractions, he says, they rely on empirical experience, changing their approach to fit what they have learned. Gilmour notes that, while today the party clearly favors the rights of the individual over the state, there have been times in the past when it has opposed a laissez-faire approach to public policy and clearly plumped for increased government power. What's more, he points out, these apparently contradictory attitudes are perfectly consistent with the fundamental Tory desire for balance. Balance, moderation, and national unity, Gilmour says, are the basic Tory goals; there is nothing the party should be against on principle except tyranny and policies that would divide the nation.

Gilmour's thesis goes a long way towards explaining what, in today's terms at least, would seem to be the anomalous behavior of Britain's prewar Conservative governments. For all their talk today of trimming back the welfare state and reducing the government's involvement in the economy, it was the Tories, after all, who in 1924 introduced old-age pensions and subsidized housing to Britain. Two years later, it was again the Tories, under Stanley Baldwin, who nationalized the electricity and broadcasting industries. And it was the Tory-dominated wartime coalition led by Winston Churchill that provided social security for all, created the National Health System, introduced family welfare allowances, adopted Keynesian budgetary techniques, and began centralized industrial planning.

It has been suggested, unkindly as well as accurately, that Margaret Roberts joined the OUCA because it was a small and sleepy group in which she could quickly shine. The facts are, however, that Oxford has always been something of a Conservative bastion, that the OUCA was a fairly large organization, and that she joined because she was a true believer. Indeed, there was something of an evangelical streak to her politics; she could understand that others might hold different beliefs, but she could never accept their doing so. "My husband disagreed with her, and she used to argue with him for hours," recalls her tutor, Dorothy Hodgkin. But though she was highly opinionated, she was not contentious—at least not with those whom she respected. "Her arguments were always on a friendly basis," Professor Hodgkin notes. "She was a strong Tory, but she was polite in her commitment." (Not everyone remembers her so favorably. "She was a blinkered little Tory apparatchik," is the judgment of a British journalist who knew her at Oxford.)

In any case, her undergraduate life consisted of more than study, choir practice, and political argument. Her political involvement was the basis of a lively social life. There was a round of teas, cocktail parties, and those once-forbidden dances. Margaret Roberts may not have been the most uninhibited socialite Oxford had ever seen, but at least, as a former classmate notes approvingly, "she never forgot the sherry."

She never had a regular boyfriend; few girls at that time did. But the pretty young coed was asked out on more than her share of dates. Her attitude towards her beaux was a curious and characteristic mixture of the romantic and the practical. Her good friend Margaret Goodrich Wickstead recalls her turning up at a party proudly bearing a carnation given her by some male admirer. She was determined to preserve it, and marched straight to the bookshelf, where she leafed through every chemistry text she could lay her hands on in hope of finding some compound that would do the trick. The search proved futile, and she wound up falling back on the old standby of aspirin and water. But at least she had tried.

Maintaining such a full life, and keeping up with her fellow-undergraduates, most of whom were far better off financially than she was, was not easy for Margaret. Even by the standards of those frugal times, her budget was tight and she rarely had any extra spending money. New clothes were out of the question, and there was little she could to to brighten up her small, dark, and cheerless room at Somerville. To supplement what little her father was able to give her, she found work at the local armed forces canteen where she dispensed coffee and biscuits to servicemen. And in 1944, her second year at Oxford, she took a part-time position at the Grantham Central School for Boys, teaching chemistry, mathematics, and general science. Her only real extravagance was, in fact, something of a necessity: a bicycle, which she bought out of the proceeds of her teaching job.

She might have had an easier time of it. Her old grammar school, Kesteven, was willing to give her a scholarship—on one proviso: that she return there to teach when she graduated. It was a tempting offer, but Margaret had no intention of going back home after she finished at Oxford. She was more determined than ever to find work as a research chemist and study law on the side. So she turned down the offer and continued to make do as best she could.

Margaret's first real experience with electoral politics came in the late spring and summer of 1945. The war in Europe now over, the Tory-dominated wartime coalition which had governed without a general election since November of 1935 decided it was time the British electorate had another chance at the ballot box. Since 1938, the MP representing the city of Oxford had been Quintin Hogg, an aristocratic young Tory and Oxford graduate whose father, the first Viscount Hailsham, had served in the cabinet of Neville Chamberlain's prewar National government. Oxford was, and remains, a reasonably safe Tory seat, but the OUCA pitched in enthusiastically nonetheless to insure Hogg's reelection. Margaret Roberts was among the most active of the undergraduate campaigners. She distributed literature, canvassed the townspeople, and delivered her first public political speeches—something, she said later, "which I quite enjoyed."

The Tories, who held 432 seats in what was then a 615-member House of Commons, went into the election quite confident of their chances. After all, they were being led by Prime Minister Winston Churchill, the defiant hero and grand old man of the Conservative party who had guided Britain through its finest hour. Surely the man who had coaxed blood, toil, tears, and sweat from his embattled countrymen during the just-concluded war could count on their support for what nearly everyone assumed would be his first peacetime government.

The British voters, however, had other ideas. They evidently felt Winnie was fine for the war, but a new era was beginning, and they wanted new policies and a new government. In one of the most astonishing upsets in modern political history, the Conservatives were crushed at the polls in July of 1945. Quintin Hogg retained his seat, but most of his fellow Tory candidates were not so lucky. In the new 640-member Parliament, Labor under Clement Attlee claimed 393 seats; the Conservatives found their numbers slashed by more than half to just 213 seats. "The decision of the British people has been recorded in the votes counted today," said a stunned Winston Churchill. "I have therefore laid down the charge which was placed upon me in darker times."

It was the first time Britain had elected a Labor government outright. The party itself was a relatively new one, founded less than a half-century earlier in 1900 out of an alliance between the fledgling trade unions (who felt they needed a political party of their own to further their interests) and British socialists (who were committed to radical change through nonrevolutionary means). In the general election of 1900, the party's first, it had won just two seats out of 670 in the House of Commons. But the workingman's movement grew swiftly, and by 1922, Labor was able to capture just under thirty percent of the total vote—and 142 seats in Parliament. It increased that total to 191 in the next general election a year later; the Tories had won 258 seats, but with the support of the still-powerful Liberal party, which controlled 159 seats, Ramsay MacDonald was able to form Britain's first Labor government.

MacDonald, a humorless somewhat aristocratic Scotsman, lasted in office just eleven months; when the Liberals withdrew their support, his government collapsed, and in the ensuing general election, the Conservatives came storming back to regain their traditional control of the Commons. Their overwhelming 223-seat majority was more than enough to keep them in power for the full parliamentary term of five years. But when they finally went to the country again, in May 1929, the Tories, who regarded themselves as "the natural party of government," were in for a shock. Rising unemployment and lingering resentments from the bitter general strike of 1926 took their toll: for the first time, the Conservatives were actually bested by Labor, which won 288 seats to their 260. It was only a plurality, however, not a clear majority; the Liberals once again held the balance of power—this time with 59 seats. MacDonald and his Labor cabinet managed to govern for two years. But then came trouble—and MacDonald found himself forced into what is still known in Labor party circles as "the Great Betrayal," an act of political heresy the party has never forgiven.

MacDonald was never a doctrinaire socialist, and when the worldwide depression threatened to undermine the British economy, he moved to cut back the nation's young and costly social security system. His cabinet refused to back him on the issue, forcing MacDonald to resign. Shortly afterward, he was expelled from the party. But his political career was not quite finished. After consulting with the leaders of the Liberal and Conservative parties, King George V asked MacDonald to form a "National Government," in effect a Labor-Liberal-Conservative coalition. That he did. But though he remained as prime minister until 1935, it was the Tories, under Baldwin, Chamberlain, and Churchill, who were to dominate the government. Labor was crushed and demoralized, its first real chance at power apparently thrown away.

The summer of 1945 brought Labor a new beginning. But the party's stunning comeback also contained the seeds of its own undoing. In one of those unpredictable rebounds that makes politics the perverse affair it is, the Conservative debacle inspired something of a Tory revival, especially on the campuses and among the young. F. A. Hayek's *Road to Serfdom*, a virulently antisocialist tract published in 1944, developed something of a cult following. Hayek, an Austrian philosopher-historian who fled to America before World War II, argued apocalyptically that any extension of state power, for whatever reasons and to whatever ends, would inevitably lead to Nazi-style tyranny. Among his readers was Margaret Roberts, who found her home-grown attitudes confirmed and reinforced on every page.

MADAM PRESIDENT

Fed both by the Tory revival and the flood of returning officers that washed over Oxford in 1946, the OUCA became the largest club on campus, with 1,750 members. That same year it elected the second woman ever to serve as its president, the committed young chemistry undergraduate, Margaret Roberts. "She became president," says Maurice Chandler, who was secretary of the OUCA at the time, "because of her obvious abilities: a good organizer, extremely capable, intelligent, and sociable." There was evidently no bias against her because she was a woman; as Chandler puts it, she was considered just one "of a number of talented people" in the association.

In her term as president of the OUCA, she presided over an all-male governing board consisting mainly of ex-officers several years her senior. They were a reasonably strong-willed group, but young Miss Roberts had no trouble handling them. She was, Chandler recalls, "very mature for her age."

The OUCA regularly sponsored speeches on campus by leading Tory politicians of the day. As president, it was Margaret's job to escort them around Oxford and introduce them to their audience. In this way, she came to meet a number of the party's most highly regarded rising stars, among them Quintin Hogg and Peter Thorneycroft, both of whom went on to become leading cabinet ministers in subsequent Conservative governments, and who currently (as Lord Hailsham and Lord Thorneycroft respectively) are among the prime minister's closest advisers.

It was also about this time that Margaret realized she could consider pursuing a career in politics. One of the first acts of the new Labor government was to raise the salaries of members of Parliament to one thousand pounds a year, the equivalent at the time of about four thousand dollars. It was a liveable wage, and for the first time it seemed possible to have a political career without a private income. Like many undergraduate politicoes at Oxford, Margaret made no secret of her budding ambitions. But the first time anyone remembers hearing her declare them was at Margaret Goodrich's twenty-first birthday party at her home in Corby Glen, near Grantham. Late in the evening, as the party was breaking up, Margaret sat in the kitchen with some girl friends, sipping cocoa, discussing the world and their likely futures in it. You know, one of the girls said to her, you should run for Parliament. Margaret paused briefly, considering the idea; it wasn't the first time it had crossed her mind, and the more she thought about it, the more she liked it. "Yes," she said after a moment, "I *ought* to be an MP."

Her term as president of the OUCA came quite close to the end of her sojourn at Oxford, and the time and energy it drained from her studies took its toll. "She had a clear head in her work," says her former tutor, Dorothy Hodgkin, "but her heart was always elsewhere—in politics." Her senior thesis on X-ray crystallography was good enough, but the round of final exams on which her entire academic career depended did not go as well as she had hoped it would. Oxford degrees are divided into three rankings, called, logically enough, First-, Second-, and Third-Class degrees. A First is a rare and distinguished accomplishment; it means that a student has done top-quality work on each of six to ten finals. A Third is also rare, as well as quite embarrassing. Most students earn a Second—and Margaret Roberts was among them.

Actually, her bachelor of science degree in chemistry was what is known as a "good" Second—meaning that on a few of her exams she turned in outstanding work, while on the rest she merely performed solidly. It was certainly nothing to be ashamed of. As Professor Hodgkin notes: "She might have done better and got a First, but she did quite nicely." Still, Margaret was slightly embarrassed; she was not accustomed to being in the second rank of anything. Margaret Goodrich Wickstead recalls walking down Parks Road in Oxford with her one June afternoon in 1947 just after she had been notified that her degree would be a Second. Chemistry, the younger girl said, was simply not a good field for a budding politician. "I think I'll get a job somewhere that will allow me to study for the bar."

She was as good as her word, though her legal studies didn't actually begin for a few years. Shortly after graduation, Margaret went to work as a research chemist for a firm called British Xylonite Plastics in Manningtree, Essex, about sixty miles northeast of London. She took Spartan digs in nearby Colchester, a drab industrial town, and commuted ten miles or so to the lab each day.

Her job did not exactly involve pushing forward the frontiers of science. She was hired to study surface tensions and help develop an adhesive for joining a recently developed form of polyvinyl-chloride to metal or wood. "She was a hard-working girl who knew her subject, but she was not the most imaginative worker," says now-retired research director Stanley Booth, her first boss at BX Plastics. "She was polite, but she was always ready for a political argument. She used to carry out debates with the staff. She was very active and obviously going to be a politician."

THE MAKING OF A CANDIDATE

Indeed, one of the first things Margaret did on moving to Colchester was to join the local Conservative Association. As at Oxford, it provided the core of her social life and filled her nonworking hours. There were teas, dinners, meetings, and plenty of speaking engagements. Years later, she recalled beginning her political life in Colchester "as a potboiler, going round village halls keeping the audience warm until the candidate arrives."

Her first real break in politics came in 1948. Selected by the Oxford Graduates Association to represent it, she went off to the annual Conservative Party Conference, held that year in the north Wales resort of Llandudno. The party conference is a vital ritual in British politics. As Anthony Sampson describes it:

> It is at the party conference that the tribal roots of the parties reassert themselves. Every autumn the party delegates assembled at one of [the]

seaside resorts with halls big enough to hold them. . . . The end-of-season atmosphere, with empty beaches, yellow leaves and stacked deck-chairs, adds to the sentimentality. The conferences tell you little about the temper of the country; they are gatherings of activists and enthusiasts from the constituencies, reassuring themselves of their party's special mission and the villainy of the others. 'Conference' with a capital C is talked about as if it were a Synod or a Curia; and conference speeches however boring they may sound to the outsider, have their own secret magic for connoisseurs which can bring the house down.

Like the conventions of any profession, party conferences in Britain not only decide upon and disseminate the Word, they also provide something of a job clearing-center for young (and, often, not so young) political hopefuls. Under the British system, a member of Parliament doesn't have to live in the constituency he represents, though it is considered politic to keep an apartment there at the very least. Thus, the local constituency party's candidate selection committee is free to scour the entire nation if it so chooses in search of a promising standard-bearer. The best place to assess the available talent is at the annual party conference.

There are two types of constituencies in Britain, the so-called "safe" seats and those that are known as "marginals." Safe seats are districts which, by dint of their economic or social character, can be counted on to vote for the same party, election after election. A heavily industrialized area will invariably return a Labor MP to the House of Commons, while an agricultural or suburban one will consistently vote Conservative. Well over 400 of Britain's 635 constituencies are considered to be such safe seats. The rest, for a variety of reasons (including a changing population or recent redrawing of district lines), are not so predictable. These marginal seats can shift their allegiances with alarming (or, depending on one's point of view, reassuring) frequency, and they are the ones that determine the outcome of general elections.

Obviously, being adopted as a Tory candidate for a safe Tory seat is tantamount to winning a lifelong ticket to the House of Commons. Such seats, therefore, are reserved for party members who have proven their worth. By the same token, while running as a Tory candidate in a safe Labor seat may be viewed as an exercise in futility, it is not so in fact, for it is in carrying the party's banner in such hopeless contests that a young would-be MP eventually earns the right to a safe seat and a career in Parliament.

KEYSTONE PRESS

SYNDICATION INTERNATIONAL/RESEARCH REPORTS

Although she was a full-time politician, Mrs. Thatcher made a point of not neglecting her housewifely duties. She had a nanny to help with the children, but she did do most of the cooking and cleaning herself. Left, posing for the press after a 1978 expedition to the grocery store. After her election as Tory leader, Mrs. Thatcher's shopping basket became something of a political prop. Right, the Thatchers at home in Chelsea, in a 1976 family portrait. Soon afterwards, daughter Carol emigrated to Australia and until the 1979 campaign the family was rarely seen together.

Loyally carrying a photo of Heath to a 1973 Tory Party meeting, Mrs. Thatcher never dreamed that she would soon be challenging him for the party leadership.

After her stunning victory over Heath in the first ballot of the 1975 Tory leadership election, pundits agreed that the answer to the newspaper's question was "no".

Mrs. Thatcher in her first formal meeting with her shadow cabinet, shortly after her 1975 election as leader of the Conservative Party. The shadow cabinet is a kind of government-in-waiting whose members are selected by the leader to "shadow" their

opposite numbers in the real Cabinet, providing a focus for the opposition's attacks on government policy. Although Mrs. Thatcher's politics were unabashedly right-wing, her shadow cabinet had a number of moderates.

Harold Macmillan was prime minister when Mrs. Thatcher first entered Parliament, and it was he who gave the fledgling MP her first job as a junior minister. Even though visiting opposition leaders traditionally don't get invited to the Oval Office, Jimmy Carter made an exception when Mrs. Thatcher came to Washington in September 1977.

Such an opportunity to prove her mettle was precisely what Margaret Roberts was looking for at Llandudno. And it is precisely what she got.

Among the thousands of Tory faithful who had come to the 1948 party conference was John Miller, chairman of the Conservative party in Dartford, an industrial area—and hence, a safe Labor seat—in Kent, just east of London on the Thames. Miller's previous candidate had grown weary of banging his head against the district's unmoveable Labor wall (in the last election he had lost by more than nineteen thousand votes out of less than eighty thousand cast), and the chairman was now looking for some ambitious newcomer to fight the good, if unwinnable, fight on behalf of his constituency's outnumbered but still loyal Tories.

Also at Llandudno for the conference that year was John Grant, a director of Blackwell's, the big university bookshop in Oxford, where he had come to know Margaret Roberts. Grant found himself seated next to Miller at a speech, and hearing of his quest, said he knew just the person the Dartford Tories were looking for.

"What's his name?" Miller asked.

"It's not a him," Grant replied, "it's a her."

Miller frowned. "That's most unsuitable."

"Nonsense," came the rejoinder, "at least meet her."

Miller did, and he was sufficiently impressed by Margaret Roberts to suggest that she apply for the Dartford candidacy. There were twenty-six other applicants for the same Tory nomination, all of them men, ranging in age from twenty-eight to fifty-five. The contrast presented by the pretty, young female research chemist was startling. "My husband was so enthusiastic over her," recalls Lucy Woollcott, with whom Margaret later came to live in Dartford and whose husband, Raymond, was a member of the Tory selection committee there. "He came home saying how she was beautiful, well-dressed, and knew what she was talking about." Another member of the Dartford Conservative Association, Margaret Phillimore, has similar recollections. "It was obvious to us that she had a marvelous brain," she says. "She was very poised, even as a twenty-three-year-old, but human and likeable and good company."

In March of 1949, the committee voted to adopt Margaret Roberts as the Tory candidate for Dartford. That night, in one of those rituals so essential to the maintenance of party loyalties, she was presented to the full constituency party for formal adoption. Her speech to the crowded hall sounded what was later to become a familiar theme: the need for tax cuts in order to provide incentive for working people. Nodding approvingly on the platform was her father, Alderman Roberts from Grantham, who gave a speech of his own on her behalf. His family had always been Liberals, he said, but as far as he could see the Conservatives of 1948 stood for all the things he believed in. When her candidacy was put to a voice vote, there was only one dissent out of a crowd of four hundred. At the age of twenty-three—younger than any other woman candidate in the nation—Margaret Roberts was ready to make her first run for Parliament.

A celebratory dinner party followed the adoption meeting. It ran quite late, which posed a problem for Margaret. How was she to get back to Colchester in time for work the next morning? The solution to this problem came in the form of one Denis Thatcher, a friend of the dinner's host, who offered to drive her back to London where she could catch a train to Colchester. Ten years older than Margaret and something of a war hero (he had been mentioned in dispatches for his performance as an officer in the Royal Artillery), Denis cut a dashing figure. But though she was grateful for the ride and shared his interest in music, she didn't appreciate his fast driving and love for powerful cars. Nonetheless, they were to see more of each other.

As a result of her adoption, the young candidate quit her job in Manningtree so that she could move from Colchester to Dartford. She found work in London with the giant food concern, J. Lyons and Company Ltd. Her job was to investigate the stability of emulsions in search of a means to preserve the foamy character of an artificial product the company insisted upon calling "ice cream." (Years later, Common Market truth-in-packaging regulations forced Lyons to change the description to something more accurate.) She also ran tests to make sure that the company's food-processing systems were uncontaminated and safe. As at BX Plastics, she was regarded as a competent, analytically minded worker. But as a spokesman for the company notes, "Even then people were aware of her intense political feelings. She had a passion for politics that was unusual for a woman in those days."

At first she stayed in a boarding house in Dartford. But before long, she moved in with Raymond and Lucy Woollcott. As Mrs. Woollcott tells the story: "She came to us because she was not living properly in the boarding house. My husband, who was the local Conservative ward chairman, used to drive Margaret home in the evening after she had been campaigning. When he took her to her room, she would point at a plate of sardines on the table and say, 'That's my supper.' Well she was only twenty-three and working sixteen hours a day, and I was scandalized. So I decided to ask her to come stay with us. Then I got cold feet—

we never had children or permanent lodgers. But she came and was the perfect guest. Of course, we never let her pay a thing."

The Woollcotts lived in a typical 1930s semidetached, three-bedroom house. Margaret's room faced east, with a big window to catch the morning sun. There was a double bed, a big cupboard and wardrobe, a chair and dressing table, green curtains, and light green wallpaper. The room was heated by an electric fire in the wall.

As it had since she started university, her day began at six thirty in the morning. She would catch the seven thirty train to London, work at J. Lyons all day, and be back in Dartford by seven in the evening. After dinner with the Woollcotts, there was political business to attend to—speeches, meetings, civic affairs. "She accepted all invitations, rubbed shoulders with all sorts of people, and got herself known and liked," Mrs. Woollcott says. "She would get home at ten or ten thirty and then work in the study until one or two in the morning."

With food in short supply in postwar Britain, the Woollcotts, like many of their neighbors, raised their own vegetables and chickens. Margaret, Mrs. Woollcott recalls, was a bit particular about what she ate. "She had a tendency to get a little plump." Nonetheless, she adored Mrs. Woollcott's chocolate biscuits, and she would devour them recklessly, without regard to their effect on her waistline.

In the eighteen months she stayed with them, real affection grew up between the ambitious fledgling politician and the childless couple. "She was always sweet-tempered and considerate," insists Mrs. Woollcott. "I can say only one thing against her: she always pried open her tins of Nescafé with my silver teaspoons, and she left her mark on every one of them."

The general election in which she made her debut as a candidate did not come until February 1950. In the five previous years, the Labor government of Clement Attlee, an Oxford graduate and former lecturer at the London School of Economics, had made good on its promise to transform battle-scarred Britain into a "socialist Commonwealth." Cradle-to-grave national insurance was introduced, family welfare allowances and workman's compensation were extended, and legislation providing for universal free medical care was passed. At the same time, the government nationalized the coal industry, the railways, civil aviation, telecommunications, the utilities, and the iron and steel industry. But these ambitious programs flew in the face of Britain's crippled economic situation. Roughly twenty-five percent of the nation's prewar capital had been swallowed up by war losses; the national debt had tripled, and exports had declined badly. As the trade balance slumped further and further into the red, inflation soared—and finally, in September 1949, sterling was devalued by thirty percent, plummeting from a rate of $4.03 to the pound to just $2.80. The Tory campaign strategy seemed obvious: "Set the people free from the yoke of Socialism," Churchill thundered.

Though her party's prospects looked good nationally, Margaret Roberts stood virtually no chance of winning in Dartford. Still, she waged a vigorous, if curiously amiable, campaign. Her Labor opponent, the incumbent MP for Dartford, was a friendly and somewhat courtly man called Norman Dodds. Though the orchestra insisted on playing "Jealousy" when they found themselves dancing together at a civic ball, the two political adversaries got on well together.

Like most holders of a safe seat, Dodds campaigned in leisurely fashion. The new young Tory candidate, however, plugged persistently away at the theme that Labor's socialist enthusiasm had destroyed the economy. "Vote right to keep what's left," she urged her generally unsympathetic audiences.

As expected, Dodds retained his seat. But Margaret Roberts managed to cut his 1945 majority of more than 19 thousand votes by nearly a third—and she had increased the Tory count by half. Nationally, the Conservative party came close to doing to Labor what Labor had done to it the last time around. Attlee's majority of 146 seats in the House of Commons was slashed to just five seats. His battered government managed to cling to power for only another eighteen months. In the election of October 1951, the Tories were voted back into power—where they would stay for the next thirteen years.

THE FUTURE MRS. THATCHER

In her second general election campaign, Margaret Roberts failed to improve on her previous performance. Nonetheless, election night at her Dartford headquarters was far from gloomy. Not only was there the national Conservative triumph to celebrate, but after the votes had been tallied, Denis Thatcher took the podium to announce that he and the defeated candidate were engaged to be married.

The announcement came as something of a shock to her friends and colleagues. "She rather produced Denis out of a hat," says Margaret

Phillimore. "She was so occupied with politics and with her job that she didn't seem to have time for a boyfriend." Indeed, not long before she got engaged she had told a friend that she didn't think she'd ever be able to fit marriage into her busy life.

Characteristically, she had an eminently logical explanation for the attraction between Denis and herself. "He was in the paint and chemicals business, I was a chemist," she told an interviewer years later. "He was on the financial side, I was interested in economics. We were both interested in politics . . . We have a lot in common." Perhaps more to the point, Denis shared her political outlook almost completely, and he had been there to comfort her after her first general election defeat.

Denis Thatcher was the grandson of an enterprising Kentish farmer who around the turn of the century discovered that sodium arsenite made a good sheep dip and an even better weed killer. The eventual result was a prosperous paint and preservatives company called Atlas Preservatives, which Denis had inherited from his father. He had been educated with indifferent success at Mill Hill, and during the war had been a captain in the Royal Artillery, seeing action in Italy and France and winning at least one mention in dispatches. He had also been married before—coincidentally, to another Margaret, whom he had met in 1942. "It was one of those silly wartime marriages which never really got off the ground," is the recent recollection of the first Margaret Thatcher, now known as Lady Hickman as a result of her 1948 re-marriage to baronet Sir Howard Hickman. Thatcher himself recalled a few years ago that he and his war bride "were never able to live together because I was in the army . . . When I came back from the war, my wife and I were strangers." They were divorced—"very amicably," said Lady Hickman, who never saw him again—in 1946. (With classic English middle-class propriety, Denis Thatcher never talked about his first marriage, and it was only in the last few years that the Thatcher children learned that their mother was their father's second wife.)

Denis and his second Margaret were married on a cold, foggy day in December 1951. The non-Conformist ceremony was performed at Wesleys Chapel, a Methodist church in London; the reception took place in the country, at the Carlton Terrace in Maidstone, Kent. Some of the guests were surprised by the bride's gown: instead of white, she wore a great plumed hat and a fetchingly Elizabethan-looking velvet dress of deep Tory blue.

The Thatchers honeymooned in Portugal and Spain and began their married life by moving to the fashionable (though more so now than then) London neighborhood of Chelsea. They took a house in Flood Street, a residential block just off Kings Road, which was to remain their address for the next twenty-eight years.

CALL TO THE BAR

Mrs. Thatcher continued working—first, at J. Lyons, then as a personal assistant to the director of the Joint Iron Council. She also continued with the law courses she had begun a few months before her marriage. Her desire to be called to the bar may have been postponed for a bit, but it had not been forgotten.

In a country where almost nothing is straightforwardly organized, the British legal system is especially Byzantine. The community of lawyers is a closed and ancient one, steeped in tradition, drenched in theatricality—and organized with a shrewd eye towards maximizing revenue. British lawyers are divided into two groups: solicitors, who take cases and give advice, and barristers, the gowned and bewigged advocates who present all cases in court. The latter are by far the more exclusive and highly regarded circle, and it was this circle that Mrs. Thatcher sought to join.

More than half of Britain's barristers work within a quarter-square-mile section of London in one of the four Inns of Court: the Inner Temple, the oldest and richest; the Middle Temple, which is slightly less posh; Lincoln's Inn, which is mainly devoted to revenue law; and Gray's Inn, the youngest and most provincial of the four. The Inns are much like colleges at a university, providing barristers with dining halls, libraries, and chambers in which groups of them can cluster, not as partners in law but as colleagues who wish to share office and secretarial expenses. (Indeed, by legal tradition, barristers are great loners who work for and with no one but themselves. It is not unusual to find two barristers from the same chamber opposing each other in court—a situation that would be regarded as an unthinkable conflict of interest if it occurred between two partners in an American law firm.)

To become a barrister, one must take two exams—an intermediate and a final—which, when passed, qualify one to be called to the bar. To pass these exams requires about two years of study which can be undertaken either at a university or at a special tutorial college. (Mrs. Thatcher chose the latter, enrolling in a course at Lincoln's Inn.) Once called to the bar, the would-be barrister must go through a twelve-month pupillage in chambers—in effect, apprenticing himself to a junior barrister whom he accompanies to court and generally assists.

Mrs. Thatcher's legal studies extended through 1952. That year she wrote a newspaper article defending unconventional women such as herself who chose to have careers even after they married—especially those who chose political careers. "Should a woman arise equal to the task, I say let her have an equal chance with the men for leading Cabinet posts," she declared. "Why not a woman Chancellor [of the Exchequer] or Foreign Secretary?"

That year she also developed an abiding personal dislike for the Labor party. Labor had won control of the Grantham Town Council, and in a display of strength, unceremoniously booted Alfred Roberts off the council after his twenty-year tenure. The proud old man took the blow stoically. He simply removed his alderman's robe, folded it over his chair, and left the chamber. The following Sunday, the Labor party was attacked from the Grantham parish pulpit for what it had done. Embarrassed, the party tried to recoup by offering Roberts his former place. But he refused. Neither father nor daughter ever mentioned the episode again, but both were affected deeply by it.

Mrs. Thatcher continued her law studies even after she became pregnant early in 1953, and was five months along when she took and passed her intermediate bar exam that spring. In August, she gave birth prematurely to twins, a boy and a girl who were named Mark and Carol. It was a long labor, and Denis was not at her side. He wasn't even at the hospital. That day England had won a major cricket tournament against Australia, and since his wife was not supposed to be due for another few weeks, Denis had gone out to celebrate. When her contractions started coming, he was nowhere to be found.

The birth of her children changed Mrs. Thatcher's life somewhat, but not nearly so much as it does many women's. She did decide not to seek elective office again until they were old enough for school. But, with the help of a nanny, she continued to work—and just four months after they were born, she passed her final and was called to the bar at Lincoln's Inn. Denis was ecstatically proud. "Bar intermediate in May, produced twins in August and bar finals in December," he went around telling people, "I'd like to meet another woman who can equal that record."

Her field would be tax law. "I was really keenly interested in the financial side of politics," she later explained, "and so I went into the revenue side of law." She did her pupillage under tax barrister Peter Rowland, who was very high on her potential at the tax bar, which was a tiny group of legal technicians specializing in one of the most arcane areas of the law. She was introduced to Rowland by the head of his chambers, an elderly and rather eccentric man who met Mrs. Thatcher at a Tory lawyers' dinner at the House of Commons. "He liked her and asked her to join us," Rowland recalls. But for no apparent reason, six months later the head decided that he didn't want any women in his chambers. So the fledgling tax barrister, with all her promise, was booted out.

She quickly found another place and began to put together a career. Colleagues remember her as a hard worker with a good brain, who was polite but not really sociable. "She was capable, but machine-like and cold," says one. "At five thirty P.M. she was out the door and on her way home. There was no lingering over a glass of plonk at a Fleet Street wine bar for her."

In part, that was because of her insistence on getting home in time for the children's dinner. The Thatchers were always able to afford a full-time nanny to look after Mark and Carol, but Mrs. Thatcher was determined that they have no doubts as to who their mother was. "Margaret talked about her children often," says fellow barrister Pamela Thomas, who was with her in chambers at Lincoln's Inn. "They were an essential part of her life." Indeed, Thomas notes that for all her career ambitions, Mrs. Thatcher was "very domesticated." "I once visited her and she was turning old nursery curtains into duffel coats for her twins." Another time, Thomas saw her buy some material to make a dress—which she completed and wore to work the next week—"an impressive achievement for a person working full-time at law."

RETURN TO POLITICS

As always, however, politics remained Margaret's ruling obsession. "We talked politics over coffee every morning at eleven," Thomas recalls. "She worshipped Winston Churchill, supported Eden over Suez, and thought socialism was extremely evil."

The 1950s were probably the years of greatest change and decision in Margaret Thatcher's life. By the somewhat arbitrary (though no less real) standards of the English class system, she had married above herself. Now she was a mother, and for the first time she was involved in a career that could take her where she wanted to go. Her contacts in the party were burgeoning. ("It was difficult to grasp what standing she had in the Conservative party," says barrister Maurice Price, who shared chambers with her. "I don't think most people knew how well-placed she was. Occasionally she would drop a remark about some conversation she had had with a top minister and I would think she was pulling my leg—but of course she wasn't.") Virtually all the major attitudes that were to shape, define, and govern her later life took final form during this time. Even her personal style was fixed then—in a brisk yet still feminine simplicity that, curiously enough, always seems to remain at just the same slight remove from current fashion. (Indeed, it is an uncanny experience to compare photographs of her today with those taken twenty-five years ago. Not only does she look and dress almost exactly the same, but in neither era is she noticeably more or less out of date.)

As she came to grips with her identity, she found herself—as many people do—embarrassed by bits of her background that didn't seem to fit in neatly with the direction she saw her life taking. "Margaret went through a spell in the 1950s of despising Grantham," says her old friend Margaret Wickstead, who to this day remains close to her grammar school and Oxford chum. "She was just very bored with it, and that put local people off." (Lucy Woollcott, who still gets personal Christmas cards from the Thatchers, recalls Margaret's telling her "that at each stage of her career she had to cut herself off from her past friends.")

While Mrs. Thatcher was grappling with the question of her place in the world, so too was Britain trying to figure out where it belonged in the new postwar scheme of things. Churchill, who had not had much success removing the so-called "yoke of socialism" from the people's necks, retired in 1955 at the age of eighty-one. He was replaced by his protegé and long-time foreign secretary, Anthony Eden, who ran smack into the Suez crisis. The crisis boiled up late in 1956, when President Nasser of Egypt seized the Suez Canal, claiming that Egypt's sovereignty required it. Despite instructions from the UN to the contrary, Nasser then closed the canal to Israeli ships—whereupon Israel attacked Egypt. Before long, Britain and France had joined the conflict on Israel's side. But the U.S. refused to go along with the Anglo-French intervention—and, using UN pressure, it forced them to withdraw. A few weeks later, ostensibly on his doctor's orders, Eden retired. Harold Macmillan moved up to take his place—and to lead the retreat from empire.

For Britain, the episode was a humiliating reminder that it was no longer a world power of the first rank. That distinction now seemed reserved for the U.S. and the Soviet Union. Churchillian Tories such as Mrs. Thatcher considered this an unacceptable state of affairs. Eden had been right to protect British interests in the Near and Far East with troops, she felt; his only mistake had been to back down under American pressure. Thus galvanized, and with her children now out of their infancy, Mrs. Thatcher resolved to return again to electoral politics in earnest. She had considered returning to active politics as early as 1955, when she had toyed with the idea of seeking her party's nomination for the safe Tory seat of Orpington, a suburban community just southwest of London. (It was just as well she didn't get it; Orpington was later to fall in an astonishing upset to the Liberals.) In any case, now, after Suez, she was more determined than ever to secure a seat in Parliament. It wouldn't be easy. She had decided to restrict her search for a constituency to the London area—the metropolis itself and the immediately surrounding counties. Her reason was simple: if she came to represent a constituency farther away, she would on occasion be forced to leave the twins overnight—and that she refused to do.

She tried first for the Kent constituency of Beckenham. It was an infuriating experience. The selection committee made it clear that it considered her talented, bright, and able—but that it also felt she really should be at home with the children. The same thing happened when she applied for Maidstone.

Then she heard that Sir John Crowder, the veteran Tory MP for the north London constituency of Finchley, was planning to retire. Along with nearly two hundred other would-be MPs, she submitted her name to the Finchley Conservative Association's selection committee. To make their job manageable, the committee asked all the applicants the same set of questions and scored the answers numerically. On that basis, the unwieldy mob was winnowed down to just four finalists—Mrs. Thatcher among them. All were to appear before the local party's divisional council, a group of fifty or so rank-and-filers who represented all the Tory party workers in the district.

The day before this ordeal, one of the four finalists was selected for another safe Tory seat, and so he dropped out. That left three, but as far as the Finchley council was concerned, there was no real choice. Recalls council member John Tiplady: "I know it may seem like hindsight, but when we interviewed the candidates, we asked ourselves, 'Is this a future Prime Minister?' Margaret clearly was and everyone thought so."

Denis Thatcher was away on a business trip in South Africa at the time. Two days later, he was on an airplane when he picked up a discarded London newspaper in which he read the news that come the next general election, his wife would almost certainly be representing the people of Finchley in the House of Commons.

4
Rising MP

"You have to build an armor round yourself . . ."

THE PALACE OF WESTMINSTER, the huge Gothic edifice that includes the famous clock tower known the world over as Big Ben as well as the Houses of Commons and Lords (which together comprise the British Parliament), sprawls along the north bank of the Thames in the heart of London like an ancient, oversized imperial barque long ago beached by some primordial tempest. Inside, it is a surrealistic combination of medieval cathedral, Victorian boys' school, and Edwardian men's club, governed by arcane though strictly enforced tradition and sustained by an overwhelming sense of history as extravagant as it is justified.

The monarch still opens each yearly session of Parliament by reading a speech—written by the current government, and outlining its legislative goals—to the ermine-robed and coroneted peers and bishops of the House of Lords. But the real power runs through the directly elected members of the House of Commons whose complexion determines the government. Although the House of Lords is not entirely without significance, it is for the most part a vestigial body, far more a source of curiosity, pageantry, and entertainment than policy or influence; on the rare occasions when it is mentioned in debate by MPs in the Commons, it is never referred to by its actual name, but invariably as "the other place"—as if it were some remote and faintly unspeakable netherworld whose activities and inmates are not really worth the attention of serious men.

Physically the House of Commons is a surprisingly small, rectangular room, just sixty-eight feet long. Down its length run long, green leather benches, built up from the clerk's table in the center in two opposing arrays of bleachers in which the governing and opposition parties sit facing each other. The party leaders and their top aides sit in the front benches, while the rank-and-file MPs are relegated to the back. Thus, all of the government's ministers—along with their counterparts on the opposition side, who are known as "shadow" ministers—are referred to as frontbenchers. By the same token, the majority of members who have not been assigned any portfolio by their party are known as backbenchers.

The chamber can be an astonishingly unruly place, sounding more like a raucous beer hall or barnyard than the distinguished "Mother of Parliaments" it happens to be. Speakers from the prime minister on down face constant interruptions: catcalls, insults, and shouts of encouragement are the order of the day every day, and major speeches invariably end amid a boisterous cacophony of intermingled cries of "hear, hear" and "shame," often accompanied by enthusiastic foot-pounding and seat-banging. Although, by tradition, members usually refer to each other as "my honorable friend" (or, if the person happens ever to have been a minister, as "my right honorable friend"), an imaginative and occasionally scandalous array of epithets can follow that gentlemanly salutation. In 1978, a Labor backbencher was ordered by the chair to apologize to the House for calling his right honorable friend, the shadow foreign secretary, a "fat-assed twit." But anything short of that is generally considered permissable.

As Anthony Sampson has noted, "It is clear as the Emperor's Clothes that all most members do about power is to talk about it. The House is like a steam-engine, hissing steam, puffing and whistling, which is secretly powered by electricity . . . [For] unless there is a temporary and zany alliance of backbenchers the vote always goes with the Government." Sampson is right, of course—though one should never underestimate the importance of talk in British politics. "Through talk we tamed kings, restrained tyrants, averted revolution, and ultimately reflected public needs in such a way as to help shape public policy," Tony Benn, once an aristocrat called Lord Stansgate and now a leader of the Labor party's left wing, pointed out several years ago. Still, though no party leader can afford to ignore the feelings of his backbenchers, the fact is that when it comes to major votes, discipline is ruthlessly enforced by the aptly named party whips.

In this sense, as in many others, the British House of Commons is quite different from the American Congress. "To get along, go along," may be the instruction given to every freshman legislator upon his arrival in Washington. But it is nonetheless possible to make a career bucking the congressional establishment. Certainly, given a faithful electorate and a shrewd turn of mind, a U.S. congressman or senator can create for himself an independent barony without necessarily toeing anybody's party line. In the House of Commons, this is not the case. One is either in the government or out of it, on the front bench or not. There are, to be sure, factions within the parties, and a young MP does not have to see eye to eye with his leader on every issue in order to rise. But in the end, there is almost no way for an MP to make his presence known and felt in the House outside of the establishment, except as a relic or an eccentric.

NEW GIRL IN THE HOUSE

This was the place to which Margaret Thatcher came for her first term as an MP in October 1959: a self-confident, secure, and somewhat smug institution. Outwardly at least, the country and the Conservative party were both in good shape. Tempered by memories of the mass unemployment of the Great Depression and his own experience of the hardships of war, Prime Minister Harold Macmillan was a popular and respected mixture of old Edwardian, Balliol College intellectualism, and humane Toryism. He led his party from the left of its center, though in the words of long-time Tory MP Nigel Fisher, "He knew when to make right-wing speeches."

Under Macmillan, Britain's Tory government tried to keep up full employment, intervened in industry when it felt it was necessary, and boosted public spending. As a result, by the late 1950s the British economy was booming, and standards of living—especially after the years of postwar scarcity—seemed on a dizzying escalator that could only go up. Inflation, however, was beginning to become a worry. In 1958, Macmillan's chancellor of the exchequer, Peter Thorneycroft, insisted that the government cut its budget by £150 million. Macmillan, along with most of his Cabinet, refused—on the grounds that "it was not politically possible." Thorneycroft (along with two like-minded junior ministers) thereupon resigned from the government and returned to the back benches. But much to the amusement of the press and public, the prime minister, who was off on a tour of the Commonwealth at the time, dismissed the flap as merely "a little local difficulty"—a nicely blasé touch that enhanced his reputation for coolness and control.

The Conservatives' 1959 budget cut taxes by £350 million, adding to the sense of prosperity. "You never had it so good," Macmillan told the nation in a famous speech—and most agreed with him. To be sure, the boom was dwindling, but it had yet to collapse. In the 1959 general election, which brought Margaret Thatcher to Westminster, the Tories widened their majority in the Commons from fifty-eight seats to one hundred seats. Cartoonists portrayed Macmillan as "Super Mac," and a 1960 Gallup poll gave him an astonishing seventy-nine percent popularity rating.

Macmillan's free-spending ways did not sit well with the new member for Finchley. But for the most part, Mrs. Thatcher was content to keep her feelings to herself. Her main concerns at the time were those of any new MP. There was the matter of her maiden speech—in effect, her debut in the House. As with any new job, first impressions are terribly important in the House of Commons—all the more because, with over 600 members (630 at the time of Mrs. Thatcher's first election), it is quite easy for a newcomer to be lost in the shuffle. Many new members have gotten their parliamentry careers off to a strong start with a good maiden speech, while others have had to work for years to overcome the effects of a dismal one.

Not only did Mrs. Thatcher have to worry about her maiden speech; she also had to contend with the fact that she had come second in the drawing for Private Member's Bills. This was an amazing stroke of good fortune for a tyro MP interested in making a name for herself. As the term implies, a Private Member's Bill is a piece of legislation introduced, not through the party machinery, but by an individual member on his or her own. Given the press of government business in the House, there is not much room on the agenda for such bills. So the House conducts a lottery of sorts among those MPs (more than 300 in all in October 1959) who have one in mind. Those whose names are among the first out of the hat, get their chance; the others must wait till next session.

Mrs. Thatcher's bill was called the "Public Bodies (Admission of the Press to Meetings) Bill." As its name indicated, the bill was designed to force local governments to admit reporters to certain official council and committee meetings. It was inspired not so much by Mrs. Thatcher's devotion to freedom of the press as by her antipathy to trade unions and Labor politicians. Earlier that year, there had been a printers' strike at some newspapers; in a show of solidarity, a number of Labor-controlled local government councils had refused to let strikebreaking reporters cover their meetings.

The bill was scheduled to be debated for the first time on February 5, 1960. What better opportunity to make her maiden speech, Mrs. Thatcher decided, than on the occasion of introducing her own piece of legislation to the House. February 5 was a Friday, a day when the chamber is usually nearly empty, most members having scattered for the weekend to their homes and constituencies. Nonetheless, more than a hundred MPs, including her old acquaintance from her days as OUCA president, former Chancellor of the Exchequer Peter Thorneycroft, turned up to hear the "new girl." (One important figure was absent from the visitors' gallery: Denis Thatcher was off on a business trip to the Mideast.) Speaking without notes, Mrs. Thatcher gave a thirty-minute explanation of her complicated and somewhat controversial bill. It was an impressive performance; even opponents of the bill conceded her speech had been of "frontbench quality."

The bill was eventually passed by the House, though her success was not precisely unqualified. Not only was the final version heavily amended, but the Tory-controlled council in her own constituency of Finchley refused to pass a motion congratulating Mrs. Thatcher on her accomplishment. Indeed, the leader of the council made a point of saying that *his* committee meetings would never be open to the press.

Still, it was an auspicious beginning. Thereafter, however, Mrs. Thatcher kept a relatively low profile in the House. To be sure, as the youngest of the twenty-five women in the Commons at the time, she was something of curiosity, and as such got more than her share of speaking invitations and press attention. In 1960, she was named as one of six Women of the Year by a London charity. At the luncheon held to commemorate the event, she revealed a penchant for romantic illusion which many commentators have since argued has always colored her politics. When asked who she would most like to be if she couldn't be herself, Mrs. Thatcher cited Ann Leonowen, the celebrated governess of *Anna and the King of Siam.* The reason, she explained, was that Anna had "a sense of purpose and the perseverance to carry out this purpose. She went to Siam with a sense of purpose and, because of her, slavery was abolished." That, of course, was the story Anna told in her own self-serving biography (and which was repeated in the hit musical *The King and I*). The fact that the story was almost totally inaccurate seems to have been either unknown or unimportant to Mrs. Thatcher.

BURGEONING FRONTBENCHER

Margaret Thatcher worked hard as an MP—so hard, in fact, that in October 1960 she collapsed in the House, apparently from overwork, and had to be rushed home. Her dedication quickly paid off. Just two years after she entered the House, she was invited into Macmillan's government as a junior minister—meaning she was a frontbencher but not a member of Cabinet—working in the area of pensions and national insurance. (Again, Denis was not around to celebrate the event; he was in Africa on another business trip.) It is not clear precisely why she was promoted so soon. "When Margaret first came into Parliament no one thought she was a particularly outstanding MP," notes a now-retired senior official in the Conservative party. Most likely it was because she was a woman. Both parties liked (and still do) to have a few women scattered through their front benches, and she was replacing one (Patricia Hornsby-Smith) who had been dropped in a minor reshuffling.

Mrs. Thatcher's ministerial debut in a Commons debate did not come for another six months, but when it did—in March 1962—she displayed what was to become her parliamentary trademark. In a forty-four-minute exposition defending the government's pensions policy, "she left MPs stunned with statistics," as one observer put it, citing everything from the cost of living in smoking and nonsmoking households to pension levels in Denmark to bolster her case. Indeed, she either stunned the House or put it to sleep—for once she had concluded, the speaker of the house, its presiding officer, had to call twice before another member jumped up to claim the floor.

Nonetheless, something of the innocent provincial still clung to Mrs. Thatcher. During one pensions debate, an aide passed some just-released statistics to her while she was in the midst of addressing the Commons. "Gentlemen," cried the attractive young frontbencher, "I have the latest red-hot figure!" The House exploded in laughter, much to her consternation and bewilderment.

By this time, things were no longer going so well for the nation. In 1960, Macmillan had shocked not only his own party but much of Britain with what in retrospect seems to have been one of the most prescient speeches by a British prime minister since Churchill's 1946 warning in Virginia that "an iron curtain has descended across the Continent." Speaking in Capetown, South Africa, Macmillan noted, "In the twentieth century . . . we have seen the awakening of national consciousness in people who have for centuries lived in dependence on some other power. Fifteen years ago this movement spread through Asia . . . Today the same thing is happening in Africa . . . The wind of change is blowing through this continent and, whether we like it or not . . . we must all accept it . . . and our national policies must take account of it."

With this address—which later became known as the "wind of change" speech—Macmillan effectively reversed the imperial expansionism that had been a hallmark of Tory policy since Disraeli. By 1962, his government had decolonized virtually all of Africa and the Caribbean, relegating to history the memory of the once-powerful British empire.

At the same time that Macmillan was dismantling the empire abroad, Britain's economy was slipping badly at home. The country that just a year or two earlier had never had it so good was now facing a run on its currency, a balance of payments crisis, and a government-imposed "wage pause" to slow inflation. "Super Mac" no longer seemed so super; his popularity plummeted to the lowest point reached by a prime minister since Chamberlain was attacked as the "appeaser" of Munich. In March 1962, a by-election (which is held when a seat falls vacant between general elections because of an MP's death or resignation) in the once safe Tory constituency of Orpington saw the Conservatives suffer one of their worst defeats ever: overcoming a previous Tory majority of fourteen thousand votes, the Liberal candidate won the contest by a healthy margin of seventy-eight hundred.

In an attempt to regain his popularity, Macmillan agreed with those in the party who were calling for an increase in government spending. But once again, his chancellor of the exchequer—this time, Selwyn Lloyd— declined to go along. So did six other cabinet ministers. To get his policy through, Macmillan was forced into what became known as "the July Massacre"—a massive cabinet shake-up that disturbed the public and angered the party.

Unfortunately, Macmillan's attempt to prime the pump didn't work. The economy continued to slump, unemployment continued to rise, and the Tories continued to lose by-elections. The end of the road for Macmillan was in sight—and it came in 1963 in the form of a one-two punch.

The first blow involved the recently formed European Economic Community—or Common Market, as it came to be known. The EEC had been organized in 1956 by six European nations, Britain not among them. On July 31, 1961, Macmillan submitted Britain's first application to join. As far as he was concerned, it marked a final move away from Britain's traditional role as a "broker" in Europe—a role whose independence was founded on Britain's possession of what was originally the empire and later the Commonwealth, as well as on its "special relationship" with the U.S.

Not everyone was so sure that joining the Common Market would be a good thing for Britain. British entry, argued Hugh Gaitskell, the articulate and moderate successor to Clement Attlee as leader of the Labor party, would mean "the end of Britain as an independent European state . . . the end of a thousand years of history"—an unfortunate bit of rhetoric which provided Deputy Prime Minister R. A. Butler with the chance to riposte: "For them a thousand years of history books, for us the future."

But though the Tories seemed to be winning the argument at home, Macmillan was at cross-purposes with himself abroad. In December 1962, he scored a great coup by persuading President Kennedy—with whom he had something of a father-son relationship—to give Britain access to the Polaris missile, at the time America's most sophisticated nuclear weapon and the key to any independent British deterrent. If anything, this agreement seemed to reaffirm the Anglo-American "special relationship." It certainly did as far as French President Charles De-Gaulle was concerned. Thus, on January 14, 1963, DeGaulle vetoed Britain's application to join the Common Market. "One day, perhaps England will be admitted to Europe," he suggested bitterly, "after it has detached itself from its ties with the Commonwealth and the United States." For Macmillan, who had made Europe the basis of his appeal to the 1962 Tory Party Conference, DeGaulle's action came as a personal blow.

But if that blow came from a cause that many regarded as sacred, the second half of the one-two punch that finished Macmillan had considerably more profane origins. The Profumo Affair—involving a model known as Christine Keeler, a junior minister in the War Office named John Profumo, and a variety of other characters including the Russian Naval Attaché and a London society osteopath—may not have compromised British security but it did destroy whatever was left of Macmillan's reputation for efficiency and good sense. In a June 1963 vote of confidence forced as a result of Profumo's resignation after he first denied and then admitted having had an affair with Miss Keeler (who had also been involved with the Russian), twenty-seven Tory backbenchers abstained from supporting the prime minister. That still left Macmillan with a majority of sixty-three in the Commons, but it was a clear indication of how badly support for him had waned.

His reputation damaged and his health failing, Macmillan faced the possibility that his party's MPs (known collectively as the Tory Parliamentary Party) might demand his replacement as prime minister before the next election, which was due in 1964. In October of 1963, just before that year's Party Conference, Macmillan went into the hospital with prostate trouble. At the same time, he sent a letter to the Tory convention in Blackpool announcing his retirement on grounds of ill health. Before the letter arrived, he summoned to his bedside Alec Douglas-Home, the fourteenth Earl of Home, a well-respected though not terribly powerful former Tory MP (he had to give up his seat when he inherited his earldom in 1951), who though now in the House of Lords, was serving as foreign secretary. To Home's amazement, Macmillan announced he should now consider himself a candidate for party leader. Macmillan did not want to be succeeded by his deputy prime minister, R. A. Butler, whom he regarded as neither sufficiently tough for the job nor capable of winning widespread support within the party. His real first choice was Viscount Hailsham, who, as Quintin Hogg in the days before he inherited his title, had been Tory MP for Oxford and now served in the cabinet as lord president of the council. But as with Butler, Macmillan feared Hailsham could not command wide support. So he was turning to Home.

In those days, the Tories did not elect their party leaders directly but relied rather on a semimystical process known as "emergence"—in effect, an unstructured though reasonably effective process of consensus. Thus, "soundings" were taken in the cabinet as to whom its members might like to see replace Macmillan. Five ministers opposed Home, and it seems clear that if Butler had put up a fight, he could have had the prime ministership. But for the sake of party unity, Butler fell in behind Macmillan's choice.

Home replaced Macmillan on October 18, 1963, becoming the first hereditary peer to serve as prime minister since the Marquis of Salisbury, who retired in 1902. Indeed, Home had to renounce his title (becoming, in the process, merely Sir Alec Douglas-Home) and wait three weeks for a by-election in order to get a seat for himself in Commons.

Though Home himself was well liked, the undemocratic nature of his succession irked many Britons, who considered it a totally inappropriate method of selecting a national leader. As a result of the flap that subsequently arose, Home later changed the Tory process for picking a leader—making it sufficiently democratic and open that years later a comparative outsider was able to unseat a distinctly uncooperative former prime minister.

Conscious that he lacked a popular mandate and encouraged by a few

Tory by-election victories, Home decided to call an election less than a year after he assumed the prime ministership. At first it seemed like a shrewd move: just two weeks before the October 1964 general election, a Gallup poll put the Tories nearly three percentage points ahead of Labor—their first lead in over two years. But the Labor party he was facing in that election was quite a different group from the bitter, divided bunch Macmillan had crushed so convincingly in 1959.

Hugh Gaitskell, the great centrist and diplomat, had tried unsuccessfully to get the Labor party to expunge from its constitution the clause that committed it to hard-core socialism. This was the famous "Clause Four," which pledged Labor to seek a society based on "the common ownership of the means of production, distribution, and exchange . . ." The attempt failed—mainly because of the opposition of the big trade unions—but Gaitskell did manage to unite his party and recapture for it the so-called "center ground" of British politics. By 1962, many in Britain, both in and out of the Labor party, expected him to be their next prime minister.

But in January of 1963, Gaitskell died. Labor had lost its last great postwar leader; its future belonged to a generation of men all of whom had grown up during the war and come into the party after V-E Day. The shrewdest, if not the brightest, of the bunch was Harold Wilson, a quondam left-winger who in fact had run against Gaitskell for the leadership in 1960. But Wilson was less a socialist than he was a technocrat—and less a technocrat than a brilliant political manipulator. And to the extent that politics is about symbols and imagery, Wilson was well equipped to claim the leadership of a nation in decline, whose old solutions had clearly failed and which was currently being led by a Scottish laird bearing an all-too-similar resemblance to a world long since gone.

In the 1964 campaign, Wilson emphasized the difference between himself and Home, arguing pointedly: "After a half-century of democratic advance, the whole process has ground to a halt with a 14th Earl" (to which Lord Home wittily retorted: "As far as the 14th Earl is concerned, I suppose Mr. Wilson, when you come to think of it, is the 14th Mr. Wilson"). But Wilson made it more than just a contest between an old aristocrat and a young meritocrat. He promised Britain the fruits of a scientific age and the benefits of rational management by an enlightened state. He hit hard on economic issues, charging the Tories with "thirteen wasted years." They were incompetent, he said, and he blamed them for a £500 million balance of payments deficit. The Conservatives countered by accusing Labor of planning massive tax increases, widespread nationalization, and the total disarmament of Britain. It was a confusing and strangely lifeless campaign.

Back in Finchley, Margaret Thatcher was having troubles of her own. Her constituency had a fairly large Jewish population, and there had been reports that the local country club was discriminating against Jews. The issue was seized upon by the Liberals, and in the May 1963 local elections, they had actually outpolled the Tories by five thousand votes. Still, she managed to hang on, though her majority was halved. Nationally, however, the Tories' huge parliamentary majority evaporated. When all the votes were counted, Labor had a four-seat edge in the House of Commons. Harold Wilson was the new prime minister.

At first, the Tories retained Home as their leader. With such a small majority, Wilson might call another election at any moment, and they did not want to be caught in the midst of an intraparty squabble over succession. But when the prime minister announced that there would be no general election in 1965, the party began to look for a new figure who could better lead them during their next chance at the polls. Under the new procedures laid down by Home after his own controversial selection, the new Tory leader would be chosen by a secret ballot of all Conservative MPs. The man they wound up electing was Edward Heath, a shy, socially uncomfortable bachelor who was nonetheless a brilliant politician.

The son of a Kent master builder, Ted Heath was an enthusiastic amateur musician and a graduate of Balliol College, Oxford, which he had attended on an organ scholarship. He had entered Parliament in 1950 and rose extremely fast. Within five years, he was chief Tory whip, a position that gave him an unmatched knowledge of the party's often unpredictable backbenchers. Macmillan considered him a trusted lieutenant (indeed, the two had dined together the night before Macmillan replaced Eden as prime minister); he brought him into the cabinet as minister for labor and then, as lord privy seal, put him in charge of Britain's 1961 EEC application. After the 1964 general election, Heath served Home as shadow chancellor, and he had impressed the entire House with his clause-by-clause dissection of Harold Wilson's first Finance Bill.

OPPOSITION SPOKESMAN

It was under Heath that Margaret Thatcher began her real rise to power. Immediately after his election, he gave her the job of the opposition's junior spokesman on housing and land. Six months later she was switched to become the party's number-two spokesman on treasury matters. In March 1967 she was brought into the shadow cabinet for the first time, serving as shadow minister for power. Eighteen months later, she was given the transport portfolio, and a year after that she got education, a controversial area which was soon to make her a truly national figure—though not quite in the way she might have intended.

The reasons for her rapid rise during this period are not immediately discernable. Tory journalist Ferdinand Mount has suggested that she might be regarded as "the Evita of the Tory party." Mrs. Thatcher, he wrote recently, moved up so quickly "not despite but because of her sex . . . It was not so much her own brilliance as the chronic shortage of Conservative women MPs that insured her rapid promotion."

Whatever the reasons, the fact was she performed creditably as an opposition spokesman, no matter what the portfolio, giving as good as she got in the rough-and-tumble of Commons debates. Indeed, she was occasionally used in areas outside her portfolio to add punch to the Tory lineup. In May 1968, for example, while serving as shadow power minister, she was assigned to wind up the opposition arguments in a censure debate on the government's inflation policy. As usual, she came formidably armed with facts and figures. ("She always wanted twice as much detail as other shadow ministers," recalls a researcher at the Conservative party's central office. "You could never cut corners with her.") Thus prepared, she proceeded to demolish Labor's argument that the previous Tory government had saddled Britain with a huge trade deficit. Such performances prompted the pro-Conservative *Daily Telegraph* to wonder: "Why has it been left to Mrs. Thatcher to do the homework?"

One of her most widely quoted remarks of the time came from a May 1965 speech she gave in London's Royal Albert Hall to five thousand members of the National Union of Townswomen's Guilds. "In politics," she told them, "if you want anything said, ask a man; if you want anything *done*, ask a woman." But the fact was there was very little she could do, politically or otherwise, as a member of the opposition. Being an opposition spokesman is an almost totally negative job. Her brief was a highly partisan one: to attack and discredit whatever her counterpart in the government had to say.

Oddly enough, for all her strongly held beliefs, she was regarded at the time as something of a Tory moderate. It's hard to see where such a reputation might have come from, for she consistently voted for the death penalty and against abortion and homosexual-rights reform, and she was also an outspoken advocate of corporal punishment in the prisons. Indeed, her Albert Hall feminism notwithstanding, she was a dogged opponent of anti-sex-discrimination legislation. At the 1968 Tory Party Conference, in fact, she led the opposition to a motion endorsing equal rights for woman, ending her speech with an often repeated quotation from Sophocles: "Once a woman is made equal to a man she becomes his superior."

Such positions no doubt came easily to her because in her own life there seemed to be no conflict between her career and her role as a wife and mother. "It depends on the kind of woman you are," she said, "whether you can play a number of different roles simultaneously and change easily from one to another." That she could certainly do. The hardheaded opposition spokesman could be found on what she called her weekend "flop days" wallowing away the morning in the bath and spending the afternoon sorting towels. It was, she said, "great therapy" for getting away from politics.

Of course, it was "great therapy" for her because she didn't *have* to be doing it. By British standards, the Thatchers were quite well off. In 1965, Denis Thatcher had sold his family's company to Burmah Oil for £530,000—roughly $1.5 million in the currency of the time. On top of that, they were pulling in a combined income—he from his job as an executive with Burmah, she from her parliamentary salary plus fees from speaking engagements and writing—of well over the equivalent of $60,000 a year. Even by American standards of the time that was a healthy income; by British standards, it was enormous. Mrs. Thatcher always insisted that they were never *really* wealthy. But though in some ways they lived modestly (she did all the interior decorating herself, for example), there was always plenty of money for a full-time English nanny—never a foreign au pair girl—to mind the children and, later on, regular Christmas skiing vacations in Switzerland. Clearly, both Mr. and Mrs. Thatcher worked hard for their money. Equally clearly, they were both amply rewarded.

She was also aided in her desire to have both a career and a family by the congenial aspects of parliamentary life. "I could never have combined family and public life had my constituency not been in London," she told Kenneth Harris of *The Observer* in a February 1979 interview. What's more, for all the occasional all-night sittings of Parliament, an MP's hours are not really all that bad. The House sits for only about thirty-two weeks a year, with a twelve-week break from August through mid-October. When it is in session, the Commons convenes at 2:30 P.M.

and adjourns at 10:30 Monday through Thursday. On Fridays, business starts at 11 A.M., but ends up usually at 4:30 P.M. Of course, ministers have a considerable amount of ministerial business to attend to; but the responsibilities of their opposition counterparts (which was Mrs. Thatcher's role for much of the 1960s) are far more limited. In any case, as she told Harris, "a great thing [about a career in Parliament] is that they provide vacations which coincide with the school holidays, so you're able to see a lot of your children then."

And her children cooperated, even saving their illnesses (through happy coincidence) for their mother's free time. It was, conveniently enough, a Saturday when Mark suffered a ruptured appendix. His mother was able to spend the weekend with him at the hospital; by Monday, when she had to be back at Westminster, the worst was over.

Like many parents of her generation, Mrs. Thatcher raised her children far less strictly than she herself had been raised. Mark and Carol were baptized, not as Methodists, but in the considerably more easygoing Church of England. And Mrs. Thatcher was never a stern disciplinarian. Such forbidden pleasures of her childhood as dances and birthday parties were for Mark and Carol an integral and normal part of growing up. The children were almost always taken along on those skiing trips to Switzerland, and there was a cottage in Kent for sunshine and fresh air on the weekends. They also were provided with a far more secure educational start than their mother had enjoyed. No provincial grammar schools would do for them. Instead, there was exclusive Harrow for Mark and the equally posh St. Paul's School for Girls for Carol. Mark and Carol weren't exactly spoiled, but they were a bit what the English call toffee-nosed. Her old friend Margaret Wickstead recalls Mrs. Thatcher's bringing the twins over for a visit when they were about ten. While the two women talked indoors, the Thatcher children, garbed immaculately in white, played outside with the Wickstead kids, who were dressed in blue jeans and T-shirts. At the end of the day, Mrs. Thatcher instructed her son to say good-by to one of her friend's children. "Oh no, mummy," Mrs. Wickstead recalls Mark saying, "I couldn't possibly say good-bye to someone so scruffy."

TIMES OF TRIAL

The mid-1960s were a frenetic and exciting time in Britain. The brash new Mersey beat that had blossomed in Liverpool at the beginning of the decade had by now spread throughout the world. British rock groups like the Beatles and the Rolling Stones were transforming popular music, and in the process, leading a global cultural revolution among the young. It was the time of Carnaby Street and hippies, swinging London and, many thought, a new Renaissance for Britain. Politically, Harold Wilson had captivated the nation with glittering talk of multi-million-pound schemes that would harness the latest technology and know-how to change century-old attitudes and conditions in a matter of years.

With Tory popularity at low tide and his own booming, Wilson decided to call another general election early in 1966. Labor's election manifesto (what Americans would call its "platform") was not much different from the manifesto of 1964. It concentrated on Tory mismanagement of the economy during the "Thirteen Wasted Years" of 1951-64, and it promised a bright new technological future under the calm and rational leadership of a Labor government. "You know Labor Government works," went the party's slogan. Wilson was at his oratorical best, slashing the Conservatives' "amateurism" and their "Edwardian" manner.

Ted Heath responded with cool stubbornness. The Tories entitled their manifesto "Action not Words," and set out five main promises to the electorate: changes in taxation and economic reform, a review of social services, trade union reform, entry into the Common Market, and improved housing. Heath hammered these points home methodically, emphasizing the growing threat of inflation under Labor as prices and wages regularly outpaced productivity. His aim was to shock the country into recognizing that beneath Wilson's upbeat rhetoric and the temporary blessings of some good trade figures and a stable pound, the British economy was in fact ailing badly.

But the country was in no mood to listen. Wilson had effectively pinned on the Tories the blame for Britain's current economic woes. What's more, there was a general feeling that Wilson had not yet been given a fair chance to deliver on his glittering promises of 1964. The campaign bored the press and public—and no one was very surprised when on March 31, 1966, Labor's four-seat majority in the House jumped to nearly one hundred seats. It was a clear mandate for Wilson to flex the government's muscles as he had promised he would. No longer would Britain suffer Tory temporizing about the free market, which invariably led to last-minute, frantic interventions in times of crisis. Under Wilson, the government would be *active*, things would get *done*, problems would be *solved*.

Labor having accepted responsibility for curing the country's problems, Heath was left to prepare for the future—a future, he was convinced, in which Labor's solutions would fail. He had predicted econom-

CENTRAL PRESS

KEYSTONE PRESS

With the prime ministership at last within her grasp, Mrs. Thatcher plunged enthusiastically into the 1979 general election campaign, happily accepting a kiss from a cheeky Cockney supporter in London's East End. Above left, riding a navy rescue rig at the London Boat Show, she wasn't averse to showing a bit of leg. Below left, talking seriously with pensioners was more her style. Below right, on election day, the candidate and her family sport confident smiles.

After casting her vote in the 1979 general election, Mrs. Thatcher finds a mob of newsmen on hand to record the event. Below, in high spirits, Mr. and Mrs. Thatcher arrive at Finchley Town Hall on election night for the vote-counting in her own constituency. Right, the results finally in, the new prime minister and her husband wave to the crowd in front of their new home in Downing St.

At the State Opening of Parliament following the 1979 election, the court official known as Black Rod appears in the Commons to summon the new prime minister and her fellow MPs to hear the Queen's Speech.

SYGMA

*Just before the opening session of the June 1979 Common
Market summit in Strasbourg, Mrs. Thatcher has a word
with West German Chancellor Helmut Schmidt as French
President Valéry Giscard d'Estaing leads them on a walk
through town. Strasbourg was Mrs. Thatcher's summit debut,
and she made a big hit with most of her European
counterparts, especially Chancellor Schmidt.*

96

ic decline and offered the hard medicine of public spending cuts and less state intervention coupled with a restoration of incentives to get the economy moving again. Though the Conservatives had been crushed at the polls, Heath's personal standing within the party had never been higher. No one had expected the Conservatives to win the election, and what many regarded as Heath's highly principled Toryism in the campaign sent his stock soaring.

In fact, Heath had good reason to look forward to the future. Wilson's oratory and his party's convincing victory notwithstanding, Britain had run up a £265 million trade deficit in 1965. What's more, production had increased barely over two percent, while wages and prices were roaring ahead. Almost as soon as the last victory toasts had been drunk, Wilson's government was faced with an economic headache that never let up.

Bread and butter issues had been at the center of every British election since the war. But Wilson's harping on Tory incompetence, the humiliating sterling crises and wage freezes, focused the country's attention as never before on the need to get things moving again. Wilson was determined to beat inflation—but without resorting to currency devaluations or wage and price controls.

His approach depended heavily upon planning and the accurate forecasting of economic performance combined with no-nonsense jaw-boning of trade unions to get voluntary wage restraint. Economic planning was not new to Britain. Macmillan had established a National Economic Development Council in 1962 to keep tabs on how the economy was doing and to make educated guesses as to where it was going. But Wilson was what the French called a *"dirigiste"*; he believed in providing strong direction, and he wanted to go a lot further than Macmillan had. So in 1964 he had established a full-fledged Department of Economic Affairs that would oversee the nation's economic future. This department set up a wide range of economic development committees at all levels of industry. Their aim: to make things work. By 1965, Wilson was organizing a National Plan designed to achieve twenty-five percent growth over the next half-decade. He was, he said after his March 1966 victory, dedicated to a "new spirit of anti-amateurism"; if he had to, he was perfectly prepared to "drag firms kicking and screaming into the twentieth century."

It was heady stuff, and the public loved it. His popularity rose even higher in June 1966 when he arm-twisted the unions into agreeing to support new legislation that would require both workers and employers to give the government advance warning of any and all wage and price increases.

But it was downhill after that. Britain's economic ailments could no longer be obscured by flashy public relations. The treasury began urging a devaluation of the pound sterling. Wilson refused. Instead, he opted for the only real alternative: massive cuts in public spending. In July 1966 Wilson announced his cuts, retracting at a stroke a laundry list of Labor election promises on housing, pensions, and medical care. He also called for a six-month wage and price freeze—something that enraged the unions and his party's left wing. When the Commons finally got to vote on the cuts early in August, Wilson's majority of nearly one hundred was slashed to just fifty-two. His left wing had deserted him. They were not about to let the Tories actually topple him, but they certainly had no intention of hiding their displeasure.

In any case, the budget cuts proved to be too little and too late. The treasury once more began to insist on devaluation. But Chancellor of the Exchequer James Callaghan was vehemently opposed to such a course, and he threatened to resign if Wilson continued to hold out. The unions and many Labor party rank-and-filers—who were, and still are, for the most part, considerably more left wing than the parliamentary leadership—grew more determined in their opposition to Wilson's wage-price freeze. As Macmillan had learned only a few years earlier, the public's affection is a fickle thing. Like the fallen "Super Mac," Wilson saw his popularity ebb with astonishing speed.

The first four months of 1967 saw Labor lose a string of by-elections. In April of that year, the Tories captured control of the metropolitan London government for the first time in thirty-three years. People were losing faith in Wilson; they were confused by his changes of direction and wondered what had happened to all his promises of a calm, decisive government that would produce results. Things grew worse still in July 1967: the trade gap widened, unemployment hit a postwar record, and exports stagnated under the weight of an overvalued pound. Still, Wilson refused to devalue.

By the fall exports had declined badly—and when a massive dock strike in early November produced the worst trade figures yet, Wilson no longer had any choice. But the devaluation was handled clumsily. Callaghan gave the game away with an inept answer to a parliamentary question the day before the announcement was to be made; it led to frenzied trading on foreign exchange markets that cost Britain some £300 million.

The Tories seized on the issue with alacrity. Just who were the incompetents now? Their lead in the polls widened to seventeen percent. Callaghan was moved out of the Exchequer, changing places with Home Secretary Roy Jenkins. Wilson himself was secure only because all the alternatives seemed worse.

It was a slim reed to cling to, but Wilson held on for all it was worth. The devaluation forced him into further spending cuts and the breaking of another promise: since the cheaper pound could no longer pay their bills abroad, British forces east of Suez were brought home. In October 1968, the powerful Trades Union Congress—the British equivalent of America's AFL-CIO—voted to condemn Wilson's wages policy; later that month, the Labor Party Conference followed suit. The prime minister was now fighting battles with his cabinet, with his party, and with his natural following in the country. The heady days of 1966 were gone for good.

Towards the end of 1968, Wilson and some of the more right–wing members of his cabinet began to consider legislation that would limit the unions' ability to strike. Work stoppages had been increasing markedly, and the prime minister hoped to restore confidence in his government by taking a firm stand. Just after New Year's Day 1969, however, the cabinet began to split over the issue. Callaghan said he would resign if the antiunion bills—which would obligate all strike votes to be secret ballots and require a mandatory pause for conciliation before a work-stoppage could procede—were pushed through. Again, Wilson refused to budge, and when his plans were presented to the House in March 1969, no less than fifty-five Labor MPs voted against them. They survived a preliminary vote only with Tory support.

In the end, Wilson was obliged to back down once more. In a humiliating compromise, he convinced the TUC that his legislation represented no more than an interpretation of their already-existing rules. As a face-saving gesture, it wasn't terribly effective. Wilson seemed a shrunken figure, a far cry from the technocratic whiz-kid who had once dazzled the nation.

Even so, he wasn't ready to be counted out. The devaluation had begun to work, and by June 1969, there was actually a trade *surplus* of some £300 million. The pound settled down, and the huge Tory lead in the polls—which had peaked at nineteen percent—began to melt away, falling to just four percent in October. In January 1970, Wilson began campaigning again even though no election had been called. He made a series of generous wage settlements to public employees and revived his old anti-Tory litany, attacking the Conservatives for favoring the rich and wanting to turn back the clock.

That same month the Tory shadow cabinet was meeting at the Selsdon Park Hotel in the London suburb of Croydon to plan strategy and draft a detailed election manifesto. Sir Keith Joseph, a clever and compassionate (though somewhat unstable) man, who was one of the party's most fervent advocates of free enterprise, stole the headlines with a series of impressive speeches on the need for "civilized capitalism." But the emphasis at Selsdon Park was on getting the state out of the economy and forcing people to depend more on their own initiative and enterprise.

For Wilson, the gathering provided a new line of attack on the Conservatives. A new creature had been born, he crowed: "Selsdon Man"— an atavistic reminder of the bad old days of Tory greed, laissez-faire government, and class bias.

It almost worked. With the opinion polls and pundits once again behind him, Wilson called a general election for June 18, 1970. The campaign seemed to go his way. Heath at times appeared slow and bumbling; the prime minister, always ebullient and confident. Nonetheless, the voters could feel the squeeze of rising inflation, and just before election day, the government had to release a new batch of statistics showing that the trade balance was once again in the red, that unemployment had hit yet another high, and that the number of working hours lost to strikes had just set a record.

With such ammunition, Heath had little trouble convincing the electorate that the economy was in bad shape. To restore it, he promised a new tax system, a streamlining of the bureaucracy, new reforms for industry and the unions, and an improvement in the way housing was subsidized. It was virtually his 1966 platform all over again, except that this time it was presented in far greater detail. In some ways, Heath seemed to be presenting himself as a Tory Wilson—a modern, managerial man facing the world in a modern, no-nonsense way. He pledged a clean break with the sorry past, a "quiet revolution" that would undo the mess created (he said) by Wilson. No more unwieldy bureaucracies, no more unworkable government-imposed wage freezes, no more socialist interference by the state. "Stand on your own two feet," was his slogan, and the country, disillusioned by Labor's unfulfilled promises, responded. Heath himself had never been all that popular in the nation at large, but the June 1970 election gave the Tories a thirty-seat majority in the Commons, more than enough to make him prime minister.

THE QUIET REVOLUTION
AND THE GREAT MILK FLAP

In all the major economic and ideological controversies of the late 1960s, Mrs. Thatcher stayed pretty much in the background, concentrating on her own highly controversial portfolio of education. As shadow education minister she had her hands full from the moment Heath assigned her the portfolio. Students were growing increasingly rebellious, and there was a fierce debate going on in Britain as elsewhere over declining standards of education. Tied to this debate was a continuing battle over Labor's desire to reorganize the country's grammar, secondary, and technical schools into vast new comprehensive schools that would eschew the academic tracking which many considered an unjust expression of outdated class attitudes. At her first press conference as the opposition's chief spokesman on education in October 1969, Mrs. Thatcher had taken pains to emphasize that she was not an extremist. "I'm not a reactionary," she insisted. Nonetheless, as a former grammar school girl herself, she was determined to resist the tide towards what became known as "comprehensivization".

When the Tories came back into power under Heath, Mrs. Thatcher retained her portfolio and became the government's secretary of state for education and science. At last she was a full member of a British cabinet. She was not the first woman ever to serve in Cabinet; indeed, she wasn't even the first woman to serve as education minister. (That honor had gone to Florence Horsburgh, who had the job in Winston Churchill's 1951–55 government.) But she quickly became by far the best known.

Though the fact that she had two children of her own in school and that she had been trained as a scientist seemed to make her well qualified to run the Department of Education and Science (DES), in many ways it was not the most felicitous assignment for this prickly and somewhat rigid woman. She detested uncertainty and made no secret of it. "I don't like watching a football match unless I know the result first, so I see only filmed reports," she told a reporter who had asked her whether she intended to watch the English national soccer team compete in the 1970 world championships. "I shall watch England's World Cup matches if I know we have won. If we haven't, I won't." Coupled with this feeling was what Anthony Sampson described as her low "tolerance of organizations over which she can have no control—a frustrating weakness in her job, for the British distaste for centralized authority has nowhere been more evident (except perhaps in the police) than in the school system." Indeed, although the central government controlled (through DES) school construction as well as the number of teachers to be hired and how much they were to be paid, the actual running of schools—their character and curriculums—was up to local authorities.

In any case, Heath had promised a quiet revolution, and Mrs. Thatcher intended to help lead it. Her first act as education minister was to repeal a controversial 1965 decision by the then Labor-controlled DES requesting local authorities to submit plans to the government for reorganizing their grammar and secondary schools into comprehensives. (Though it was only a request, the education ministry applied a bit more pressure the next year by announcing it would refuse to give building grants to any school system that didn't comply.) Mandatory or not, comprehensivization clearly had the Labor government's seal of approval—and that seal Mrs. Thatcher was determined to revoke. "Everyone is born with some combination of talents," she argued, "so we want a society, and an education system, that enables people to develop whatever talents they have to fulfill." Grammar schools were under attack, she felt, simply because they were good. Most important, however, local authorities should be able to choose freely the sort of school system they wanted without having to contend with heavy-handed government pressure.

But though she insisted she wasn't against comprehensivization on principle—opposing the idea only when it was forced down local authorities' throats—the fact is Mrs. Thatcher used her power as education minister to prevent many school systems that wanted to go comprehensive from doing so. Under provisions of Britain's landmark 1944 Education Act which had established the tri-partite school system that comprehensivization sought to unify, the education minister had the power to abort the reorganization of an entire school system merely by objecting to the plans for a single school within it. Mrs. Thatcher used this power, critics charged, to "sabotage" dozens of comprehensivization schemes; in fact, out of proposals to reorganize more than four thousand schools, she vetoed less than four hundred, but it was enough to prevent the vast majority from going comprehensive.

Her attachment to grammar schools inevitably brought accusations that she was an elitist determined to keep the poor and disadvantaged in their place. Such attacks grew more virulent when she made one of the worst political blunders of her career. Heath was hoping to cut government spending by something on the order of £300 million, and a good part of it—as much as a third—was to come from the education budget.

One suggestion was to end the £8 million-a-year free-milk program for primary-school students aged seven to eleven (Labor had earlier ended the practice of providing free milk to secondary school students.) Reportedly, Mrs. Thatcher opposed the idea in Cabinet. But cuts had to be made somewhere, and rather than lose funds for school construction or the famed Open University (Harold Wilson's "university of the airwaves" whose broadcast lectures and free correspondence courses had brought advanced education to tens of thousands), Mrs. Thatcher gave in on free milk. She evidently felt it was the most sensible and politically viable option.

A more wrongheaded political judgment has never been made by any modern cabinet minister. In one of those irrational outbursts that so often determines the course of politics, the British public went wild at the thought that its children were losing their free milk (even though poor children were exempted from the decision). "Mrs. Thatcher, Milk-Snatcher," demonstrators chanted, and she was shouted down at more than a few public meetings. To make matters worse, the DES also raised school-meal charges, adopted the Continental practice of imposing admission charges at museums and galleries, and asked university administrations to take over the finances of their student unions (something which, with the campuses already in turmoil, they had no desire to do). What's more, unlike other ministers who could implement their cuts by executive fiat, the education minister was obliged by law to submit hers to Parliament—thus prolonging the agony. The catcalls she had to endure in the House were unbearably cruel. "Ditch the bitch!" Labor backbenchers shouted every time she rose to speak.

As editor Edward McClure of the influential *Times Education Supplement* notes, the milk flap was to a great extent "a spurious issue." But that was of little consolation to the beleagured education minister. By November 1971, the 1.5 million-circulation *Sun* was calling Mrs. Thatcher "the most unpopular woman in Britain." Her children were being taunted at school, and she came home from the ministry each night pale and ill. "In Cabinet," recalls Peter Walker, who was then Ted Heath's environment minister, "she became emotional and angry." Things grew so bad that her husband began to suggest perhaps she should quit politics.

But Mrs. Thatcher hung on, growing increasingly defensive and isolated. Her relations with the press and the educational establishment, never good to begin with, broke down almost completely. "She got on badly with the education world," says McClure. "She believed all educationalists were socialists and they rightly believed she was an aspiring right-wing Chelsea lady. She was hopeless at mustering support or goodwill. She lacked sympathy for the world with which she had to deal."

Indeed, as far as she was concerned, the press was her enemy. "She was so upset," an aide recalls, "she refused all contact with the press for a while." Adds an education reporter who covered her at the time: "She treated us as an Opposition frontbench. She considered every question hostile, never on its merits." Even the ostensibly nonpolitical civil servants at DES felt her wrath. "It was impossible to hold a rational conversation with her," says one.

An unadmiring former senior Tory official recalls a meeting held at DES at about this time. Some department staffers were arguing that voluntary youth agencies should be given a part to play in community policy. Mrs. Thatcher would have none of it. Such groups, she reportedly raged, were "literally for the birds—an untidy, ragged left-of-center army." Says the now-retired official: "Her doctrinaire stance took us away from a policy of persuasion and separated us from the whole world of people and ideas who could help us put future generations in touch with the party."

She even became an object of ridicule within the cabinet and at 10 Downing Street. Many of her fellow ministers' wives detested her. Once, when a member of the cabinet tried to make light of the ill-feeling, saying: "Oh you smart middle-class ladies can't stand her," his wife snapped back: "It's no wonder since the only thing she talks about with us is the price of beefsteak." And at a formal lunch given by Heath at No. 10, an eminent guest was caught out by one of those sudden lulls in conversation just as he facetiously asked, "Is there any truth in the rumor that Mrs. Thatcher is a woman?" The subject of this cruel jest, sitting just a few places away, pretended not to hear it, but the rest of the table, a participant recalls, was "caught between mortification and hysterical laughter." Heath had a chuckle himself, though he chastised the offender with a black look, telling him, "You simply cannot conduct yourself this way at a formal luncheon."

In most cases, a minister in her position would have been forced out by the controversy, just as James Callaghan had lost his job at the Exchequer after the devaluation debacle. Ironically, it was Heath's obstinancy that saved his future rival's neck. There was even then little love between the prime minister and his strident education minister. But the louder the calls for her ouster grew, the more determined Heath was to keep her on.

In fact, Mrs. Thatcher's tenure at DES, the longest of any education minister, was not nearly as right-wing as it may have seemed. By 1970, education spending as a proportion of the British gross national product had reached an all-time high, rising to six and a half percent of GNP—higher, for the first time ever, than the proportion spent on defense. Mrs. Thatcher pushed education spending up still further, increasing DES's budget by more than £150 million in her time there. "She talks right-wing, but when she acts she plays it safe, right down the middle," is the judgment of a journalist who has known her since her Oxford days. In any case, as political editor Simon Jenkins of the influential and conservative British weekly *The Economist* notes: "The whole structure of central government in Britain is based on the politics of spending money." In other words, the more funds a minister can win for his or her department, the more successful that minister is regarded to be, and by that reckoning, Mrs. Thatcher did well indeed at DES. "The important thing was to protect *education*," she said later, "and that's what we did."

Still, the experience hardened her. "Iron entered her soul at that stage," suggests Anthony Sampson. She confessed later that she was nearly broken, and afterwards preferred to be described as "resilient" rather than "tough." When at last the worst of the milk controversy had died down, she issued her own evaluation of the experience: "The criticism had been vicious," she said; to cope, she added, "you have to build an armor round yourself, knowing the things they say aren't true."

HEATH'S U-TURN

Mrs. Thatcher's problems at DES soon paled into insignificance alongside Heath's problems with the nation. In 1972, with inflation rising and seemingly nothing able to stop it, Heath committed an about-face every bit as shocking as President Richard Nixon's surprise announcement the year before that he was now a Keynesian. After vowing in the 1970 campaign to break with Labor's economic policies in general—and absolutely to avoid freezing wages or limiting pay increases in particular—Heath in 1972 dusted off that desperate measure of last resort used by the two previous governments and announced a compulsory incomes policy. What's more, he increased state involvement in industry. Rolls-Royce was nationalized, and a number of other ailing companies got massive government bail-outs.

Mrs. Thatcher, among many others, was shocked by this policy U-turn. Privately she considered resigning over the issue, though publically she kept a discreet silence. Finally she decided to stay in the government, telling friends she was afraid that if she resigned, she might never get back into the front benches again. Her stance may not have been hypocritical; certainly, had she resigned she would not be prime minister today, with a chance to implement what she considers a truly Conservative approach to public policy. But it did open her to the charge that if Ted Heath's government had trampled Conservative principles in the mud, Margaret Thatcher was among the tramplers.

Heath's policy reversal did not stem Britain's slide into what quickly became economic chaos. Heath's government had passed a hotly disputed Industrial Relations Act, designed—as Harold Wilson's unsuccessful bill a few years earlier had been—to limit the ability of the trade unions to strike. In the fall of 1973, the National Industrial Relations Court—which had been created by the act to judge disputes—levied a £75,000 fine against the 1.2 million-member Amalgamated Union of Engineering Workers for refusing to comply with an order banning strike activity. AUEW president Hugh Scanlon, an intelligent and highly militant former communist, responded by calling what *The Times* described as a "blatantly political" one-day work-stoppage on November 5. The strike closed newspapers, shipyards, automobile factories, and many power stations, and it left the nation uneasily wondering whether the winter would bring a new series of confrontations between the government and the unions.

The AUEW continued pulling one-day strikes through the autumn, supplementing them with a ban on overtime. Lacking engineering technicians, power stations began to reduce their output, and Britain began to face a severe shortage of electricity. Charitable groups distributed leaflets telling the old and sick how to keep warm in unheated apartments, while one of London's biggest candle factories increased production by several hundred percent.

With all this going on—and the Arab oil embargo which followed the Yom Kippur War in the Middle East adding to the trouble—Britain's coal miners joined the uncooperative engineers by rejecting a thirteen percent pay increase and declaring an overtime ban of their own. Heath reacted angrily, but miners' leader Joe Gormley struck back at what he called a "smear campaign" directed against miners who were only pursuing their legitimate right to strike for higher wages. When Gormley added that his members would "break the Government" if necessary to win their claim, the stage for massive confrontation was set.

On November 14, Heath responded to the growing turmoil and worsening fuel shortages by declaring a state of emergency—surprising the nation with his quick action. To conserve fuel supplies in the face of the strikes as well as the oil embargo, Heath found legislation authorizing him to ration fuel to industry. That night, floodlights and advertising displays in London and around the country went dark in compliance with new government restrictions. Long queues formed at filling stations, people talked of a return to wartime petrol rationing and the government initiated what it called the SOS campaign—for "Switch Something Off." *The Times* began warning of "this critical winter" which would put British democracy and the government's strength to the test. Hospitals built up stockpiles of vital supplies, and thermostats in official buildings were turned down to sixty-three degrees.

At the end of November, the miners rejected another, higher pay offer. As *The Times* put it, they were "on a collision course with the Government"—a prediction that was confirmed when Heath began to insist that the miners' "clash is with the people." Despite the chill winter winds and the lack of fuel, Britain's political temperature was rising fast.

In December, the government imposed a fifty mph speed limit. Shortly afterward, the country's train engineers, following the depressing pattern, imposed their own overtime ban for higher pay. Speaking in the House of Commons on December 13, Heath told the country to prepare for a three-day work-week to be imposed as of New Year's Day 1974 in a final effort to conserve fuel and ration scarce supplies to industry. Within a few days 544,000 workers had been laid off in anticipation of the new restrictions, and the stock market plummeted.

By January 8, the pound was at a postwar low. Nearly a million workers had been idled by the three-day week—the largest number of layoffs since the General Strike of 1926. Labor called for voluntary wage restraints and government arbitration to bridge the impasse. But Heath refused to budge. The TUC tried to convince Heath to consider the miners a special case, far more deserving than most of higher wages. Its leaders met with Heath at 10 Downing to press their case, and when the talks broke down, influential *Times* columnist Bernard Levin echoed the feelings of many by noting that Heath had picked the wrong group of workers with whom to have a showdown. The miners suffered the most unhealthy working conditions and worst working hours of almost any group in the country. They had been too long neglected and abused, and the feeling began to grow throughout Britain that Heath was being unreasonably harsh and stubborn with them.

More than 2.2 million Britons were out of work by the end of January—the most since the Great Depression. On February 2, Heath decided he had to go to the country for a new mandate. He announced he would be holding an election on February 28. His slogan was "Who Governs?"—and two days later, the miners gave their answer, voting overwhelmingly to transform what had up to then been merely an overtime ban into a full-scale strike.

The Tories entitled their manifesto "Firm Action for a Fair Britain" and argued that the election centered on a "clear choice between moderation and extremism." Heath offered himself and his party as the only alternative to "militants out to wreck society." Labor, he insisted, was a "pushover" that would "surrender" to the wreckers. If it sounded more like the language of war than industrial relations, it was no accident.

At first, the opinion polls gave the Tories a lead of two to six percent over Labor. But then disaster struck. First, Enoch Powell, the influential and brilliantly articulate right-winger who had been dropped from the Tory shadow cabinet in 1968 after predicting in a famous speech that continued black and Asian immigration to Britain would lead to a bloody race war, announced he was refusing to run as a Conservative. Compounding the felony, Powell went on television to urge the country to vote Labor. (The particular reason for Powell's break with the party was his fierce opposition to the Common Market, which Heath had championed. But Powell had long been unhappy with the Conservative leadership in general, considering it far too left wing.) Then, the monthly trade figures were released by the treasury—and they showed the worst deficit since the government began keeping such records. With inflation now running at better than twenty percent a year—the highest rate since 1947—Heath was in trouble.

For its part, Labor claimed to be offering a "way out of the crisis." It promised to reject "the policies of confrontation and conflict and fight-to-the-finish philosophies." In their place, Wilson offered what he called a "Social Contract" with the unions, a working understanding that would be based on "justice, equality, concern for the low-paid, the needy and pensioners." Specifically, Labor pledged to cut taxes for the poor, raise them for the rich, and repeal the Industrial Relations Act.

The electorate had a hard time making up its mind, and the results of the February 28, 1974 election showed it. For the first time since 1929, there was no clear winner. With 37.1 percent of the popular vote, Labor had won 301 seats, while the Tories—with 37.9 percent—had just 297 seats. The balance of power was held by fourteen Liberals and twenty-three other minor-party MPs. In an effort to retain power, Heath met with Liberal Party Leader Jeremy Thorpe to see if a Lib-Con coalition could be arranged. As his price for support, Thorpe insisted on a Tory commitment to proportional representation—a key issue for the Liberals, who held less than three percent of the seats in Commons even though they had won nearly twenty percent of the popular vote. Heath refused and tendered his resignation. Thus, lacking a majority but controlling more seats than anyone else in the House, Harold Wilson moved back into No. 10. He made a new, higher offer to the miners which they accepted. By March 11, they were back at work, and the crisis was over.

Without a majority, however, Labor couldn't really govern. Wilson was trying to get new union and labor relations bills through the House, but the Tories and Liberals combined to defeat him twenty-nine separate times in the months of June and July alone. On September 20, he asked the Queen to dissolve what had turned out to be the shortest Parliament in the twentieth century.

The second election of 1974, held on October 10, was as clearly defined—and nearly as ambiguously decided—as the first. Labor argued that it had "inherited the three-day week, unlit streets and unheated homes"—and had put Britain back to work. The Tories countered that the huge wage increases granted by Wilson to get things going again had set the stage for an even more massive inflationary surge. Where Labor promised more nationalization and increased centralized planning, Heath spoke of another "National" government that would include non-Conservatives in its cabinet and avoid Labor's "divisiveness and extremism." The Tories would cut spending, he added, though not across the board. The exceptions were in housing and food.

By this time, Mrs. Thatcher had given up her education portfolio and had been made shadow environment minister, which included responsibility for housing. As such it fell to her to promote the Conservatives' plan for controlled mortgage rates and subsidized housing. It was an astonishing proposal for an advocate of free-market, monetarist economics to make. Not only did it involve state intervention in the economy, it required a huge increase in public spending. Clearly it was not her idea. But once she was convinced of the political necessity of such a plan, she pushed it hard and enthusiastically—only to hear it denounced, correctly, by Wilson as a blatant "electoral bribe."

In the end, Labor won a working majority—though a tiny one of only three seats. Still, it was enough to keep Wilson in office. The Tories, with just 35.8 percent of the popular vote—their lowest poll in recorded history—were to remain in opposition for the next five years. But not under Ted Heath. A leadership challenge was shaping up that would change the face of British politics—and the course of Margaret Thatcher's life.

5

Victorious
Upstart

*"I am just Margaret Thatcher.
You must take me as I am."*

 EVER SINCE 1922, when Tory MPs staged a startling revolt that dethroned Austen Chamberlain as party leader, Conservative backbenchers in the House of Commons have been organized into what, in homage to their never-forgotten upstart victory, they call the 1922 Committee. This group is run by an elected eighteen-member Executive, whose job it is to take care of administrative matters affecting backbenchers—handling committee assignments and the like—as well as to make sure that the views of backbenchers are considered by the leadership. On the morning of October 14, 1974, four days after the Conservative party's second general election defeat in less than eight months, the 1922 Committee's Executive found itself and the party smack in the middle of a full-fledged leadership crisis.

Early in September, the Executive had decided to schedule an October 14 meeting at the London home of its chairman, Edward du Cann, a respected backbencher who also happened to be chairman of a big London merchant bank called Keyser Ullmann. Originally the purpose of the meeting was to deal with all the normal bureaucratic business that comes up just before the birth of a new Parliament. But by the time the Executive had gathered at du Cann's house, it found itself with a different order of business. For in the three days following the October 10 general election, the Executive's members had been deluged by demands from their fellow-backbenchers that something be done about the man many blamed for the party's sorry state, its leader Ted Heath.

Whatever his gifts as a prime minister and an international stateman, the fact was Ted Heath was never very popular with his fellow Tories in the House of Commons. As longtime Conservative MP Nigel Fisher has noted, Heath was "admired, but he was not loved. His colleagues in Parliament accorded him the loyalty due the leader of their party; but few felt any great personal loyalty to him as a friend." In part, this was the result of his politics. His abrupt policy U-turn in 1972, when he abandoned his so-called "quiet revolution" and reverted to a compulsory incomes policy and increased government intervention in the economy, had outraged many in the Conservative party. But mainly it was Heath's personality that was the problem. A cold, aloof man, he was uncomfortable in social situations and incapable of the bonhomie essential to electoral politics. He seemed indifferent to his colleagues' personal problems, and on occasion he could be gratuitously cruel.

The first real stirrings of discontent with Heath began sweeping through the Tory ranks at Westminster late in 1973. But they were vague and inchoate, and when Heath decided to go to the country the following February, they all but disappeared, swallowed up by the obligatory unity that descends on a party at election time. Some in the Conservative backbenches felt Heath should have called the election sooner, while others were convinced he should have tried to ride out the storm a bit longer. Everyone, however, agreed that this was not the time to raise such questions publicly.

This pragmatic discretion prevailed through the first half of 1974, precisely as it had a decade earlier, after Harold Wilson had ousted Sir Alec Douglas-Home from 10 Downing Street. Then, as now, Labor and Wilson lacked a clear mandate; another election might be called at any moment, and the Conservatives couldn't afford to be caught in the middle of an unseemly squabble over the leadership.

For some Tories, however, the demands of party loyalty were becoming increasingly difficult to live with. Chief among them were Mrs. Thatcher and Sir Keith Joseph, who by now had become her political and economic guru. As education minister and minister for health and social security respectively, the two had not been able to play a conspicuously active role in the great economic policy debate of 1972–73, and both were extremely unhappy about what they regarded as the inadequacy of Heath's approach to controlling inflation. Thus, when the Conservatives went back into opposition after the February 1974 election, they agreed to continue serving in the shadow cabinet only if Heath agreed to provide party money to help set up a "Center for Policy Studies," separate from the party's official Research Office, that would explore and promote the virtues of what Joseph liked to refer to as a "social market economy"—in essence, his free market "capitalism with a human face."

Through this vehicle, Sir Keith and Mrs. Thatcher began to challenge Heath's Tory pragmatism with a more ideological monetarist approach to economic policy. They picked up some support early on, winning over Sir Geoffrey Howe, who had been Heath's minister of trade. But while most of the shadow cabinet was willing to agree that public spending should be cut and the growth of the money supply contained, the majority didn't view this monetarist prescription as anything more than a part of what had to be some larger solution to inflation. Nonetheless, Thatcher and Joseph continued to press their argument. Indeed, that summer and fall, Sir Keith went on a nationwide speaking tour that was, in effect if not in fact, the beginning of the first real challenge to Heath's leadership.

The Tories have a reputation for being brutal with losers—especially with a loser who happens also to be the party leader. But even though the Conservatives had lost two out of the last three general elections under his leadership, Heath could claim with some justification in the spring and summer of 1974 that he wasn't quite the loser he might have seemed to be. After all, no one had expected the Tories to win the 1966 election, and the surprising 1970 Conservative victory was in many ways a personal triumph for Heath. As for the February 1974 election, the outlook had once again been for a Labor victory—even a landslide—and yet neither had happened. True, the Tories had been turned out of office. But they had won a higher popular vote than Labor and had managed to deny Wilson a clear majority in the House. At the very least, Heath's supporters argued, he had led the party to a moral victory in this last go-round.

But was Heath entitled to take personal credit for whatever joy could be extracted from the Conservatives' latest showing at the polls? Many Tory MPs thought not. In fact, the campaign experience of a large number of them had been quite the opposite. If anything, Heath had appeared to be an electoral liability, an albatross without whom they might actually have won the election. As Nigel Fisher described his own campaign: "On nearly every doorstep, if a conversation developed, one's constituent—whether man or woman, Conservative, Liberal or Labor—would say, 'I'd vote for you except for Heath' . . ."

BACKBENCHERS' REVOLT

After Wilson won a clear majority in the second 1974 general election, this feeling about Heath hardened into widespread conviction. And the October 14 meeting of the 1922 Committee's Executive quite inadvertantly provided a focus for the growing dissatisfaction.

The meeting was supposed to be private. But when members of the Executive turned up at du Cann's house, they found it surrounded by reporters and photographers eager to know whether another 1922-style backbench revolt was in the making. In fact, at that point at least, the Executive had no such plans in mind. All its members knew was that Heath's standing among the backbenchers had sunk low indeed, and that decisive action was needed if he was to restore it. Their meeting lasted only an hour, but it was long enough for every member of the Executive to agree that a new leadership election was required, not immediately perhaps, but soon. The object of the election wouldn't be so much to replace Heath as to reconfirm him, and in the process oblige him to reassure the backbenchers that he understood their problems. Du Cann was instructed to carry that message to Heath, Deputy Party Leader William Whitelaw, and the party's chief whip, Humphrey Atkins. He was to report back to the Executive the next morning.

Du Cann's meeting with Heath did not go well. As usual, Heath was remote and peremptory. It sounded to him as if the backbenchers were getting ideas above their station, and he didn't like it one bit. Du Cann left feeling he hadn't been given a chance to explain fully the Executive's position.

To avoid another mob scene with the press, the Executive decided to hear du Cann's report in a secret meeting at his bank, Keyser Ullmann, in Milk Street in the heart of London's financial district. But once again, the newspapers had been tipped off. The next day the front pages were filled with pictures and stories about the nefarious doings of what headline writers quickly dubbed "the Milk Street Mafia" which was conspiring to bring Heath down. (In retrospect, it seems clear that it was Heath's supporters who leaked news of the meeting, apparently in an effort to discredit any attempt to question Heath's fitness as party leader.)

The irony, of course, was that all the Executive wanted to do was to clear the air. So when du Cann told the group of his frustrating encounter with Heath, they decided to write him a letter asking for a face-to-face meeting. The letter was sent privately, but Heath answered it publicly. The current Executive had been elected in the previous Parliament, he said, and he had no intention of meeting with a group whose qualifications for representing the Tory backbenches were so questionable. He would agree to a meeting only after the new Parliament's 1922 Committee had elected a new Executive.

It was a perverse response. Had Heath simply asked the 1922 Committee for a vote of confidence, he probably would have gotten it immediately, and the matter would have been settled. Instead, he temporized, perhaps out of an unshakable belief that the party's respectable showing in the election had left him above such pandering.

In any case, the full 1922 Committee met on October 31 to discuss the leadership flap. According to the accounts of most participants, du Cann took great pains to run the meeting fairly, letting it drag on for hours to insure that everyone who wanted to speak got a chance. The next day, however, the newspapers were full of stories that the session had been rigged, with only anti-Heath MPs getting the floor. It was apparently another attempt by Heath's supporters to undermine what they considered the opposition. As such dirty tricks go, however, this was an astonishingly shortsighted one which immediately backfired. After all, the people Heath had to influence—the Tory MPs—were all at the meeting and knew for themselves how it had been run. They were outraged at the inaccurate press accounts and insulted by what seemed to them such transparent attempts at manipulation.

Thus it was hardly surprising that a week later, the 1922 Committee reelected its Executive en masse. It was the first time in memory that an entire Executive had been returned to office, and it should have provided a clear warning to Heath to start taking the Executive's messages a bit more seriously. But he chose to disregard it. In his own mind there was no question that he was by far the best qualified person in the party to serve as its leader, and he had no intention of entertaining any suggestions to the contrary.

The situation was rapidly turning into a standoff—all the more so because the leadership selection rules (which had been devised in 1965 after the experience with Home convinced Tory MPs it was time to dispense with "emergence") didn't anticipate that an unpopular leader would try to stay in office against the will of his fellow MPs. As a result, backbenchers began demanding new rules. Faced with a full-scale revolt if he didn't go along, Heath agreed. He appointed a ten-member rules committee headed by Lord Home himself and consisting of Tory MPs, peers, and party officials, to make recommendations.

The rules committee issued its report just before the Christmas 1974 parliamentary recess. It recommended several changes in the leadership selection process, among them that when the party is in opposition, Tory MPs be required to hold new leadership elections every year. It also suggested that for a candidate to be elected leader on the first ballot, he or she must not only command a clear majority (meaning the votes of at least 139 of the 276 Tories then in the House of Commons), but must also win by a margin of at least fifteen percent of the total eligible vote.

Tory MPs endorsed the recommendations in mid-January 1975. By this time, they wanted to get the mess over with as soon as possible. Heath felt the same way; he too accepted the committee's report and called for an election as soon as it could be arranged. A date was quickly proposed and fixed: the first leadership election under the new rules would be held on February 4, 1975.

PICKING UP THE CHALLENGE

Even at this relatively late date there remained a real question of just who, if anyone, was going to run against Heath. The mercurial and often appallingly insensitive Sir Keith Joseph had been the first real candidate. But he was forced to drop out of the running after the two speeches he gave in the fall of 1974 raised an enormous storm of protest and more than a few questions about his fitness for high office. In the first, he spoke somewhat cavalierly about the seriousness of unemployment; in the second, he made some ill-advised and rather lofty comments about unmarried working-class mothers having too many babies, appearing to suggest—though it seems he had no such intention—that contraceptives ought to be doled out on a class basis.

Mrs. Thatcher had been one of Sir Keith's most enthusiastic supporters. When he withdrew his candidacy for the leadership late in November 1974, she announced hers. Before she did so, however, she went to inform Heath of her plans. Their meeting in his office at Westminster lasted precisely ninety seconds, and it was not cordial. He merely acknowledged her message and dismissed her without thanks for the courtesy. "These things are usually done by stealth," notes Tory MP David Howell, who is currently in Mrs. Thatcher's cabinet as energy minister. "It was a very, very courageous thing for her to do, and typically straight."

Mrs. Thatcher wasn't exactly an enthusiastic candidate for the leadership. Her personal goal was to be the first woman chancellor of the exchequer (traditionally the number two position in Cabinet), not party leader or—heaven forbid—prime minister. Indeed, just a few months earlier, in June 1974, she had told the *Liverpool Daily Post* that it would be unrealistic for her to aim any higher than chancellor. "It will be years before a woman either leads the party or becomes Prime Minister," she said. "I don't see it happening in my time."

Ladbrokes, the big English betting firm, agreed. Around the time Mrs. Thatcher announced her candidacy for the Tory leadership, they were quoting fifty-to-one odds against her ever unseating Heath.

A much better chance was given Edward du Cann, the chairman of the 1922 Committee—and Mrs. Thatcher was so diffident about seeking the leadership that she agreed to drop out of the race if he would run. The case for du Cann's candidacy was impressive. As chairman of Keyser Ullmann, his managerial and financial expertise was considered unquestionable, and his evenhanded behavior throughout the backbench crisis of confidence in Heath had earned him the respect of most Tory MPs. With Joseph out of the picture, he seemed to many to be the only credible challenger. Heath recognized this and tried to coopt du Cann by offering him a post in the shadow cabinet. Du Cann refused it. But in the end he too declined to throw his hat in the ring. For one thing, his wife was not eager to be subjected to the intrusions, risks, and attention that would inevitably come their way if he were to win. Perhaps more important, there was the matter of his association with Keyser Ullmann. There had been rumors that the bank's activities would not stand up to close scrutiny. They had been firmly denied, and an informal check by some Tory MPs with connections in the financial world appeared to confirm the denials. Still, it was felt that if du Cann became party leader—and, hence, a potential prime minister—he would have to sever his connections with the bank. This he was not willing to do. (As it turned out, Keyser Ullmann's affairs *were* rather questionable. A May 1979 Department of Trade report accused the bank's directors, who were headed by du Cann, of incompetence over an improper £17 million loan made in 1973 to a young wheeler-dealer.)

In any case, when du Cann announced in mid-January 1975 that he would not run, that left only two candidates willing to challenge Heath: Mrs. Thatcher and Hugh Fraser, an aristocratic and engaging backbencher who had never served in any cabinet or shadow cabinet. Fraser didn't mount any real campaign for the leadership; he seemed in the race solely to provide an alternative for anti-Heath MPs who couldn't bring themselves to vote for a woman.

With less than three weeks to go before the first ballot, Margaret Thatcher had only two declared supporters out of the 276 Tory MPs eligible to vote. That quickly changed after du Cann dropped out. On January 15, Airey Neave, a somewhat obscure backbencher who had been a member of the committee of twenty-five or so MPs actively supporting du Cann, suggested that the group transfer its allegience to his old friend Margaret Thatcher, whom he had known and liked ever since she entered the House. This unexpected development was perhaps the most crucial event in Mrs. Thatcher's entire political career.

To be sure, Neave wasn't much of a force in the House. A much decorated war hero, he was the first Allied officer to break out of the supposedly "escape-proof" German prisoner-of-war camp at Colditz. He later returned behind the lines to organize a highly successful exit route for other escaped POWs. After the war, Neave served as a junior prosecutor at the Nuremberg war-crimes trials, where he personally served arrest warrants on such high-ranking Nazis as Rudolf Hess and Albert Speer. He wrote several popular books about his wartime experiences, and in 1950 he entered Parliament. Shortly after Harold Macmillan came to power in 1957, Neave was made a junior minister. But in 1959, a mild heart attack forced him to return to the backbenches. (Heath, who was chief Tory whip at the time, reacted in typically callous fashion when Neave explained his problem to him. "Well," he said, "that's the end of your political career, then.")

But though Neave did not have much political influence, he was a superb organizer. He persuaded fifteen of the twenty-five du Cann activists to join him in working for Mrs. Thatcher, and with William Shelton, one of her two original supporters, he masterminded a brilliant campaign for her.

As Mrs. Thatcher's manager, Neave had two big advantages. The first was Heath's own ineffectiveness as a campaigner. The obligatory back-slapping and cajoling necessary in such contests both bored and embarrassed the stiff, somewhat shy party leader. Moreover, Heath's cause wasn't helped by the penchant of some of his more enthusiastic aides for dirty tricks. The early attempts to discredit the 1922 Committee's Executive had irked many MPs. Still more were offended by the transparent smear campaign that erupted soon after Mrs. Thatcher emerged as the main contender. Suddenly the newspapers were filled with stories reviving memories of her "milk-snatcher" days at the education ministry.

And an interview she had given the year before to a small pensioners' magazine in which she suggested that old folks could beat inflation by stocking up on special offers at the grocery store was brandished as a shocking endorsement of hoarding.

For her part, Mrs. Thatcher professed to be unfazed by it all. "They broke Keith," she said, recalling the controversy that had forced Joseph out of contention the previous autumn, "but they won't break me."

Neave's other main advantage was Mrs. Thatcher herself, or more precisely, what she had made of the surprising opportunity Heath had given her in November 1974, when he appointed her co-shadow chancellor. It was a starring role Heath had given her. Whether he did so in the hope that she would fall on her face, or because he believed his own position was so impregnable that there was nothing she could do to weaken it, no one can say. All that's certain is that it kept Mrs. Thatcher in the headlines throughout December and January as Harold Wilson and his chancellor of the exchequer, Denis Healey, tried to push their latest budget through Parliament.

As one of the main Tory speakers, Mrs. Thatcher jousted frequently with Labor ministers in the Commons, building a reputation as a fearsome infighter with an astonishing command of statistics and an awesome ability to grasp the fine-print implications of complicated tax legislation. Her greatest moment came, fortuitously enough, just two weeks before the first leadership ballot, when she finally went head-to-head with the formidable Healey, a brilliant parliamentary tactician and debater whose considerable intellect and devastating sarcasm had undone more than a few of her predecessors. Labor had tended to avoid personal attacks on Mrs. Thatcher, inhibited perhaps by the fact that she was a woman. But on January 21, she savagely attacked Labor's proposed Capital Transfer Tax, telling Healey, "You apparently do not understand the effect your tax will have on the lives of individuals, the economy, or indeed on a free society in general." The next day, Healey came roaring back, gloves off.

"Mrs. Thatcher has emerged from the debate as La Passionaria of Privilege," he told the House, in a sly reference to a fiery Communist woman orator of the Spanish Civil War. "She has shown she has decided . . . to see her Party tagged as the party of the rich few, and I believe she and her Party will regret it."

If Healey expected that he had put his opposite number in her place, he was mistaken. Brandishing that combination of sarcasm, invective, and insult on which the House of Commons thrives, Mrs. Thatcher made it clear she was not about to be intimidated. She would like to say that Healey's remarks hadn't done him justice, she began by way of reply, but unfortunately they had. "Some Chancellors are micro-economic," she continued, gathering steam as she went, "some chancellors are fiscal. This one is just plain cheap. When he rose to speak yesterday, we on this side were amazed how one could possibly get to be Chancellor of the Exchequer and speak for his Government knowing so little. If this Chancellor can be a Chancellor, anyone in the House of Commons could be Chancellor. I had hoped that the Right Honorable Gentleman had learnt a lot from this debate. Clearly, he has learnt nothing. He might at least address himself to the practical effects because it will affect . . . everyone, including people born as I was with no privilege at all."

Her remarks galvanized the House and brought the Tory benches to their feet with a rapturous roar. It was a brilliant performance, delivered at precisely the right moment. As Macmillan had said years earlier, mastery of the country begins with mastery of the House of Commons. She had clearly mastered the House, and for the first time it seemed genuinely possible that she just might oust Heath.

Riding the crest of her self-generated wave, Mrs. Thatcher continued to hammer away at the theme that she was no out-of-touch suburban matron but a true and responsive child of the hardworking middle classes. On February 1, four days before the leadership election, she met with party officials from her own constituency of Finchley and delivered what was, in effect, her only campaign speech. "Forget that I am a woman," she told them. "Forget the accusations that I am a right-winger demanding privilege . . . I had precious little privilege in my early years . . . I am still trying to represent the deep feelings of those many thousands of rank-and-file Tories in the country—and potential Conservative voters, too—who feel let down by our Party and find themselves unrepresented in a political vacuum." She went on to admit that as a minister in the 1970–74 government she shared some of the blame for Heath's erring ways. But, she added: "I hope I have learned something from the failures and mistakes of the past and can help to plan constructively for the future . . . There is a widespread feeling in the country that the Tory Party has not defended [its] ideals explicitly and toughly enough and that Britain is set on a course towards inevitable Socialist mediocrity. That course must not only be halted, it must be reversed. The action by the Tory Party must begin now."

In the meanwhile, Heath's inept campaign continued to bumble along. While Heath himself undertook a totally out of character attempt to drum up support by appearing in the Members' Bar at Westminster to buy drinks for astonished junior backbenchers to whom he had never even spoken before, his aides were compiling a wildly overoptimistic assessment of his chances—and compounding their mistake by telling everyone who would listed that Heath was a shoo-in. In part, this unrealistic, self-defeating optimism stemmed from the Heath camp's fundamental conviction that their man was simply too good, too right for the job to be unseated. To make matters worse, as many as forty backbenchers who were planning all along to vote for Mrs. Thatcher misleadingly told his whips—out of playfulness, spite, or fear of retribution—that Heath had their support.

Neave, on the other hand, was playing it extremely close to the vest. His soundings showed that Mrs. Thatcher stood a good chance of besting Heath, but in a shrewd effort both to strengthen the resolve of her declared supporters and to win what was called the "what the hell" vote, he wasn't about to admit it. "Margaret is doing well," he would tell anyone who asked, "but not quite well enough." As the campaign neared its conclusion, he even instructed his operatives around Westminster to look as glum as they could.

On February 3, the day before the first ballot, officials of the national party organization informed the 1922 Committee that no less than seventy percent of the rank and file were in favor of retaining Heath as leader. Tory peers said the Conservative members of the House of Lords were also overwhelmingly in favor of Heath's staying on. Later that day, Lord Home, the former prime minister who himself had been ousted by the man Mrs. Thatcher was now seeking to replace, added his enormous prestige to the Heath effort. Of the entire shadow cabinet, only Keith Joseph was for Margaret Thatcher. The rest, with the exception of one member who intended to abstain, would be voting to reelect Heath.

But it wasn't the rank and file in the country, the Tory peers in the House of Lords, or even the shadow cabinet that would decide the election. It was the 276 Conservative MPs in the Commons, the people who knew Heath best and liked him least.

THE BALLOTING BEGINS

On February 4, the Tory Parliamentary Party gathered at Westminster to vote. Committee Room 14 was set aside for the purpose, and starting at noon, Tory MPs began filing in one at a time to be handed a paper ballot with the names of the three candidates—Heath, Thatcher, and Fraser. Having scrawled their X next to their choice, the MPs would, under the watchful eyes of a representative of each of the candidates, stuff the ballot into a black box and leave the room.

Mrs. Thatcher voted early and then went off to the financial district for lunch, returning later to wait for the result in Neave's office. Heath, who also voted early, retired to his own office, where his old friend Lord Aldington kept him company.

Both opposing camps professed confidence. Heath's men had told their boss he had a good chance of winning a clear victory on the first ballot, and should expect 138 to 144 votes. Neave told Mrs. Thatcher to be ready for a 122-122 tie, which would force a second ballot. Sir Timothy Kitson, who was supervising the vote on behalf of the Heath team, offered to bet William Shelton, his opposite number in the Thatcher camp, one pound that Heath would win at least 130 votes. Shelton took the bet and offered a wager of his own in return: one pound that Mrs. Thatcher would get more than 110 votes.

At 3:30 P.M., the balloting was declared closed. While a crowd of eighty or so MPs and the entire parliamentary press corps waited anxiously in the wide corridor outside Room 14, the ballots were counted and checked. After about twenty-five minutes, an ashen-faced Kitson hurried out followed by Shelton, looking noncommittal. To the crowd, it seemed clear that Heath had not polled the 139-vote minimum necessary for a first ballot victory. The question remained just how big a lead over Mrs. Thatcher he had managed to amass. At four P.M. precisely, Edward du Cann emerged to announce the result:

Margaret Thatcher—130

Edward Heath—119

Hugh Fraser—16

Abstentions—11

Not only had Mrs. Thatcher kept Heath from winning, she had actually outpolled him. There was a moment of stunned silence as the implications of the totally unforeseen upset sank in. Then the corridor exploded in a gasp of disbelieving chatter and speculation.

Heath, still in his office, heard the news from Kitson. "So," he said quietly, "we got it all wrong." After a few moments, he began drafting his resignation statement, the first Tory leader in 53 years to be forced out of office before he was ready to go.

The honor of telling Mrs. Thatcher of her triumph belonged to Neave. "It's good news," he told her. "You're ahead in the poll. There will be a second ballot, but you got 130 votes." Not surprisingly, she was delighted—and enormously relieved. She had run "alone, regardless of the consequences," she later said, but the fact was—as she recognized—that had she lost, "it might have put me in the backbenches for life—or out" of Parliament entirely. In any case, Nigel Fisher recalls that when he came into Neave's office a few minutes after the announcement to offer his congratulations, Mrs. Thatcher jumped up, kissed him firmly on both cheeks and squealed, "Isn't it exciting, Nigel, isn't it exciting?"

That it was. "This is a great victory for the ordinary backbench MP," remarked Peter Emery, an ordinary backbench MP who had supported Heath a decade earlier only to discover, somewhat to his disappointment, that occasionally virtue really *is* its own reward. Suddenly, anything seemed possible, and the upstart Tory ranks were thrown into confused and happy turmoil. Writing in the left-wing *New Statesman* the next week, political commentator Alan Watkins likened the scene to "a Labor Party Conference after the Left has inflicted an unexpected defeat on the [leadership]. Everyone was highly excited and no one knew quite what to do next."

What Mrs. Thatcher had to do next, of course, was to prepare for the second ballot, which was scheduled for February 11, a week away. With Heath out of the picture, a new wave of candidates came forward, men who had coveted the leadership but who, out of loyalty or fear, had chosen not to contest their now-fallen leader directly. Foremost among them was the party's popular deputy leader, Willie Whitelaw, who declared his candidacy within two hours of Heath's resignation. A bluff, hearty, Scottish squire, the affable Whitelaw was one of the few politicians in British history to serve as minister for Northern Ireland and emerge from that quagmire with both his sanity and his reputation intact. Many MPs had urged Whitelaw to stand in the first ballot, but his loyalty to Heath had prevented that. Now it seemed he had waited too long. Not only did his lack of oratorical skills and almost complete ignorance of economics weigh against him, but there was a widespread feeling that, having bested Heath, Mrs. Thatcher had clearly earned the right to succeed him as party leader. What's more, Whitelaw's close association with Heath was hardly an asset at this point. "I did not vote Ted out in order to have Willie thrust on me," insisted one backbencher—and he spoke for many.

The only real question was how much of the first-ballot vote for Mrs. Thatcher was really more anti-Heath than pro-Thatcher. In retrospect, it seems clear that if either Joseph or Whitelaw had stood in the first round, either one could have beaten Heath handily. The fact that Whitelaw's politics were virtually identical to Heath's leads to the conclusion that the vote for Mrs. Thatcher was not particularly ideological. "Though it is hard to separate doctrine from personality," says Lord Blake, the provost of Queen's College, Oxford, and a leading historian of the Tory party, "I tend to think that the Party voted against Heath personally—not *for* her right-wing views."

Ideological or not, the support was there. And when former Heath backer and fellow shadow cabinet member Norman St. John Stevas threw in with Mrs. Thatcher, bringing with him much of the party's moderate center, it seemed nothing could stop "the Blessed Margaret," as the Catholic St. John Stevas liked to call her.

The week-long second campaign for the party leadership was a curiously amiable affair. Three of the five candidates seem to have entered the race less to win than to make ideological points or get their names better known for the sake of future contests. And when the two front-runners turned up to speak at the same Young Conservatives meeting— at which Whitelaw dutifully stuck to his assigned topic of home rule for Wales and Scotland, while Mrs. Thatcher cheerfully ignored hers and gave instead a rousing stemwinder—photographers had no trouble persuading the two to pose together. They even induced Whitelaw to give his rival a kiss on the cheek. When the resulting photograph appeared the next morning on the front page of virtually every newspaper in Britain, Whitelaw professed bewilderment. "I don't know what all the fuss is about," he said mildly. "After all, we've done it before lots of times, in hotels and halls, on staircases and in the streets."

LEADER OF THE OPPOSITION

February 11, the day of the second—and, as it turned out, final—leadership ballot, also happened to be the day Carol Thatcher, who shared her mother's interest in the law, was to take her bar examination. That morning, as she left their Flood Street home for Westminster, Mrs. Thatcher had some words of commiseration for her daughter. "Good luck, darling," she told her. "You can't be as nervous as me."

The balloting procedure was the same as it had been the week before, but this time the result was far more conclusive. Mrs. Thatcher polled 146 votes, with Whitelaw, her closest rival, trailing far behind with 79.

"It's all right," Neave told his candidate. "You're Leader of the Opposition."

It was a heady moment. Margaret Thatcher had become not only the first woman leader of the Conservative party, but the first woman opposition leader in any major Western democracy, and she had done so with a convincing personal victory. The romantic St. John Stevas, who had been a close friend of Mrs. Thatcher's ever since he served as her number two when she was running the Department of Education and Science, was a bit carried away by it all. "It wasn't an election," he declared a few days later, reaching for yet another religious metaphor. "It was an assumption."

Mrs. Thatcher was herself a bit stunned by her upstart victory. "To me," she told a post-election press conference, "it is like a dream that the next name in the list after Harold Macmillan, Sir Alec Douglas-Home and Edward Heath is Margaret Thatcher." But as she and Neave agreed even before the shouting had time to die down, there was plenty of work to do.

Her first task as leader was to call upon the man she had replaced. Like all the candidates for the leadership, she had pledged to offer Heath a post in her shadow cabinet. Just what post was never specified. Given their deep differences over economic policy, shadow chancellor seemed out of the question. Shadow foreign secretary was the likeliest job, the pundits agreed; after all, Heath's big issue had always been the Common Market, and Mrs. Thatcher wasn't known at the time to have any particularly strong feelings about foreign policy.

The morning after the final leadership ballot, Mrs. Thatcher called upon Heath at his London home to make good her promise. Since Heath hadn't yet given up the official car that is one of the perks of party leadership, Mrs. Thatcher—who herself owned a ten-year-old Vauxhall—had to be driven to the meeting in a friend's unprepossessing old Mini.

There are two accounts of how her session with Heath went. Mrs. Thatcher told associates that she came to the point quickly. "I have said publicly that I would ask you to join the shadow cabinet," she was reported to have said. "Will you do so?" Heath supposedly turned her down flatly, explaining that he would prefer to return to the backbenches. Mrs. Thatcher is then said to have asked him if he would lead the Conservative party campaign in the upcoming referendum on Common Market membership. (Britain had finally been admitted to the EEC in 1972 but was now having second thoughts, and a referendum had been called to resolve the dilemma.) Heath reportedly turned down that offer too, saying he would take an active but nonofficial part in the referendum campaign.

For his part, Heath later claimed that Mrs. Thatcher never offered him any specific post in her shadow cabinet. Strictly speaking, he was probably correct—Mrs. Thatcher never offered him any *specific* post. In effect she offered him any post he wanted. That he was not included in her shadow cabinet seems at least as much his doing as hers.

It was just as well Heath stayed on the outside. Although Mrs. Thatcher reappointed Whitelaw as deputy party leader, her chief adviser and number two in the shadow cabinet was Sir Keith Joseph, and he and Heath disagreed strongly about almost everything.

Nonetheless, Heath was a remarkably sore loser. It was years before he could bring himself to mention Mrs. Thatcher by name in public. Over a year later, when a television interviewer asked him if he had anything nice to say about his successor, the best Heath could do was to reply somewhat peevishly, "When she became leader of the party, I wished her well and I wished her every success. I don't think anyone can do more than that." And when he would show up in the Commons, in the corner seat traditionally reserved for former prime ministers alongside the government frontbench, he would studiously and ostentatiously ignore her. "He takes his place not ten feet from her," reported Labor MP Joe Ashton in December 1975, "he stares silently as the Sphinx, aloof and remote and looking constipated with the injustice of it all."

But as embarrassing as it may have been, Heath's behavior was not necessarily bad for Mrs. Thatcher. "She was helped by what many Tories felt to be Ted's rather boorish attitude towards her," recalls one of her advisers. "This helped to strengthen support for her in the first few months."

In any case, Mrs. Thatcher quickly found herself much too busy to worry overmuch about Heath's deportment. To dispel her reputation as a narrowly focused figure of limited and mainly suburban appeal, she plunged headlong into a grueling round of speaking engagements and personal appearances designed to establish her once and for all as a truly national politician. Within days after her election, she journeyed up to the north of England and to Scotland, heavily industrialized working-class areas thought to be hostile to her and everything she stood for. Nonetheless, she drew huge, enthusiastic crowds. Whether it was her politics they liked, or the fact that few people can resist a triumphant underdog, the fact was Mrs. Thatcher seemed clearly on her way to mastering the country.

On March 5, 1975, she gave her first political broadcast on television as leader of the opposition. Though she showed up at the studio carrying a book menacingly entitled *Invective & Abuse,* her message was a cheery one. "To yesterday's men," she trilled, "tomorrow's woman says hello."

She even managed, at least partly, to win over the all-male Carlton Club, the traditional London club of Tory party leaders. Though the club couldn't quite bring itself to end its centuries' old practice of excluding women from its lists, it did offer Mrs. Thatcher an honorary membership. Unfortunately, she had little time to make use of it—or to engage in many other social or semi-official affairs.

Shortly after her election as leader, Mrs. Thatcher insisted that "no, I'm not ruthless." At the same time, she added, she recognized that "some things have to be done and I know when they are done one will be accused of all kinds of things." One of the first changes she made was not terribly controversial: she redecorated the rather shabby leader's office, bringing in some upholstered settees and an armchair, a pink-shaded brass lamp, and a chrome-and-glass table. But after that cozy start, things got a bit stickier.

As expected, she reshuffled the shadow cabinet, dropping (predictably enough) a half-dozen Heath supporters. Somewhat less predictably she also promoted two Heath men—Sir Geoffrey Howe (who had actually run against her on the second ballot) and Sir Ian Gilmour—to the senior posts of chief Tory spokesmen for treasury and home affairs respectively. The howls came when she cleaned house at the Conservative Central Office, purging a good many of its passionately pro-Heath staff and appointing her old friend Lord Thorneycroft as party chairman. In addition to the chairman, Mrs. Thatcher replaced in fairly short order no less than nine other key party officials, including the deputy chairman, four vice-chairmen, a treasurer, the head of research and the director-general. Housecleaning or purge, her uninhibited hatchet-wielding outraged much of the Tory establishment. It was, snorted *The Times,* no less than "the act of a downright fool"—to which *New Statesman* columnist Alan Watkins gleefully riposted, "Those that live by patronage shall surely perish by patronage."

Although she had held a number of major portfolios in previous shadow cabinets, Mrs. Thatcher had been in an actual cabinet only once—and the fact was that education minister was rather low in the pecking order. But if her more experienced colleagues in the new shadow cabinet thought their new leader would be easily dominated, they were in for a rude shock. She brooked no nonsense. If she felt a question had been settled, there was no reopening it. She would listen to her colleagues but was far happier lecturing them. One member of her shadow cabinet said her approach to policymaking was "like a little terrier, yap-yap-yapping at the issues."

In the House of Commons, she displayed rather less control—at least at first. Harold Wilson had welcomed her warmly, if a bit cheekily, when she made her first appearance in the chamber as opposition leader. "I look forward," he said, referring to the customary consultations between party leaders, "to the meetings behind the Speaker's chair, and to the informality and intimacy they afford." But he was not about to make life easy for her. A master of parliamentary sparring, Wilson flicked and jabbed relentlessly at Mrs. Thatcher, never attacking her personally, but making her appear snappish rather than witty. When, for example, he chided her for her inexperience, the best she was able to come back with was the rather nasty retort: "What the Prime Minister means is that he has been around for a long time—and he looks it."

Mrs. Thatcher complained constantly that Wilson would never give her a straight answer at Question Time—which one reporter compared to complaining that Muhammad Ali would never stand still to let you hit him. She seemed uncertain in her first weeks as leader and at times appeared not to grasp the implications of her elevation. One of the first times under her leadership that the Tories introduced a motion to censure Wilson's government, she told her colleagues that she didn't want to open the debate. Instead, she would rather speak towards the end, after she would have had a chance to hear how the prime minister intended to defend himself. It was left to her most trusted friend, Airey Neave, who was now in the shadow cabinet as chief opposition spokesman on Northern Ireland, to set her straight. "But Margaret," he told her, "when you're Prime Minister you'll have to open debates quite often."

Her private life had changed considerably too. Denis had by now retired from Burmah Oil (though he remained on the boards of two other companies and continued to serve as chairman of a family-owned weed-killing firm called Chipmans Ltd). The children were out of school— Carol working as a law clerk and Mark as a trainee accountant. Despite Mrs. Thatcher's new fame, all were determined to keep out of the public glare, Denis Thatcher most of all. An inveterate golfer, occasional sailor, and fanatic rugby fan (he had played the game himself and was for twelve years one of the country's top referees), Mr. Thatcher had no intention of letting his wife's skyrocketing career disrupt his comfortable life. "They say I am the most shadowy husband of all time," he told reporters just after the leadership election. "I intend to stay that way and leave the limelight to my wife." Still, there were inevitable intrusions. Government security men, for example, insisted he exchange the personalized license plates on his car ("DT 3") for something more anonymous.

Despite the demands of her new job, Mrs. Thatcher tried to continue keeping house herself at Flood Street. Inevitably, however, standards slipped. "The house is not as perfect as I would like," she confessed in an October 1975 interview, "because I haven't time to make it so." And the family routine was destroyed, just as it had been when she was a child. "We rarely sit down together for a meal, except breakfast, during the week," she reported. "If, during the Parliamentary recess, I am working at home, the house becomes an office and people are constantly in and out." A good cook who once enjoyed pottering about in the kitchen, Mrs. Thatcher now found herself reduced to seeing "that there is enough food in the fridge for the family to help themselves."

BROADENING THE ARENA

It was a challenging time for Mrs. Thatcher. She had to establish herself not only throughout Britain as a credible national leader, but in the international arena as well. Lacking any real experience in foreign affairs, and being something of an unknown quantity to her foreign counterparts, she set out to remedy that state of affairs by scheduling a hectic round of foreign travel. In addition to the more than two dozen trips around Britain that she made in 1975, Mrs. Thatcher also found the time to visit Turkey, Luxembourg, France, Germany, Rumania, Canada, and the U.S.

The most important foreign trip was her journey to America in September 1975. She was a bit uptight at the start, turning up her nose at a hot dog offered to her in New York, but by the time the visit was over she was totally in command. Arriving in New York at a time when the headlines were dominated by three other (albeit rather less distinguished) women—Patty Hearst, "Squeaky" Fromme and Sara Jane Moore—she stole the show and raised a few political and diplomatic eyebrows by dropping the guise of nonpartisan neutrality customarily supposed to envelop all politicians when they go abroad.

In New York, Chicago, and Washington (where she drew a bigger crowd at the National Press Club than the recently departed Japanese prime minister), she hit hard at Wilson's Labor government and what she said it was doing to her country. Britain, she warned, was an "eleventh-hour nation" dedicated to "the relentless pursuit of equality" in which democracy itself was on trial. Such outspokenness in foreign parts angered many at home. The pro-Labor *Daily Mirror* ran a front-page "Letter to America" in response, arguing that "the British sickness is class" not socialism—and that "Margaret Thatcher is the embodiment of that system." Foreign Secretary James Callaghan had some sharp words too. "It seems to me," he said severely, "that when we are abroad, all of us submerge our individual party policies in the interests of the country we come from." Mrs. Thatcher was characteristically unabashed. "It's not part of my job to be a propagandist for a socialist society," she retorted.

Americans, however, were less interested in Britain's ideological problems than in the fact that its opposition leader happened to be a woman. As a result, Mrs. Thatcher was deluged by questions about feminism and women's liberation wherever she went. The questions seemed to annoy her, and her answers did not always go down well with America's more liberated females. When a Chicago woman incautiously asked Mrs. Thatcher whether she owed her position at least partly to the influence of the feminist movement, she snapped, "Some of us were making it long before Women's Lib was ever thought of," adding that all the political leaders she had so far met have "just accepted me as a politician and got on with business." The fact that she happened to be a *woman* leader, she insisted, "is something that never bothers or concerns me." And when another Chicagoan asked whether she preferred "Mrs." or "Ms." Thatcher, the answer was as acerbic as it was sincere: "I am not sure I fully understand the significance of your question," she replied. "I am just Margaret Thatcher. You must take me as I am."

That America did, and it seemed fascinated by her. CBS commentator Eric Sevareid observed that "Wilson is the passing figure and she is the arriving one." He lauded her "combination of dignity and the common touch," and concluded that Britons were "looking for a break and she may be it."

The trip, which included meetings with President Gerald Ford and Secretary of State Henry Kissinger, was an important breakthrough for her. As she noted when it was over, "I feel I have been accepted as a leader in the international sphere—the field in which they said I would never be accepted." And the adulation continued back home as well. By the time she returned, the polls indicated that forty-seven percent of all Britons expected her to be their next prime minister, versus just thirty-one percent for Harold Wilson.

Such sentiments can be ruthlessly ephemeral, however, and Mrs. Thatcher still had a major task before her. She had inherited the leadership of a divided, demoralized party. If she was truly to be its leader, she had to master the annual Party Conference, meeting in October 1975 in the gaudy resort town of Blackpool.

It was a tense scene at first. Heath showed up the day after she did, winning a tumultuous ovation from the assembled delegates as he strode into the main hall where he conspicuously avoided the new leader. To make matters worse, over drinks that night with a group of journalists, he lambasted Mrs. Thatcher and Keith Joseph. They were, he said, fanatics who would hurt the country and ruin the Conservative party. The next day his comments were headline news. Heath issued the obligatory denial, but it was not a very convincing one.

For her part, Mrs. Thatcher pretended not to notice any of it. And at the Conference's final rally (by which time Heath had gone), she left no doubt as to who was in command. Dressed in Tory blue, she began her speech by praising her predecessors: Churchill, who was leader at the first Conference she had ever attended, then Eden, Macmillan, Home, and yes, Heath, too. She went on to look to the future. "Let me give you my vision," she told the vast hall. "A man's right to work as he will. To spend what he earns. To own property. To have the state as servant and not as master. These are the British inheritance." The Tory faithful cheered themselves hoarse. As she said later that evening, "Now, I *am* Leader."

6

Waiting for
the Call

*"[The Prime Ministership] belongs to
the courageous, not to the timid."*

FOR ALL HER POLITICAL AMBITION, aptitude, and success,
Margaret Thatcher was never really at home in the glare of
public life. It made her nervous and uncomfortable, and, as
a result, she often seemed every bit as cold and remote as
Ted Heath. (Indeed, just before the 1975 leadership election, the influential *Times* columnist Bernard Levin compared what he
regarded as the similarly frosty personalities of the two main contenders
and wondered what point there was in the Tories' jumping "out of the
igloo and onto the glacier.") In fact, she could be—and often was—astonishingly warm. She continued to be particularly considerate to the
people she worked with, remembering birthdays, apologizing for the increasingly lengthy workday and, on one occasion, asking aides to go easy
on a colleague because he was having marital problems. When an old
friend, Tory MP Fergus Montgomery, was charged with shoplifting in
1977, creating a serious potential embarrassment for the party, she
stood by him staunchly, spending the better part of an afternoon walking him round and round the corridors at Westminster until she was satisfied that virtually everyone there had seen them together. And when
he was finally acquitted of the charge, she startled MPs by dashing into
the Members' Bar at the House (where she was virtually never seen) to
give him a congratulatory hug and kiss and share in a celebratory drink.

But though in private she would display a friendly and even affectionate streak that invariably surprised people meeting her for the first time, this side of her nature never came across in public. Major speeches terrified her, and to compensate she would fall back on her acquired middle-class mannerisms—the high-pitched, annoyingly deliberate lecturing tone of a schoolmarm (which one Scottish MP tagged her "Margaret-the-moralist" style)—that evidently had impressed her as a child. She distrusted the press and disliked talking to reporters. "Interviews," she once complained, "come out devoid of flesh and blood, full of artifice, full of cynicism, full of the epithets of their writers." And she despised appearing on television. "Winston was never on television," she observed somewhat enviously, "certainly never interviewed on it." What bothered her the most was that the image she had of herself wasn't the image she saw projected on the small screen. "It's not really me you are seeing," she insisted shortly after her election as leader, "because so far I don't feel natural on television."

Unfortunately, now that she was leader, the spotlight of public and press attention shone on her more intensely than ever. Her wardrobe was publicly dissected, her penchant for outlandish hats made fun of, and her relatively affluent life-style criticized—all in a manner which none of her predecessors had had to contend with. In part, this was because she was a woman, and hence a figure of more than usual curiosity. It also had to do with the growing personalization of politics, the increasing treatment of political figures as celebrities akin to pop singers or movie stars, whose every action and preference, no matter how trivial, seems worthy of comment. And it was partly Mrs. Thatcher's own fault, the result of her continuing insistance that she was no different from the great mass of people. Of course she was different, and if she refused to admit it, the press and her opponents were determined to prove her wrong.

For her part, Mrs. Thatcher felt she owed no one any apologies for the way she lived. When critics sniped at the Thatcher family's annual skiing vacations, a luxury far out of the range of the vast majority of Britons, she snapped that she and her husband had "worked jolly hard for that." Her circumstances, she insisted somewhat defensively, were comfortable, but no more than that. "We're not wealthy, Denis and I," she said. "Wealth to me means a great deal of heavy capital. Saving is a great worry to us." Indeed, coming from a generation that (as she put it) did not believe in borrowing unnecessarily, she never owned even a single credit card. (When one bank foolishly sent her one unsolicited, she tore it up and threw it away.)

A VOICE FOR HUMAN RIGHTS

Wealthy or not, Mrs. Thatcher had more important concerns on her mind than how her bank balance compared to the national average. Politically, she was wading into waters far deeper than she had ever known. As party leader and a potential prime minister, she had to demonstrate her expertise—or at the very least, her interest—in every aspect of statecraft. By this time, her economic and social views were well known. But despite her successful trips abroad, the same could not be said about her approach to foreign affairs.

Characteristically, she set out to rectify this embarrassing gap in her image by tackling the touchiest and most important foreign policy of the day—détente. The largely American effort to initiate a new era of more relaxed relations between East and West, signalled by the signing of the Helsinki Accords in 1975, was—and remains—the subject of intense debate and violent disagreement in Europe. Many diplomats and political leaders wondered whether Washington, in its enthusiasm, was being a bit naive in accepting the assurances of the Soviets about their regard for human rights. Harold Wilson, whose Labor government was firmly behind détente, was not among them. But Mrs. Thatcher was, and in her first eighteen months as leader she set out on a determined campaign to make sure the world knew it.

She dated her concern for human rights back to her childhood, to the time when the Austrian refugee who had been her sister's pen pal came to live with their family in Grantham and appalled the young Margaret Roberts with her account of life under the Nazis. Years later, in an airport book shop while on a trip as education minister, Mrs. Thatcher picked up a copy of Solzhenitsyn's novel, *The First Circle*. It fascinated and gripped her to the point where she neglected reading her official briefs in order to get through it, and it inspired in her a special and continuing interest in the state of human rights within the Soviet Union.

As Tory leader, her first official foray into the area of détente and human rights came in April 1975, when Harold Wilson returned from Moscow to announce the signing of a new Anglo-Soviet trade agreement. During Question Time in the Commons, Mrs. Thatcher challenged him about the desirability of such a pact. As usual, Wilson deflected the question, suggesting she leave foreign policy to those with more experience in the field. His hauteur infuriated her, and she decided to carve out for herself an unchallengable role in the debate over détente. She would give a series of well-researched, carefully considered speeches on the subject that would leave no doubt as to where she stood on the issue or her qualifications to address herself to it.

Her first such speech was delivered three months later, in July 1975, to the Chelsea Conservative Association. "Détente," she told the group, "sounds a fine word. And, to the extent that there has really been a relaxation in international tension, it is a fine thing. But the fact remains that throughout this decade of détente, the armed forces of the Soviet Union have increased, are increasing, and show no signs of diminishing." Not surprisingly, her maiden effort didn't set the world on fire. In fact, it inspired very little comment at the time, though it may have influenced Wilson to make a tougher than expected speech at the Helsinki Conference a few days later.

She returned to the subject the following January, in a speech whose uncompromising, hard-line tone was deliberately designed to attract the maximum possible press attention. "The Russians," she flatly declared, "are bent on world dominance, and they are rapidly acquiring the means to become the most powerful imperial nation in the world has seen ... They put guns before butter, while we put just about everything before guns. They know that they are a superpower in only one sense—the military sense. They are a failure in human and economic terms." If Britain didn't understand that, she went on to warn, "if we cannot draw the lesson ... then we are destined—in their words—to end up on 'the scrap heap of history.' "

The Wilson government attempted to dismiss the speech as the inconsequential outburst of an unqualified woman. Much to its embarrassment, however, the Soviets took it quite seriously. Tass, the official Soviet news agency, labelled Mrs. Thatcher an "Iron Lady"—an appellation she was to wear quite proudly and to great political effect—and Moscow undertook a vigorous propaganda campaign to discredit her, portraying her in cartoons quite literally as the wicked witch of the West.

Encouraged by this response, Mrs. Thatcher returned to the theme for a third time on July 31, 1976, the first anniversary of the Helsinki signing. Quoting the "Iron Lady" tag with evident relish, she lambasted Moscow for "flagrantly" ignoring the spirit of the year-old agreement. "In spite of Helsinki," she said, "the Soviet Union remains a closed and repressive society." And she repeated her earlier pledges that when in power she would step up Britain's declining defense spending. The speech placed her in the forefront of Western doubters of détente and earned her an immediate invitation from Peking to visit China. (She went the following spring, and later justified her apparent approval of a state every bit as totalitarian as the Soviet Union by arguing, "In philosophical terms, we are different from her as much as we are from Russia. But we can recognize that China is not an expansionist power like Russia and she does not pose a threat to us.")

WILSON STEPS DOWN

Domestically, too, the pot was boiling over. By early 1976, a series of by-election losses had cut Labor's majority to just one seat. For a time, that seemed not to matter much. Wilson was a shrewd operator and his "Social Contract" with the unions seemed to be working. Crippling strikes of the sort that had toppled Heath had all but vanished, while the unions' voluntary agreement to limit pay increases to six pounds a week had halved the rate of inflation, which the year before had broken thirty percent. On March 16, 1976, however, the domestic political situation in Britain was thrown into turmoil.

At a gathering of the cabinet at No. 10, Harold Wilson startled his fellow ministers by opening the meeting with an eight-page statement. "I have just returned from the Palace where I had an audience with the Queen," he began—and in his flat Yorkshire accent he proceeded to announce his unexpected and totally "irrevocable" decision to resign as prime minister. He intended, he said, to return to the backbenches; his abdication of power would be complete. In precisely the same words that Stanley Baldwin had used when he turned the government over to Neville Chamberlain on the eve of World War II, Wilson promised, "Once I leave, I leave. I am not going to speak to the man on the bridge and I am not going to spit on the deck."

Just why Wilson quit is still a mystery. His love for the job and for the perks of power was legendary. Indeed, it had been said of him that the reason he was always so keen to fly to America was that it enabled him to be prime minister for another five hours that day. At the time, he claimed to have decided in March 1974 to stay in office no more than two years. He had hoped to step down after the 1975 Party Conference, he said, but then changed his mind in order to direct the first stage of his government's anti-inflation policy. He added that he had informed the Queen in December 1975 that he would be giving up the prime ministership in three months' time.

Wilson had just turned sixty, and though he insisted that his health was not a problem ("I am fit as flea," he said), he felt he had "a clear duty" to step aside in favor of someone else. Some of his associates believed that Wilson, who had held the office longer than any other peace-time prime minister in this century, had his eye on the history books. He was said to have rated the Tories' chances of winning the next general election quite highly—and, a Labor MP suggested at the time, "He was determined never to get beaten again." His wife may also have been a factor. Mary Wilson was a shy, sensitive woman who, in the words of a close friend, "loathed every minute of Harold's time in office." None-theless, rumors persist that Wilson quit so abruptly because he had something to hide—something that, if he hadn't resigned, would have come out into the open and destroyed him. If so, he has kept his alleged secret well hidden. To this day, no skeleton has been discovered in Wilson's closet that would be of sufficient magnitude to account for his astonishing decision.

In any case, Wilson insisted he was going at a time when Britain's economic fortunes had reached what he described as "the turn of the hinge." Thus, he argued, there was no need to call a general election to pick his successor; certainly, the unwritten British constitution didn't require one. He would leave it to his fellow Labor MPs to select the next prime minister.

That decision did not please the Tories. Labor was trailing badly in the polls and in a general election almost certainly would have been voted out of power. What's more, Mrs. Thatcher guessed that Labor MPs would ultimately vote to replace Wilson with his foreign secretary, James Callaghan, and she felt that of all the possible contenders, he would prove the toughest adversary for herself and her party. Thus, when Wilson appeared in the House a few hours after his decision to resign had been announced, she greeted him with a pointed question. "Are you aware," she asked, "that the best way to resolve the uncertainty and give the new prime minister the authority required would be to put the matter to the people for a vote?" As usual, Wilson sidestepped her.

As Mrs. Thatcher had predicted, Callaghan emerged from a six-man field a week later to win the Labor party leadership, and with it the keys to 10 Downing Street. In some ways, he was not all that different from his opposite number. The great-grandson of an illiterate weaver who fled Ireland during the nineteenth-century potato famine, Callaghan, like Mrs. Thatcher, had come from humble surroundings. His father, a chief petty officer in the Royal Navy, had died when he was nine, leaving his Baptist mother a meager pension. "My mother had only one idea," Callaghan recalled years later, "to get me into an absolutely safe job that guaranteed a pension at sixty—and can you blame her?"

During World War II, Callaghan enlisted in the navy himself, and rose to the rank of lieutenant. He entered Parliament in 1945, representing the Welsh constituency of Cardiff South. Two years later, Clement Attlee brought him into the government as a junior transport minister. Though he never went to a university, in the 1950s he became a disciple of Harold Laski, the left-wing political scientist. His first real cabinet post was as chancellor of the exchequer under Wilson in 1964. Three years later, after the devaluation debacle, Wilson transferred him to the Home Office, where he remained as home secretary until Labor's defeat in 1970. When Labor and Wilson came back to power in 1974, Callaghan was made foreign secretary, a job in which he drew mixed notices. While at the Foreign Office, he was accused of botching a 1974 attempt to mediate a settlement between the Greeks and Turks on Cyprus, an episode that led U.S. Secretary of State Henry Kissinger to dismiss him as a "boy scout."

Callaghan won the leadership—in the process, beating off a determined challenge by Labor's left wing—because he was regarded as a Wilsonian moderate, a reliable caretaker figure who could keep the ship of state on a reasonably steady course. Like Wilson, he was a shrewd political operator, so flexible, in fact, that many considered him little more than an opportunist. ("It is frightful that we are . . . stuck with a Prime Minister who has never taken a line on a damn thing in his life," grumbled Lord George-Brown, a former Labor foreign secretary who had quit the party shortly before Wilson's resignation.)

Operator or opportunist, Callaghan certainly had his work cut out for him as prime minister. Within hours of his taking office, Labor lost its one-seat majority in the House when forty-six-year-old Brian O'Malley, the government's minister of health and social security, suddenly died of a stroke. The next day, a Labor backbencher changed his party allegiance, going over to the Conservatives, and leaving Labor with just 314 seats in the Commons, versus the 316 controlled by the Tories and the minor parties. "Two days ago, I'd have thought we could go on for another two years without an election," said one Labor MP. "But now I'm not so sure. What a hell of a housewarming present for Jim Callaghan."

As was the case between the two 1974 elections, Labor's lack of a clear majority did not mean the government would automatically fall. As long as it could get a handful of minor-party MPs to support it on votes of confidence, Labor could continue governing until it deemed the moment propitious for a general election.

Callaghan's first task was to come up with a replacement for the voluntary six-pound-a-week ceiling on pay rises that Wilson had persuaded the unions to accept. The agreement to honor the guidelines ran only until July 1976, leaving the new prime minister with less than four months to sell the unions a new package. Determined to come up with something just as effective as Wilson had, Callaghan and Denis Healey (who remained as chancellor of the exchequer) drafted a new government budget that proposed a three percent limit on wage increases in exchange for £1.3 billion in tax cuts. The tax cuts on top of the allowable three percent pay raise, Healey argued, would still permit workers to increase their take-home pay by that familiar six pounds a week. Unfortunately, the unions weren't convinced about Healey's arithmetic, and without their cooperation the plan couldn't work. Thus, in a move as tactically astute as it was politically unprecedented, Callaghan and Healey tossed their plan into the unions' laps. If they didn't like it, Healey said, they should come up with an alternative. It was up to them either to accept or reject the government's offer.

To the Tories, this somewhat cynical manuevering represented an outrageous government sellout to union power. "I do not think the chancellor of the exchequer can abdicate his responsibilities to anybody outside Parliament," Mrs. Thatcher lectured Healey in the Commons. "That seems to be taxation without representation."

Whatever it was, it seemed to work, though only after a fashion. Healey was forced to compromise on a 4.5 percent pay ceiling, and the pound-sterling proceeded to crash—hitting an all-time low of $1.70 in June 1976. But Callaghan did persuade the militant coal miners, who had been instrumental in bringing Heath down, to moderate their wage demands. And by postponing his planned nationalization of Britain's shipbuilding and aircraft industries, he was able to convince the U.S. and ten other industrialized nations to put up $5.3 billion in credits to help the beleaguered Bank of England support the pound in foreign exchange markets. As a result, when Mrs. Thatcher accused the prime minister of presiding over "drift, debt and decay" and introduced a motion of no-confidence in his government that June, Callaghan had no trouble rounding up enough minor-party support to turn back the challenge by a comfortable 309–290 margin. "Now, now, little lady," he gibed at her in the House after his victory, "you don't want to believe all those things you read in the newspapers about crisis and upheavals and the end of civilization as we know it. Dearie me, not at all."

Such condescension infuriated her, and Callaghan knew it, which is why he continued to employ it against her for the next three years. To her immense frustration, Mrs. Thatcher felt constrained from fighting back in kind. "As a woman Leader," she explained (in a rare concession that sometimes her sex *did* make a difference), "if I do that, the danger is it will become shrewish." Not surprisingly, given her combative nature, she quickly grew to detest her opposition (and, hence, inherently limited) role. "When I first became Leader," she said a few years later, "I thought: Oh Lord, I hope to goodness we're not in Opposition for more than eighteen months. It's such a *tough* job being in Opposition." For one thing, as she noted, "so long as you are in Opposition, and can only talk and can't act, you are misrepresented." What's more, because of the government's power to set the agenda and have the last word, it was possible—indeed, quite easy—for a skilled parliamentarian like Callaghan to avoid a showdown almost indefinitely. To the feisty Mrs. Thatcher, this sort of thing was almost unendurable. "I'm fine in a roughhouse," she said. "It's when they sit there like suet puddings that I find it difficult."

Callaghan's smugness notwithstanding, Britain's economic situation continued to deteriorate through 1976. Though inflation was coming down and North Sea oil held out the promise of a golden future, unemployment was rising towards the 1.5 million mark, the pound remained weak, and the trade deficit was widening. By the fall, Healey was forced to beg the International Monetary Fund for an emergency $3.9 billion loan to keep the British economy afloat. The IMF agreed, but on the proviso that the Labor government adopt a series of tough austerity measures to get its books back into order.

MRS. THATCHER STRIKES BACK

The Conservatives' popularity was rising fast, and Mrs. Thatcher continued to flail away at what she called "the fallacy of Socialism . . . the idea that profit is somehow wrong." Callaghan responded by attempting with some success to switch the main public debate from Mrs. Thatcher's increasingly effective theme of "freedom vs. Socialism" to an argument over the virtues of an incomes policy.

It was a shrewd tactic. The notion of an incomes policy, under which the government seeks by persuasion or coercion to limit pay increases to a stated amount, had long been popular in Britain. And though its track record hadn't been very good in the past, it certainly seemed to be working now, judging by the declining inflation rate. Mrs. Thatcher had no use for the incomes policy approach. It amounted to "getting central bargaining by the state on behalf of everyone," she argued. "It can't take account of the variety of difference between companies, between places of work . . ." But the public thought otherwise; certainly they weren't attracted to the alternative she proposed: a strict, austere monetarism, involving a lower level of government spending and a slower growth of the money supply (meaning, in effect, a probable increase in unemployment and an almost certain jump in interest rates).

Callaghan's advantage was only a temporary one, however. Labor was having serious troubles of its own. The party was pledged to support what was known as "devolution"—Britain's version of what Americans call "states rights"—in this case the establishment of representative assemblies in Scotland and Wales that would assume some of the powers the Westminster Parliament was used to wielding over the entire United Kingdom. Labor moderates led by Callaghan were not prepared to go quite so far in this direction as some activists would have liked. As a result, in March 1977 the prime minister suffered a humiliating setback when his own party's left wing deserted him to form an unlikely alliance with antidevolution Tories that ultimately defeated the government's watered-down devolution bill. A few days later, another left-wing revolt made it doubtful that he could muster enough support to pass some public spending cuts required by the conditions of the IMF loan. To avoid further embarrassment, Callaghan refused to allow the controversial measure to come to a vote. Infuriated by his desperate maneuvering, Mrs. Thatcher introduced her second motion of no confidence.

She came to the battle in a remarkably optimistic frame of mind, buoyed by her party's fifteen-point lead in the public-opinion polls and by a series of by-election victories. She had just returned from Zurich, where she had been invited to address the Zurich Economic Society, one of the most influential and prestigious forums in Europe. "Had I spoken to you last year," she told the group, "I should have expressed faith in our nation and civilization and its capacity for survival. But today, I can offer you more than faith. I bring you optimism rooted in present-day experience." Her reading of events, she went on, had given her "reason to believe that the tide is beginning to turn against collectivisim, socialism, statism, *dirigism,* whatever you call it . . . It is becoming increasingly obvious to many people who were intellectual socialists that socialism has failed to fulfill its promises, both in its more extreme forms in the Communist world and in its compromise versions." What she termed "a revulsion against the sour fruit of socialist experience" was turning people back to the realization that freedom of choice—and, by extension, a free-enterprise economy—was the basis of the only system of ethics that made any sense. "Choice," she argued, "is the essence of ethics: if there were no choice, there would be no ethics, no good, no evil; good and evil have meaning only in so far as man is free to choose." And quoting her favorite poet, Kipling, she held out her vision of the Conservative Second Coming:

> *So when the world is asleep, and there seems no hope of waking*
> *Out of some long, bad dream that made her mutter and moan,*
> *Suddenly, all men arise to the noise of fetters breaking,*
> *And everyone smiles at his neighbor, and tells him his soul is his own.*

Back in London, however, such poetry had little effect. As it had so many times in the past, the balance of power lay with the Liberal party, and Callaghan was determined to win the support of its thirteen MPs. He couldn't consider inviting them into a full-fledged coalition; that had been anathema to all Labor party leaders since "the Great Betrayal" by Ramsay MacDonald in 1931. Nor could Callaghan agree to the laundry list of conditions presented to him by the Liberals' boyish leader, thirty-nine-year-old David Steel. In addition to the Liberals' perennial demand for proportional representation, Steel was insisting as the price for his party's support that Callaghan commit himself to lower taxes, a new devolution bill, and a promise of no more nationalization—all of which would, if implemented, result in a massive and irrevocable defection by the Labor left.

But Callaghan knew that Steel was not dealing from strength. Though the polls showed that a spring general election—which would be required if the government lost the vote of confidence—would probably go against Labor, they also indicated that the Liberals would fare even worse. So in a series of private talks, Callaghan called Steel's bluff. In the end, Steel agreed to instruct his troops to vote against Mrs. Thatcher's no-confidence motion and to participate for at least the next six months in what Callaghan called an "experimental collaboration." What Steel got for all this was little more than Callaghan's promise to consider some of his legislative proposals as well as a firm commitment to establish a joint committee wherein Liberals would "consult with Labor on Government policy." Thus was born what the newspapers quickly dubbed the "Lib-Lab Pact." "This," crowed a top Labor official after the agreement was formally adopted, "was Jim's finest hour."

It may well have been. With the thirteen Liberal MPs now pledged to vote with the government, Labor had no trouble beating off Mrs. Thatcher's motion of no confidence. She was angry and frustrated, but there was nothing she could do.

Within a week, however, the Lib-Lab Pact began fraying at the edges. Restive Labor backbenchers made it impossible for the government to write a new devolution bill. And the Finance Bill, which enables the government to implement its budget, and is thus the linchpin of the government's entire economic policy, was sabotaged in committee by two Labor MPs who ignored the instructions of their whips and voted with the Tories to push through extra tax cuts that would cost the government an additional £340 million. Labor, Steel complained, had become "a difficult, fragile and internally divided partner."

In an effort to keep the troops in line, Labor party leaders began mounting something of a scare campaign, making dire predictions as to what might happen if the government fell and Mrs. Thatcher came to power. Unless everyone got behind Callaghan, warned Trade Minister Eric Varley, "the alternative would be too horrible to contemplate."

Finally, late in June, Callaghan was forced to read the riot act to his unruly backbenchers. Speaking to some two hundred Labor MPs who had crowded into a House of Commons committee room, he put the issue clearly and succinctly. "Either this Government governs or it goes," Callaghan declared angrily. "Our present difficulties are not caused by the Tories, they are caused by ourselves." It seemed to do the trick, at least for a while. Still trailing badly in the polls, though not by quite as wide a margin as a few months earlier, neither Labor nor the Liberals wanted to be forced to go to the country. Not only did it seem almost certain that a general election would sweep the Tories back into power; there was also a widespread feeling that the economic advantage provided by North Sea oil, which was expected to be flowing at capacity within a very few years, would keep them there for a decade or more.

But the differences within Labor were only papered over; nothing fundamental was resolved except the near universal desire of MPs to retain their seats. The mildly left-wing *Guardian,* no friend of the Tories and the only one of Britain's four serious national dailies to support Labor with any degree of regularity, said as much in an editorial, sounding a theme that the Conservatives were later to pick up and use with great effectiveness. "No electorate," the newspaper counselled, "is likely to invest its trust in a Party whose Government has been content simply to drift from expedient to expedient, its legislation progressively collapsing around it with little objective left but to stagger through somehow, hoping for salvation through North Sea oil."

Nonetheless, Labor continued to stagger on. But the going grew rough again early in July 1977 when two of Britain's biggest unions, the two million-member Transport and General Workers Union (TGWU) and the 260,000-member National Union of Miners (NUM), tore up the by now tattered "Social Contract." Though British trade unionists have a worldwide reputation for bloody-mindedness, the TGWU and the NUM were not acting simply out of spite or pique. Their willingness to keep wage increases below 4.5 percent for the previous two years—a period during which inflation had stayed well into double figures—had in fact reduced their members' real income by nearly 5 percent. Now they were demanding a return to what they called "unfettered collective bargaining"—no pay ceilings, incomes policies, or government guidelines, just old-fashioned negotiating for whatever they could win. Having little choice but to acquiesce to the unions, the government decided to try to put the best possible face on what was unmistakably another humiliation. Thus, Denis Healey rose in the House of Commons to praise the unions' "restraint and patriotism" (they had, after all, honored the Social Contract for two years) as well as to hint that from here on out the government could live with wage increases on the order of ten percent a year.

ON THE GO AGAIN

Mrs. Thatcher was not surprised by this latest development. But as long as the Liberals continued to support Callaghan's government, she and her party were impotent. She continued to attack Callaghan, of course, crisscrossing the country to lambaste what she considered to be his ineffectual leadership. She kept to a gruelling pace and came to rely heavily on the assistance of her close friend, Lady Guinevere Tilney, who had volunteered to act as a sort of lady's maid to the Tory leader. "Gwynney," as she was known to her friends, was the wife of Tory backbencher Sir John Tilney and something of a politician herself. She had gotten to know Mrs. Thatcher when the two served as co-chairmen of Britain's National Women's Commission from 1969 to 1971. (They were in some ways an odd choice to head the organization: both were firmly opposed to equal-rights legislation, Mrs. Thatcher out of her Sophoclean belief that it would make women superior to men, Lady Tilney because she felt "it stamps women as second-class.") Now Gwynney traveled everywhere with Mrs. Thatcher, packing and unpacking her clothes, selecting the right handbag and accessories, in short, supervising every aspect (including the buying) of her friend's wardrobe.

It was a big job, for Mrs. Thatcher was now almost constantly on the go. In 1977, her travels took her not only throughout Britain, but abroad as well. In the spring, she made her first trip as Tory leader to the Far East, stopping in Japan and Hong Kong, and taking up the anti-détente-inspired invitation to come to China, where she was treated more like a visiting head of state than the mere opposition leader she was.

The China visit fostered the impression that Mrs. Thatcher was being taken more seriously than ever by foreign governments—and so she was. Nowhere was this clearer than on her second official visit to the U.S., a nine-day trip she made in September 1977. In New York, she drew large crowds as she spoke with characteristic confidence about the inevitability of another Tory government in Britain. "The question is not whether we will win," she asserted, "but how large the majority will be." She also went to Houston, where she was given a VIP tour of the space center, managing to retain her aplomb even when the tight linen suit she was wearing forced her to duck-walk awkwardly through the small door of a mock-up of the space shuttle. "One tries not to be inelegant about these things," she grinned, grasping an outstretched arm to steady herself and then striding off with a purposeful look to see the moon rocks.

Her biggest moment of the trip—and possibly of her entire diplomatic career to date—came in Washington. Just a few weeks earlier, White House aides had turned down a request by François Mitterand, the leader of France's socialist opposition, for a White House meeting with President Carter. Such meetings, they explained, were reserved for heads of state only. But when Mrs. Thatcher showed up, Carter quickly invited her to the Oval Office—the clearest signal possible that the U.S. government shared her view of the Conservative party's bright prospects.

Carter may have gotten a bit more than he bargained for when he asked Mrs. Thatcher in for a chat. Though she was grateful for the invitation, she was no more reluctant about lecturing the American president than she was her own shadow cabinet. When Carter asked her if a Tory government in Britain could get along with the unions, she enthusiastically responded, "Let me put it the way I put it in my campaign speeches"—whereupon she proceeded to launch into a campaign speech, making the familiar points that high taxes stifle incentives and that many British workers thus support the Conservatives. She also irked some senior U.S. officials by flatly telling Carter, who professed to be putting American foreign policy on a moral basis, that "foreign policy is simply a matter of national self-interest." In fact, she was doing no more than echoing a traditional British view of the matter that dated back to Lord Palmerston, the mid-nineteenth-century prime minister who pragmatically maintained: "We have no eternal allies and no perpetual enemies. Our interests are eternal and perpetual and those interests it is our duty to follow."

Still, it was a highly successful trip. Unfortunately, it did not give her the boost at home that her first American triumph had generated. The combination of a steadily declining (though still double-digit) inflation rate, the government's apparent ability to placate the unions, and Callaghan's reassuringly avuncular manner had enabled Labor to narrow dramatically the gap in the polls. From a 14.5 percent lead in July, the Tories had seen their advantage dwindle to just 4.5 percent in September. "We are going to win the next election," a newly confident Denis Healey told the annual Labor Party Conference which met that October in Brighton. "The only thing that can defeat us is ourselves."

The Tory faithful who gathered for the annual Conservative Party Conference a week later were a dispirited lot. Standing beneath a giant blue banner proclaiming them "The Party of the People," they listened eagerly as Mrs. Thatcher tried to rally their enthusiasm with an upbeat vision of the future. "One Thursday," she cried, "a day like any other Thursday and yet, I believe, a day that will prove the turning point of our time, the Labor party will have to keep their appointment with the voters. It is a prospect I relish. 'Either back us or sack us,' says Callaghan. Just give the people the chance, Jim . . . give 'em the chance."

It was a good performance, but the tide was clearly running against the Tories. By late October, Labor had pulled even in the polls. Partly because of the stringent conditions imposed by the IMF, and partly because of North Sea oil (which had more than tripled Britain's foreign currency reserves since the beginning of the year), the economy had improved to the point where Healey was able to announce a tax-cutting budget—in the process, stripping the Tories of one of their main issues. "If Margaret Thatcher is looking chilly this week," observed left-wing Labor MP Dennis Skinner, "it's because Denis Healey has stolen her clothes."

Labor was also winning the argument about how best to control inflation. The trouble with Mrs. Thatcher's monetarist approach, as she and her advisers recognized, was that the impact of cutting spending and tightening up the money supply would be uneven, at least at first. Big unions would still be able to win big pay increases, and some businesses would be forced to the wall, pushing unemployment up without bringing inflation down quickly enough to make the trade-off seem worthwhile. How could the government get workers and employers to limit wage increases until the harsh medicine had time to work? There was no easy answer. The best the Tories could come up with—and it was a reluctant conclusion—was the suggestion that the government advise the unions and employers on what level of pay increases the nation could afford.

They weren't really happy with this idea; it smacked too much of an incomes policy in disguise. Their ambivalence showed clearly in the diffident wording and tortured grammar of "The Right Approach to the Economy," the October 1977 Tory policy document that first put the idea forward. "In framing its monetary and other policies," it stated in a passage as noteworthy for its execrable style as for its convoluted logic, "the Government must come to some conclusions about the likely scope for pay increases, if excess public expenditure or large-scale unemployment is to be avoided, and this estimate cannot be concealed from the representatives of employers and unions."

Translated into plain English, what the Conservatives were saying was that the government would always know what sort of pay increases it hoped to see, and it might as well share that knowledge with the folks who were actually sitting at the bargaining table. Just how such an approach might actually differ from the traditional—and, to the Thatcher-Joseph way of thinking, heinous—practice of setting voluntary pay guidelines was a matter best left to the semanticists.

But though they were winning the argument, Callaghan and Healey were not all that enthusiastic about pursuing an incomes policy. Nor were they necessarily opposed to a quasi-monetarist approach. It was just that the notion of an incomes policy had an almost mystical appeal to the voters, perhaps because the idea of suspending the laws of economics by government fiat seemed so attractively simple. In any case, given Labor's so-called "special relationship" with the unions (the idea that it could get along with them while the Tories couldn't), plus the undeniable fact that the inflation rate *was* falling, Callaghan and Healey could—and did—easily argue that the incomes policy approach was working.

In fact, over the winter of 1977–78, Callaghan and Healey began cautiously edging their way towards what had been Mrs. Thatcher's position. They weren't about to abandon incomes policy, but they did start talking up the virtues of reducing government borrowing and slowing down the growth of the money supply. It was just as well, for their "special relationship" with the unions was deteriorating rapidly. The firemen wanted a 30 percent pay increase—and when they didn't get it, 33,000 of them walked off the job, forcing the government to use troops to fight fires. Meanwhile, the miners began their annual negotiations by demanding a 90 percent wage hike. And power-station workers wanted more money, too; to bolster their case they began a job action that blacked out four million homes.

Nonetheless, Labor's popularity continued to grow. By January 1978, it had actually overtaken the Tories in the opinion polls. Where six months earlier, voters said they preferred the Conservatives by a 49–34½ margin, now they favored Labor by 46–44.

THE ISSUE OF RACE

Despite her conviction that she was right and Labor wrong on the economy, Mrs. Thatcher knew she had to find another issue to regain her once-comfortable lead. At the end of January, she found what she was looking for, and though it plunged her into the most intense controversy she had experienced since her days as education minister, in the short-term at least it paid off.

The issue she chose was immigration, which in Britain is virtually a euphemism for race. The British like to pride themselves on their racial tolerance, but the fact is there is hardly a country in Europe where ethnic jokes, slurs, and distinctions are made more openly, frequently, or unselfconsciously. In a sense, it is not really discriminatory, for everyone is fair game. As the joke goes, the English make fun of the Scottish, the Scottish make fun of the Welsh, and everyone makes fun of the Irish. But a special disdain is reserved for the non-British. The insular notion that "the wogs begin at Calais" is still far more widely and deeply accepted than most Britons would care to admit. Stereotypes such as the lazy Spaniard, the over-emotional Italian, and the clockwork German are considered by many to be self-evident facts of life; they figure with astonishing frequency in television situation comedies, Parliamentary debates, and barroom conversations.

It can be argued that such attitudes are not terribly consequential, that they are a trivial, amusing, and particularly British idiosyncrasy. Perhaps they are. Unfortunately, the same cannot be said of the growing hostility in Britain towards blacks and Asians, who currently comprise about 3.5 percent of the UK's population of 56 million. To be sure, Britain has never experienced anything approaching the virulent racial discrimination and violence that has wracked America for most of its history. But that may be changing. Higher than average birthrates and the now-subsiding wave of immigration from the "New Commonwealth" nations of India, black Africa, and the Caribbean have swelled the proportion of dark-skinned Britons in recent years. And as their numbers have risen, so too has the degree to which many white Britons feel themselves threatened, culturally as well as economically.

In some ways the situation is reminiscent of America in the 1960s and early 1970s, when many white Northern liberals enthusiastically supported the civil rights movement in the South—until the blacks they so earnestly championed began moving into their neighborhoods and competing for their jobs. It is complicated in Britain by that hangover of empire, the lingering nineteenth-century notion of "the white-man's burden," as well as by the fierce, self-protective clannishness of many Asian immigrants—mainly Indians and Pakistanis—whose desire to maintain their cultural identity is often matched by their intense drive to succeed economically. The result has all too often been a volatile mixture of condescension, envy, and resentment, particularly, though certainly not exclusively, among working-class whites who see themselves suddenly forced to compete in a declining economy with people they don't know or understand.

In the mid-1970s, such feelings were reflected in the rise of racist fringe groups such as the neo-Nazi National Front. The Front was a largely working-class movement that wore uniforms copied from those of the storm troopers and preached that Britain's national salvation lay in the "repatriation" (that is, forced expulsion) of all nonwhites. It never had more than 14,000 or so actual members, but its leaders quickly learned how to grab headlines, and in 1977 the group startled the country by winning an average of five percent of the vote in a series of parliamentary by-elections—and up to twenty percent in some local council contests.

In mainstream politics, Britain's growing racial uneasiness made itself felt in the form of increasingly widespread demands for tighter controls on immigration. This was hardly a new issue. It had first surfaced in the early 1960s, after Harold Macmillan's Tory government had over-enthusiastically promoted immigration—mainly from the Caribbean—to fill Britain's need for bus conductors, menials, and other relatively low-status workers. Macmillan's encouragement had led to a sharp increase in the number of Commonwealth citizens moving to Britain; between 1959 and 1961, Commonwealth immigration jumped more than sixfold, skyrocketing from a relatively modest 21,600 to more than 136,000. By 1962, the government was beginning to worry that the situation might be getting out of hand, and thus it enacted legislation to limit the inflow, bringing Commonwealth immigration under systematic control for the first time.

The new legislation served its purpose. Within five years, the net annual inflow of Commonwealth immigrants had been reduced to just over 36,000. But late in 1967, another floodtide loomed when Kenya suddenly threatened to expel 150,000 of its Asian residents—virtually all of whom, as citizens of the Commonwealth, held British passports. With domestic unemployment at a record level and the British economy ailing, Harold Wilson's Labor government of the time was in no mood to extend open arms to the about-to-be-homeless Asians. Home Secretary James Callaghan, who was just getting over the embarrassment of his abrupt transfer from the exchequer following the devaluation debacle of 1967, was thus handed the awkward assignment of drafting and pushing through legislation designed to keep the hapless Kenyan Asians out of Britain.

The resulting Commonwealth Immigration Act of 1968 pleased the trade unions, who were worried about protecting jobs. But it outraged Labor left-wingers, who wondered loudly what had become of their party's supposed concern for the downtrodden. Under the new act, only those UK passport holders who had at least one British-born parent or grandparent would be automatically allowed to settle in the mother country. That effectively permitted white immigration to continue, while barring the vast majority of nonwhite Commonwealth citizens from ever coming to live in Britain. And sure enough, when Kenya made good its expulsion threat early in 1968, only a handful of the 150,000 displaced Asians were permitted to settle in the UK.

When the Tories returned to power under Ted Heath in 1970, they undertook to restrict immigration even further. But in 1972, after Idi Amin expelled Uganda's entire Asian population (a move reportedly aimed more at embarrassing the British than discomfiting the Asians), Heath took a more humanitarian stance, announcing that Britain would take in all Ugandan Asians with UK passports—no matter what their parentage—who could find nowhere else to go. By mid-1973, nearly 30,000 Ugandan Asian refugees had resettled in Britain. And at their annual Party Conference in 1976, the Tories, now under Mrs. Thatcher, reaffirmed their commitment to Heath's pledge. By this time, the net inflow of immigrants to Britain was running at about 45,000 a year—a level many experts considered reasonable.

But with unemployment once more on the increase, and, along with it, violent crime and the welfare rolls, immigration again became a cause célèbre. Racial clashes between loutish white youths out for a night of "Paki-bashing" and increasingly militant West Indians, Sikhs, and other minorities were beginning to occur with ominous frequency. A decade earlier, Enoch Powell had been thrown out of the Tory shadow cabinet by Ted Heath for predicting race war if Britain did not take steps to limit immigration severely. ("As I look ahead, I am filled with foreboding," he said in that what became known as the "rivers of blood" speech. "Like the Roman, I seem to see 'the River Tiber foaming with much blood'.") Now many were beginning to think he might have been right.

Over the winter of 1977–78, Mrs. Thatcher and her aides took note of this growing feeling and came to the conclusion that it could provide them with just the opportunity they needed to regain the ground they had lost to Labor. A poll of voter attitudes commissioned by the Tory party the previous October had yielded the not very surprising result that when it came to inflation, unemployment, and the unions—the issues those polled considered most important—most Britons preferred the Labor party's approach. On noneconomic issues, however, the Conservatives came out ahead. Thus, at a meeting of the Tory leadership held during the Christmas 1977 parliamentary recess, Mrs. Thatcher decided that for the first five months of 1978 the Tories would leave economics alone and concentrate on social issues—starting with immigration, an issue of special urgency to them since it had been siphoning off some Conservative votes to the National Front.

Her new strategy surfaced for the first time on January 30, following a weekend riot in the industrial town of Wolverhampton in which nearly 200 unemployed West Indian youths threw bricks at police and smashed shop windows after being insulted by young whites. Appearing the next day on a top-rated television interview program called "World in Action," Mrs. Thatcher responded to a question about immigration by asserting that many Britons were afraid of being "swamped by people with a different culture"—and that for the sake of good race relations, as well as to maintain the "fundamental British characteristics which have done so much for the world," the government "must hold out the clear prospect of an end to immigration."

It was the strongest statement ever by a Tory leader on this touchy issue. Quoting official estimates that the continuation of current immigration practices would boost Britain's black and Asian population to four million by the end of the century, Mrs. Thatcher declared: "Now, that is an awful lot and I think it means that people are really rather afraid that this country might be rather swamped by people with a different culture. And, you know, the British character has done so much for democracy, for law, and done so much throughout the world, that if there is any fear that it might be swamped, people are going to react and be rather hostile to those coming in. So, if you want good race relations, you have got to allay people's fears on numbers."

Her home town of Grantham, she noted, had a population of 25,000. With 45,000 to 50,000 immigrants coming to Britain annually, she noted, that "would be two new towns a year and that is quite a lot." She insisted she had no intention of abandoning the 1976 Tory commitments to East African Asians who held UK passports and to the dependents of immigrants already in Britain. But massive migrations must be ruled out. "We are a British nation with British characteristics," she declared again. "Every country can take some small minorities and in many ways they add to the richness and variety of this country. The moment the minority threatens to become a big one, people get frightened."

National uncertainty about immigration—and the refusal of political leaders to deal forthrightly with the subject—was, she maintained, "driving some people to the National Front. They do not agree with the objectives of the National Front, but they say at least they are talking about some of the problems." To preempt the Front's appeal, she had decided to tackle the issue head on. "We are not in politics to ignore people's worries," she argued, "we are in politics to deal with them."

Mrs. Thatcher's remarks touched off a political firestorm. Critics—and there were many, not all Labor—called her everything from a "racist" and an "opportunist" to "a muddled woman." "This is simply a way of winning an election—she thinks," snapped Home Secretary Merlyn Rees. "If this is the way she wants to proceed, that a vote is worth it at any price, then good luck to her." Added an immigrant leader, Secretary-General Sibghat Kadri of the Standing Conference of Pakistani Associations: "This kind of talk can only bring us closer to racial war in this country."

In the House of Commons the next day, Prime Minister Callaghan challenged her to spell out just how she intended to reduce immigration without going back on the Tory pledges to East African Asians and dependents. "I hope Mrs. Thatcher is not hoping to appeal to certain elements in the electorate," he said. "I hope we shall not play on the fears of the people if they are not based on accurate expectations or figures."

The furor might have died down except for a by-election that had been scheduled for March 2, 1978. On that day, the voters of the constituency of Ilford North, a barren lower-middle-class commuter suburb just north of London, were due to go to the polls to elect a successor to Labor MP Minnie Miller, who had died the previous October. Ilford, which numbered some 7,000 Jews and 3,000 Asians among its 85,000 residents, had been a safe Tory seat for most of the 1950s and 1960s. In 1974, however, Mrs. Miller, a local Jewish leader with a large personal following, had squeaked by the Conservative incumbent with a margin of 778 votes. Given its polyglot population and the timing of its by-election, Ilford provided a perfect opportunity for everyone concerned with the immigration controversy to test the political waters.

The National Front, plainly delighted by the prominence the immigration fracas had given it, seized on the Ilford by-election as a chance to demonstrate its strength, announcing it would hold a mass march through the center of the town the weekend before voters were due to go to the polls. In response to the outraged protests of Ilford's Jewish community, and to prevent violence, London Metropolitan Police Commissioner Sir David McNee blocked the march by banning all political demonstrations in the Greater London area for two months. As a result, the Front had to settle for a program of house-to-house campaigning. Roughly a thousand Front supporters turned up for the effort—only to be outnumbered by twice as many antifacist demonstrators, and five times as many police.

Labor never expected to hold the seat, which was its most marginal in the country. But it did want to keep the Tory victory margin as low as possible. Thus, it was in Ilford—and not at Westminster as normally would have been the practice—that Prices Minister Roy Hattersly made the long-awaited announcement that the inflation rate had finally fallen back into single figures. More to the point, the Labor party leadership launched an aggressive and personalized anti-Thatcher campaign that grew increasingly vitriolic as the election date approached. Home Secretary Rees accused her of "moving towards the attitudes and policies of the National Front"—thus "making respectable racial hatred." Social

Services Minister David Ennals charged that "her utterances have given a push to division and conflict," while Energy Minister Tony Benn added that she seemed bent on pitting "one group against another." Even the prime minister joined in. Dropping the chiding tone of paternal condescension with which he customarily addressed Mrs. Thatcher, Callaghan complained angrily in the Commons that her statements on immigration were "totally meaningless, full of froth and with a kind of spurious gentility we have come to associate with her."

For her part, Mrs. Thatcher gave as good as she got, branding Labor's charges "absolute nonsense." She "wholeheartedly" condemned the "racist" policies of the National Front. But she insisted heatedly that it would be "absolutely absurd" not to discuss race and immigration. "The media raised it, not me," she said. "I have given my views and I have been bullied and intimidated."

SUNNY JIM VS. THE IRON LADY

Labor had good reasons for responding to her in such a fashion. While the Conservatives as a party had until recently been running ahead of Labor in the polls, Mrs. Thatcher's personal popularity had always lagged far behind Callaghan's. Thus, Labor strategists felt they had much to gain by trying to personalize the rivalry between the two leaders. Given a choice between Labor and Conservative policies, the voters might well choose the latter, they reasoned. But if they could make the choice appear to be between the avuncular "Sunny Jim" Callaghan and the schoolmarmish "Iron Lady," there seemed little doubt that the electorate would opt for the former.

But the attacks on her were not all the result of rabidly partisan calculations. Many moderate Tories felt uneasy about what they considered to be her extreme right-wing approach. Just a month earlier, Sir Ian Gilmour, who had started out as her shadow home secretary but had been moved to the defense portfolio as a result of his opposition to capital punishment, wrote in *The Times* that "the center is still the right place for the Tory Party." Now Ted Heath felt obliged to break his long-standing silence on her performance, complaining that she had caused "an unnecessary national row." And two bishops of the Church of England mounted their pulpits to criticize Mrs. Thatcher. "You are playing a dangerous game," warned the Right Reverend David Young, Bishop of Ripon. "You are fostering emotions and feelings of prejudice, fear and hatred which can only be destructive to our society." Added the Bishop of Lichfield, the Right Reverend Kenneth Skelton: "Fantasies and lies and hatreds are being sedulously spread." (These ecclesiastical outbursts drew swift and withering comment from the Tory backbenches. "If there is one thing the British public can do without," snorted MP Eldon Griffiths, "it is high-minded humbug from the Bishops.")

Still, for all the furor she had provoked, it was clear Mrs. Thatcher had stuck a responsive chord. "The British public—and this is not a nation of racialists—ARE worried about further immigration," editorialized the tabloid *Sun,* Britain's top-selling national daily. "If the big parties will not heed the worries of the electors, the electors may turn elsewhere." Within two weeks of her immigration statement, the Tories went from a two-point deficit in the polls to an eleven-point lead over Labor. Perhaps more significant, they won the Ilford by-election by a convincing margin, piling up 50 percent of the vote to Labor's 38 percent. The immigration fracas had paid off; roughly 6,000 Ilford voters who had cast their ballots for Labor in 1974 went for the Tory candidate this time. And according to an election-day survey, more than half of them crossed over because of what they perceived to be the Conservative party's position on immigration. "If this pattern continues to the next general election," chortled Deputy Party Leader Willie Whitelaw, "Margaret Thatcher will be the next prime minister."

The pattern did continue. Meanwhile, Mrs. Thatcher was growing more sophisticated in her exercise of power, becoming increasingly autocratic with her shadow cabinet. "All we talk about is next week's business," griped one member. It wasn't that she was shortsighted; it was just that she regarded her shadow cabinet as too moderate for her taste, and rather than provoke an intraparty ideological dustup by attempting to reshuffle it, she simply chose to work around it. Just as Callaghan had become a master at sidestepping his party's National Executive, which he considered too left wing, so Mrs. Thatcher learned to cut all but her most trusted advisers out of the Tory party's policy-making process.

She did this by preempting the shadow cabinet with two other, more important policy-making groups. The first was an informal Monday lunch group, chaired by Keith Joseph. It would summon shadow ministers, singly or in groups, to discuss specific areas of policy. Its recommendations would either be passed on to the full shadow cabinet directly or to the second group, a formal steering committee which set the shadow cabinet agenda, winnowing out "inappropriate" items. In this way, Mrs. Thatcher was able to put her personal stamp on Tory policy while avoiding potentially divisive splits within the official leadership. A moderate member of the shadow cabinet would have a hard time arguing against well-briefed advocates of Thatcher-Joseph proposals he was seeing for the first time.

That is not to say she had a totally closed mind to policy initiatives that clashed with her own instincts. In 1978, for example, Lord Carrington, a hereditary peer with long diplomatic experience, managed to persuade her that Tory policy should favor a continuation of economic sanctions against the breakaway colony of Rhodesia. It took some doing, but once Mrs. Thatcher was convinced, she undertook to bring the entire Conservative frontbench along with her. And when junior defense minister Winston Churchill—the grandson of the great man himself—refused to go along, she did not hesitate to drop him as an opposition spokesman.

Nor was she totally inaccessible. She made a point of lunching in the Commons dining room at least once every two weeks, and she would occasionally make a foray into the once exclusively male Members' Smoking Room. But unlike most of her predecessors (except for Heath), Mrs. Thatcher had little use for the late-night sessions over brandy traditionally favored by Tory leaders to take the temperature of their backbenchers. "Margaret's more of a luncher," a Tory MP reported at the time. "Like Ted, she doesn't much care for small talk. She enjoys a bit of a gossip, but than she likes to get down to a good serious discussion."

By June 1978, a general election seemed imminent. Disgusted at his inability to influence Labor policy, and concerned that his apparent sell-out might cost his party heavily at the pools, Liberal Leader David Steel announced just a few weeks before the end-of-July summer recess that the Lib-Lab Pact would not be renewed when Parliament convened again in October. Unless Callaghan could work out a deal with one of the other minor parties, the fourteen Scottish and Welsh Nationalist MPs or the ten Ulster Unionists in the Commons, he would have no choice but to go to the country in the fall. As if in anticipation of an election, the Labor frontbenches closed out the session with a blistering series of attacks on Mrs. Thatcher, calling her speeches "a rallying cry to prejudice" and her policies "a recipe for anarchy in this country." Perhaps the most cutting assault came from Callaghan himself, who began his final speech of the session by quoting from Dryden's poem "Absa-

lom and Achitophel" to characterize the Tory leader and her shadow
cabinet:

> Stiff in opinions,
> Always in the wrong,
> Was everything by starts and nothing long;
> But in the course of one revolving moon,
> Was chemist, fiddler, statesman and buffoon.

CREATING AN IMAGE

Mrs. Thatcher had by this time hired a full-time media adviser to help
improve her image. Gordon Reece was a former television producer
who had made his reputation working with some of Britain's top come-
dians. He taught Mrs. Thatcher how to lower the pitch of her often annoyingly shrill voice; he steadied her fidgety speaking style; and to the
dismay of political cartoonists, persuaded her to abandon her beloved
garden-party hats. To the suggestion that he was trying to remodel his
client in a Nixon-style "selling of the prime minister," Reece angrily responded, "We are not doing anything remotely like that." In fact, he
had a point. His goal was to bring out as much as possible the private
Margaret Thatcher that the voters never saw. Nixon's media men had
rather the reverse in mind. In any case, under his tutelage Mrs. Thatcher
began attempting to show her more human side in public. It wasn't always easy. Though she was persuaded to tell an interviewer that there
were times when she would cry "silently, alone, when I feel I have not
done something well enough," she couldn't resist adding that the last
time she was so overcome was "not recently. I've got used to criticism."

The results of such image-tending were not immediately apparent. By
the end of the summer of 1978, Labor was four points ahead of the
Tories in the polls. By itself, this wasn't terribly significant; in Britain,
the party in power always tends to improve its standing over the summer
when Parliament is not in session and it is easier for government spokesmen to command the headlines than it is for their opposition counterparts. But coupled with the fact that Callaghan's personal popularity was
fully twenty points ahead of Mrs. Thatcher's, neither was it terribly reassuring.

August is traditionally a quiet month at Westminster. With the Commons in recess and its members scattered about Britain on their summer

holidays, the uncharacteristic hush that fills the ancient palace at this time of year is usually disturbed only by workmen taking advantage of the summer lull to get at the building's deteriorating innards and by the crowds of tourists who daily file wide-eyed through its grand corridors and ornate central lobby. But August 1978 was different. A surprising number of MPs and their staffs were to be seen on the premises. The reason was simple: virtually everyone expected a general election to be called for early in October.

Certainly, the portents were all there. Not only was Labor enjoying its widest lead in the polls for quite some time, but the economy was riding the crest of what some experts felt might be a short-lived boom. The pound was strong, inflation was well below ten percent and still falling, and living standards had risen eight percent over the year before. The fact that this rosy-cheeked flush wasn't expected to last very long—unemployment had just topped the 1.6 million mark and most analysts were in agreement that a sharp downturn was in the cards for early 1979—only confirmed the belief that this was clearly Labor's time to be heard. Indeed, just about the only major politician not to go on record predicting a fall general election was the man whose decision it actually was: Prime Minister Callaghan, who remained ensconced at his Sussex farm, insisting he had yet to make up his mind and reminding persistent questioners that he wasn't obligated to go to the country for another full year.

The Tories were convinced an election was in the offing. Acting on Gordon Reece's advice, they hired Britain's hottest advertising agency, Saatchi & Saatchi, to put together a multi-million-pound media campaign trumpeting the Conservative message. By the end of August, Britain was blanketed with huge billboards posters proclaiming, in a pointed reference to the mounting jobless figures, that "Labor Isn't Working." Except for a brief sailing holiday—which she characteristically cut short—Mrs. Thatcher had been working the hustings all summer. Now she kicked off what pundits labelled "the Conservatives' run-up campaign" by visiting two constituencies in Kent that just happened to be among Labor's most marginal seats.

Taking its cue from the prime minister, Labor was being a bit more laid back—but not much. The powerful Trades Union Congress, whose affiliated unions represented more than 11 million working people in Britain, organized a "Committee for Labor Victory" that pledged to provide union manpower to aid Labor candidates in one hundred of the party's most important races. Meanwhile, the sniping at the Tories—and their leader—had resumed. The hiring of Saatchi & Saatchi, sniffed Denis Healey, reflected an "attempt to sell Mrs. Thatcher as if she was a soap powder."

In September, Labor's confidence was shaken more than a bit when the TUC, meeting in Brighton for its annual convention, voted overwhelmingly to reject Callaghan's pay policy. The prime minister had proposed setting a five percent limit on wage increases as part of what he promised would be the final phase of the government's four-year-old anti-inflation program. But the TUC wanted no part of it. Still, when Callaghan took the podium to address the assembled TUC delegates, the betting was heavy that he would use the occasion to announce an October general election.

As it turned out, he didn't. Instead, he delighted the crowd by half-singing an old music hall ditty about a bride left at the alter, to which he added, "I have promised nobody I shall be at the altar in October."

Nonetheless, the conviction persisted that an election had to be in the cards. Labor was eight seats short of a majority in the House of Commons, and it was hard to see how it could win the first major vote of the fall session. This vote, technically on a motion of thanks for the Queen's Speech (which is written by the government and sets out its upcoming legislative program), would be in effect a vote of confidence without which Labor could not govern.

For their part, the Tories were gearing up for a fall campaign. An airplane was chartered to carry Mrs. Thatcher around the country, and the dozen or so reporters who planned to accompany her were invited to an informal reception in her offices at the House of Commons. Mrs. Thatcher appeared at the gathering in dazzling spirits, keyed up and ready to go, much like an actress on the eve of an opening night. Earlier that day, Callaghan had hurriedly summoned his cabinet to No. 10, and the BBC later announced that he had requested five minutes of air time for a ministerial broadcast the next evening. It seemed clear to everyone that the election date was finally going to be set. "I don't know what he's going to say," Mrs. Thatcher grinned, "but I don't imagine he is making a Ministerial broadcast to say he *isn't* going to hold an election."

A reporter at the reception was intrigued by Mrs. Thatcher's certainty. "What if the prime minister doesn't call an election?" he asked her, somewhat perversely.

She smiled indulgently. "Of course he will," she said, "He has to."

"But just suppose," he persisted. "What if he doesn't do it?"

"He has to," she repeated. Her smile was gone now, as if she were considering the question seriously for the first time. "My God, if he doesn't, it would be a disaster," she finally said. "We're all ready to go."

LABOR HANGS ON

The next day, at five minutes to six in the evening, the prime minister took to the airwaves as promised. With a playful smile betraying his obvious delight at confounding the experts, Callaghan once again reminded the nation that the current Parliament was entitled to go on for another full year, and he announced that he would "not be calling for a general election at this time." Arguing that problems such as inflation, unemployment, and low productivity required a government that "will continue to carry out policies which are consistent, determined and do not chop and change," Callaghan told his nationwide audience that "we go on because we feel that is best for Britain."

Not many shared his opinion. David Steel called the decision "truly astounding"—and even some senior Labor ministers had to agree. "I was canvassing in my constituency when the call came to go to No. 10," said one. "I assumed, as I think we all did, that Jim was going to give us our marching orders. This has to be one of the biggest surprises in British political history."

Mrs. Thatcher was beside herself with fury. "The real reason Mr. Callaghan isn't going to have an election is because he knows he will lose," she fumed. The only "reasonable and honorable thing" a minority prime minister such as Callaghan could do, she insisted, was to go to the country. The prime ministership, she added bitterly, "belongs to the courageous, not to the timid."

Most pundits and more than a few Labor party strategists agreed with TUC chairman Tom Jackson, who complained that by postponing the election, the prime minister had set the stage for a "winter of discontent" over his wage policy that would hurt Labor's chances in the spring. But Callaghan, who had left virtually the entire Labor party leadership in the dark until the last minute, wasn't nearly as confident about Labor's fall prospects as most of his colleagues were. Although the published polls put Labor on top of the Conservatives with their highest rating in a year, private soundings submitted to Callaghan by pollster Robert Worcester, who met with him two days before the surprise announcement, showed Labor actually trailing the Tories by four points.

Callaghan "would have been foolish" to risk an October election, Worcester maintained. At best, he felt Labor would have "squeaked home" with no more than the minority standing it currently enjoyed.

With the election now put off for the time being, Callaghan's task was to round up enough parliamentary support to get his government through the Queen's Speech, which would open the fall session at the end of October. With the Liberals on record as aiming to bring down the government at the earliest opportunity—and the Tories, as Callaghan himself noted, bound to "vote against us even if we produced the Sermon on the Mount"—his only hope lay in winning the votes of at least a third of the twenty-four Ulster Unionist and Scottish and Welsh Nationalist MPs.

Such hopes were based on more than wishful thinking. Shortly after Callaghan's announcement, the Scottish National Party (SNP) made it known that a formal pact with Labor was out. But, added their deputy leader, Margaret Bain, "It would be difficult to vote against the Queen's Speech if it included a date for a referendum [on home rule] or for elections to the [proposed Scottish] assembly." What's more, the fiercely independent Ulster Unionists, who represented Northern Ireland's Protestant majority, passed the word that they, too, might be induced to support Labor on the Queen's Speech.

Before the Queen's Speech came up, however, there were the Party Conferences to get through. As usual, Labor held its conference first, this time in Blackpool. The atmosphere was not good. In addition to their uneasiness over Callaghan's gamble, the delegates shared the TUC's distaste for his latest incomes policy. Galvanized by a massive strike by 57,000 autoworkers at British Ford—who termed the five percent ceiling "insulting"—they disregarded Denis Healey's warning that if Labor couldn't keep inflation under control, "we shall not win the next election" and voted two-to-one to reject their leader's proposed five percent guideline.

But Callaghan was nothing if not resilient. Taking the podium, he charmed the hostile crowd with a virtuoso speech that was by turns folksy, firm, conciliatory, and statesmanlike. He manfully—and disarmingly—offered a mea culpa for Labor's failings and sternly lectured the delegates on basic economics. The government, he promised, would interpret the pay policy "as easily as possible." But he gently reminded the conference that it bore a responsibility to keep wage increases from sending the inflation rate back into double figures. And he pledged—diplomatically but firmly—that the government would impose tight credit and higher taxes if wage increases got out of hand over the winter. Callaghan even offered his troops a few sweeteners such as promises of improved public housing and health systems and job-training for young drop-outs. When he finished, the prime mover in the party's pay policy revolt—General Secretary Moss Evans of the giant TGWU—leapt to his feet to lead the huge conclave in an enthusiastic standing ovation. Callaghan had managed to avert a potentially calamitous intraparty split such as the one that had cost Labor the 1970 election.

When the Tories met the following week, there was little they could do except fulminate. With the Ford strike still in progress—and the Labor rank and file, despite its apparent personel affection for Callaghan, still volubly against his five percent guideline—Mrs. Thatcher decided she could once again afford to take on the prime minister in a head-to-head confrontation over inflation and incomes policy. "It is time," she told a television interviewer at the conference, "to return to bargaining between the employee on the spot and the employer."

But the incomes policy was still evidently an idea whose time had not yet passed. Despite all the problems, the polls showed that the voters continued to prefer government wage guidelines to the free-for-all both she and the unions seemed to want. And when Ted Heath publicly reaffirmed his belief in the efficacy of incomes policy, Gallup reported that his personal popularity leapt ahead of Mrs. Thatcher's.

In the weeks before Parliament convened, Callaghan and his aides had been laboring over a Queen's Speech designed to offend as few as possible of his own backbenchers (eight of whom had threatened to abstain in the voting if it were not to their liking) while attracting the minor-party MPs whose support he so desperately needed. The result was predictably bland. "It reminded me of a very large sedative," said Liberal MP Emlyn Hooson. Indeed, it barely touched on the issues most likely to decide any general election, the problems of unemployment and inflation.

What it did do was hold out a number of carrots to the Ulster Unionists and the Scottish and Welsh Nationalists. The government said it hoped to increase Northern Ireland's representation in the Commons, and it promised extra funding for local Scottish and Welsh development programs. What's more, after the speech, Callaghan announced a date for the long-awaited devolution referendum. It would be held on March 1, 1979—appropriately enough, St. David's Day (St. David being the patron saint of Wales).

In the debate that followed the speech, Mrs. Thatcher kept up her attack on Callaghan's five percent wage ceiling. "A rigid incomes policy won't hold, and there's no use arguing as if it will," she told the House. "The Prime Minister knows it and we all know it." But in one major way her position had changed; the message of the polls, it seemed, had finally gotten through to her. It was no longer incomes policy per se that she was against, only rigid limits. "Pay policies of course are extremely important," she said. It was just that the prime minister's approach resembled a battleship which carried all the right guns and armaments but simply would not float.

In the end, however, what counted wasn't the government's economic policy or even its fitness to continue governing. What mattered was whether it had offered enough to the Nationalists and their Northern Irish counterparts. Within a few days, it seemed clear that it had, and at the end of the Queen's Speech debate, Mrs. Thatcher angrily conceded that she and her Tories would not be able to bring Callaghan's minority government down. "If the Prime Minister wishes to go on to the bitter end," she said, frustration etching her voice, "so be it."

7

To the Hustings

"What Britain needs is an Iron Lady."

 JAMES CALLAGHAN MANAGED TO BRING his minority Labor government through the fall 1978 Queen's Speech and continue on into the winter with relative ease. By simply lying low, by sticking to an innocuous legislative program, Labor was safe for the time being; it could even hope to prolong its lease on No. 10 through the following summer, until October 1979, when the Parliament's five-year term would finally end and a general election would be an unavoidable constitutional necessity.

Mrs. Thatcher kept campaigning, and there was no shortage of grist for her mill. As she told a reporter who asked her to comment on the accusation that she was a reactionary: "Well, there's a lot to react against—prices doubling in five years, unemployment doubling in five years." In particular, Callaghan's five percent pay policy had become, like most New Year's resolutions, more honored in the breach than in the observance. When Ford settled its strike by agreeing to grant workers a seventeen percent wage hike, Callaghan attempted to punish the company by imposing government sanctions against it. But the Parliament refused to let him—in effect, making it clear that unions were free to demand (and managements free to grant) whatever pay increases they deemed appropriate. In short order, disgruntled workers from miners to hospital orderlies were asking for raises three, four, and five times Callaghan's suggested five percent limit.

This sort of frenzied wage push was not exactly what Mrs. Thatcher had in mind when she had called for a return to free collective bargaining. But was there any alternative? The austere monetarist approach she had been preaching may have won the support of some economists, and even of Callaghan and Healey themselves, but the voters certainly wanted no part of it. Late in 1978, Mrs. Thatcher hit upon a solution to her dilemma. In a speech in the London neighborhood of Paddington on December 18, she suggested a way to dispense with incomes policy yet still control inflation: reform the unions in such a way as to limit their power to win big pay increases. "Today union power is feared sometimes even by union members," she asserted. "And there is grave public distrust about their willingness to bargain responsibly. It's as much in the interests of the unions themselves as of the public that a start should be made towards finding a remedy for these problems which are daily becoming more pressing. We intend to make that start."

The methods by which Mrs. Thatcher proposed to limit union power were not new ones. The ideas of outlawing so-called secondary picketing (the use of "flying pickets" to disrupt businesses other than those actually involved in the dispute) as well as discouraging closed shops and encouraging the use of secret ballots in union strike votes had all been tried, in one form or another, by Wilson and Heath in their earlier, unsuccessful attempts at union reform. But public attitudes had changed since the early 1970s and within a few weeks, events were to win Mrs. Thatcher and her proposals massive support.

A COUNTRY IN CRISIS

Through the fall of 1978, British tanker-truck drivers, the men responsible for delivering gasoline, heating oil, and other vital fuels, had been negotiating for a fifteen percent wage increase. The oil companies that employed them were willing to grant the raise but only if the men agreed to a program of productivity increases. The drivers refused, and early in January 1978, several thousand of them walked off the job in an unofficial strike. In short order, Britain's petrol pumps began to run dry, while homes and factories grew chilly as heating-oil supplies ran out. As the army feverishly began trying to train soldiers to handle the huge, unwieldy tank trucks, panic buying by nervous motorists rapidly drained gasoline stocks. Price-gouging and fistfights on lengthy petrol station queues became a depressingly familiar phenomenon. Dozens of schools were forced to close as a result of unheated classrooms.

Jan. 1978

A few days after the tanker-men struck, they were joined on the picket lines by 100,000 long-haul freight truckers (known in Britain as lorry drivers). The 15,500 trucking firms that made up the Road Haulage Association had offered the lorry drivers a fifteen percent raise over their basic fifty-three-pound weekly wage, but the men—who complained that unskilled office clerks earned more than they did—were holding out for twenty-two percent.

With more than two-thirds of all the goods in the UK transported by road, and squads of "flying pickets" disrupting deliveries by nonstriking drivers who worked for companies not involved in the dispute, the lorry drivers' walkout affected virtually every sector of British industry. Uncollected cargo piled up on the docks at Liverpool, Southampton, and a half-dozen other ports, forcing incoming freighters to be diverted to the Continent. Limited deliveries plus more panic buying stripped supermarket shelves of meat, vegetables, and dairy products. The large Tesco chain warned it might soon have to start rationing sugar, and the National Farmers Union reported that with feedstocks running out, livestock breeders might be forced to destroy millions of chickens and pigs. Even newspapers were affected; as newsprint deliveries faltered, most of Britain's national dailies found themselves with no choice but to trim press runs and cut editions to half their usual number of pages. (Provincial newspapers were unaffected since most of them had already been shut down by a strike of provincial journalists.)

With no way of bringing raw materials in or shipping finished products out, scores of factories had to shut down, and thousands of workers were laid off as a result. The "winter of discontent" predicted by the TUC's Tom Jackson had arrived with a vengeance.

While the storm clouds gathered, Prime Minister Callaghan was getting a winter tan on the sunny Caribbean island of Guadeloupe, where he was attending a four-nation summit meeting with his counterparts from the U.S., France, and West Germany. He returned to chilly London after six days away, and no sooner had he stepped off his Royal Air Force VC-10 than reporters besieged him with questions about what he planned to do about what one of them called the "mounting crisis." Callaghan was in no mood for such talk. "We've had strikes before, we've come close to the brink before," he snapped with uncharacteristic testiness. "There is a need for a great deal of industrial self-discipline . . . but please don't run down your country by talking about mounting chaos."

If Callaghan's idea was to reduce tensions by trying to minimize the seriousness of the situation—and it probably was—it backfired awesomely. "Crisis? What Crisis?" read the next day's headline accounts of his airport press conference. To increasingly frazzled Britons—their children shut out from unheated schools, their cars idled by a shortage of gasoline, their supermarket shelves emptied by panic buying and their nerves frayed by worry over whether they might be laid off at any moment—Callaghan's apparently cavalier attitude was hardly reassuring.

In the Commons, Mrs. Thatcher demanded that the prime minister declare a national state of emergency. "There comes a time in the life of a country," she asserted "when a Government . . . has an overriding responsibility to keep essential supplies and services running." But Callaghan refused to be panicked into what he considered precipitate action. "There is no point in declaring a state of emergency," he insisted—though he did concede that "plans for that are always ready."

Callaghan's apparent refusal to accept that there was indeed a crisis did not reflect simply Panglossian optimism. His government was obliged to hold a general election sometime in the next ten months, and one of Labor's main campaigning points would be the tattered but still saleable notion that it enjoyed a "special relationship" with the unions. "Now how can we possibly argue that," one of Callaghan's aides pointed out, "if the Leader of our Party, the Prime Minister, is going around saying that industrial relations are in a state of deep crisis."

But crisis it was, and it continued to deepen. The tanker drivers went back to work after a week when their employers caved in and agreed to give them their fifteen percent without any productivity demands. But the lorry drivers stayed out. And by stationing squads of "flying pickets" at depots and factory gates throughout the nation, they were able to magnify the impact of their walkout to a point where they were close to paralyzing the entire British economy. Within two weeks, nearly £2 billion in potential exports had piled up in factory storage yards, unable to get to the docks for shipment abroad. At the same time, 4 million tons of recently arrived food, raw materials, and general cargo were rotting in pierside warehouses. "This is the worst snarl-up we've ever had—and that includes dock strikes," reported a spokesman for the National Ports Council.

To make matters worse, rival unions of railroad workers involved in an internecine dispute over pay parity halted all British train service for two days. Millions of commuters were stranded. In London alone, nearly 300,000 workers who depended on the trains were unable to get to their jobs. The Automobile Association reported most main roads "bursting at the seams" as thousands took to their cars; traffic jams five miles long and worse were common.

By the middle of January, Saatchi & Saatchi had come up with a cheeky new ad campaign for the Tories designed to capitalize on the nation's increasing frustration. "Cheer up!" exhorted posters that appeared throughout the country, "Labor can't hang on forever." Callaghan evidently agreed. In a closed-door meeting with Labor MPs he warned that unless the unions could be brought back into line—and brought back quickly—"the consequences may be a Conservative Government."

In what turned out to be a vain effort to restore some semblance of labor peace, Callaghan summoned two of the country's most powerful union leaders—TUC general secretary Len Murray and TGWU boss Moss Evans—to what nearly stretched into an all-night session at 10 Downing Street. The prime minister tried to set the stage for a truce by offering a series of major concessions on his pay policy. But as far as the unions were concerned, Callaghan's offer was too little too late.

In fact, the union leaders well appreciated that the growing turmoil would only increase the already good chance that Britain's next government would be a conservative one. As much as they dreaded that prospect, however, the unsettling truth was that in large part they had lost control of their frustrated, angry, and beleaguered rank and file. "If we cannot afford the food, why should anyone else have it?" asked an embittered lorry driver in Manchester in a well-publicized outburst that reflected the feelings of many strikers. Most of the walkouts had not been ordered by union bosses; they had begun on the shop floor, and the leadership found itself forced to race madly to keep up with its determined troops.

Meanwhile, Mrs. Thatcher was almost joyfully on the offensive. On January 16, she introduced a motion to adjourn the House of Commons. It was not quite a no-confidence motion, but if passed it would have much the same effect. She followed it up with a series of passionate television and parliamentary speeches, widely regarded as among the most brilliant of her career, in which she argued forcefully that if Britain were "to avoid not just disruption but anarchy," the unions must be brought to heel. Her approach was ostensibly bipartisan. "This is no time to put Party before country," she maintained. But she left no doubt as to where she felt the blame for Britain's worsening troubles should be placed. "Whatever view the Prime Minister may take about the situation in Britain," she told the House, "we take the view that there is a possibility of grave trouble of crisis proportions. It is a very grim picture indeed." Flying pickets, she declared angrily, "have no right to intimidate any citizen in this country"—and she accused Callaghan of being concerned only with "the convenience of the trade unions." Britain, she said, "is practically being run" by the striking lorry drivers. "They are 'allowing' access to food," she went on, in an acid reference to their program of permitting deliveries of what they deemed essential supplies, "they are 'allowing' certain lorries to go through. *They have no right to prevent them going through.*" She went on to assert that if, as the government maintained, the law restricting secondary picketing was unenforceable, then "we have got to change it. If the Prime Minister wishes to embark on that course, we will certainly support him."

Denis Healey quickly denounced Mrs. Thatcher's words as "inflaming fear, hatred and greed." But he undercut his own rebuttal with an injudicious bit of over-reaching. As he catalogued Labor's virtues, he got a bit carried away and referred to 1978 as a year of "exceptional achievement." The chamber, including the Labor benches, dissolved in laughter at this burst of rhetorical excess, and whatever impact Healey might have had was lost.

With a hastily-taken opinion poll showing that eighty percent of those questioned backed Mrs. Thatcher's proposals to tame the unions, Callaghan realized that some swift back-pedalling was in order. Thus, when he rose in the House to defend himself, he began by praising Mrs. Thatcher's speech. She might have been "exploiting short-term resentments," he chided her mildly, but he found himself unable to dispute the notion that the unions had gone too far. "The situation," he conceded at long last, "is serious." As Labor left-wingers sat in sullen silence, Callaghan told the House that "the trade union movement must operate within the parameters of public opinion." He roundly condemned picketers for imposing "indefensible hardship . . . on innocent people" and he asked the striking lorry drivers "to measure your sense of grievance against the effect your actions are having on the community at large."

Reassured by his apparent return to realism, and still hoping to postpone a general election for as long as possible, the Scottish and Welsh Nationalists, along with the Ulster Unionists, stuck by Labor. Thus, Callaghan was able to turn aside Mrs. Thatcher's motion to adjourn the House by a comfortable twenty-four-vote margin.

But the situation in the country continued to deteriorate. Talks between the lorry drivers and the Road Haulage Association broke down completely, the railway men staged two more twenty-four-hour train strikes, and on January 22, in the biggest job action Britain had seen since the General Strike of 1926, 1.5 million public employees held a massive one-day walkout for higher pay. They followed it up with a continuing series of smaller "lightning" strikes that crippled ambulance service, halted garbage collections, closed schools and even led to a backlog of unburied bodies in the Liverpool morgue when municipal gravediggers laid down their shovels. To add insult to injury, an official of NUPE, the big public-employees' union, ordered his members to stop smiling on the job. "Many of our members are disgruntled over their continuing low wage," he said with a straight face, "and they have nothing to smile about."

As if all this man-made trouble weren't enough, Mother Nature conspired to turn 1979's winter of discontent into one of outright misery for Britons. The worst Arctic gale in sixteen years dumped a foot of snow across much of England and Wales, tying up what little industrial activity had so far managed to escape the effects of the strikes. "If you are in bed, stay there," a London radio announcer advised his listeners on the morning of the blizzard. "If not, go back."

By the end of January, the situation had grown so bad that even the archbishop of Canterbury, Dr. Donald Coggan, was moved to a rare comment on a secular issue. "Enough is enough," he proclaimed. "The right to strike is being used far too soon and far too regularly and far too irresponsibly."

On January 26, the Tories once again tried to bring the government down. Challenging him "to assert the right of ordinary people to carry on working without interference," Mrs. Thatcher minced no words in demanding that Callaghan step down. "You no longer have the courage to act," she told him in the House, "Will you not then at least have the courage to resign?"

But with the Tories a comfortable 7.5 percent ahead in the polls and even April seeming too soon to risk a general election, Callaghan was not about to rise to Mrs. Thatcher's bait. Instead of taking up her dare, he chose to commit a remarkable act of heresy for a Labor prime minister. After warning the unions that "there do come times when a nation's patience runs out," he startled the Commons by asserting that he fully supported workers who wanted to cross picket lines. "They are not sacred objects," he lectured disbelieving MPs. "I would not hesitate myself [to cross them] if I believed it right to do so." Thus, he was able once again to turn back Mrs. Thatcher's challenge, though this time his margin had shrunk to just sixteen votes.

By early February, the worst seemed to be over. The lorry drivers accepted the Road Haulage Association's offer of a twenty percent pay increase, and before long the economic situation had returned to normal.

But time was running out for Callaghan's Labor government. The March 1 referendum on devolution was fast approaching, and the Scottish National Party had linked its continuing support of the government to passage of the home-rule proposition. "Unless Callaghan makes sure the referendum is 'yes', he's out," warned an SNP official. Unfortunately for Callaghan, in order to insure that devolution could procede only if it had widespread support, the referendum legislation said that even if a majority of those voting were to cast their ballots in favor of the plan, it would not be considered adopted unless the number of 'yes' votes also exceeded forty percent of Scotland's total electorate of 3.8 million. With pollsters and pundits alike predicting a low turnout, it seemed unlikely that the forty percent requirement would be met, and that even though more people would vote for devolution than against it, the proposition would still fail.

Sure enough, on March 1, devolution was defeated, not by "no" votes, but by a low turnout. Two weeks later, the SNP made good its threat. Party Leader Donald Steward introduced a motion to bring down Callaghan's government. Shortly afterwards, the Liberals announced they would support the motion. And at the end of March, Mrs. Thatcher introduced her own motion "that this House has no confidence in her Majesty's Government." Determined to avoid a repetition of her humiliating setback the year before, when Callaghan defeated her no-confidence motion by coming up with the Lib-Lab pact, she decided not to act until the crucial minor parties had irrevocably commited themselves to an anti-Labor vote.

Still, Callaghan had a chance. If he could win over the three Welsh Nationalists in the House as well as the twelve Northern Irish MPs (the Ulster Unionists and two others), Labor would survive. Thus, he and Denis Healey began the most blatant Parliamentary horse-trading Westminster had seen in years.

THE MOMENT OF TRUTH

On March 30, 1979, Mrs. Thatcher opened the no-confidence debate by declaring, "The Government has failed the nation. It has lost credibility and it is time for it to go." She charged Labor with "doubling the prices in the housewife's shopping basket" and blamed Callaghan for a long list of failures including inflation, general economic policy and, above all, union unrest. "People expect rubbish to be collected, schools to be open, hospitals to be functioning—and they are not," she asserted. In fact, her speech reads better than it sounded. She was nervous and as a result, came across badly in what should have been her finest hour, sounding stiff when she should have been stirring, appearing hectoring instead of heroic. The Tory benches cheered her lustily, but out of obligation, not passion.

Callaghan's delivery, on the other hand, was masterful. He began his response sarcastically, taunting Mrs. Thatcher for waiting until the minor parties had acted before introducing her own motion of no-confidence. "She found the courage of their convictions," he gibed. He then turned on the Liberals and Scottish Nationalists for attempting to bring about a general election which in all probability would cost them dearly. "It's the first time," he observed, "that the turkeys have been known to vote for an early Christmas." In a more serious vein, he went on to accuse Mrs. Thatcher of following the discredited policies of confrontation which under Heath had "led to the ignominy of the three-day candle-lit week." He then finished with a double flourish, announcing a new four-pound-a-week increase in government pensions, and dismissing Mrs. Thatcher's proposed cuts in welfare spending as a reversion to "soup-kitchen social services."

In all, the debate lasted seven hours. Before it was over, many MPs drifted out to a pub just across the road from Westminster Palace (the Members' Bar inside having been shut down by a strike of parliamentary catering staff). The whips of both major parties watched them go nervously, fearing that some might have a bit too much to drink and forget to come back for the final vote.

They needn't have worried. When the vote came at ten P.M., the chamber was filled to overflowing, with twenty-five MPs forced to stand in the doorways. After an inconclusive voice vote (both sides shouted equally loudly), the speaker called for a "division": MPs voting for the no-confidence motion would troop out into the right-hand lobby, while those opposing the motion would gather in the left-hand lobby.

Some seventeen minutes later, their heads having been counted, they crowded back into the chamber to await the result. Mrs. Thatcher sat motionless, apparently calm. Callaghan, grinning bravely, leaned forward nervously, clapping his hands lightly in anticipation. At 10:18 P.M., a Tory vote-counter came in smiling broadly, and the Tory benches erupted in a huge roar. A moment later, the Speaker called for order and boomed: "Ayes to the right lobby, 311. Noes to the left lobby, 310."

For the first time in fifty-five years, a government had lost the confidence of the House. Conservatives shouted and danced for joy. In the Labor benches, some MPs rose to sing the socialist anthem "The Red Flag," while others bawled out the old civil rights standard "We Shall Overcome."

Mrs. Thatcher's 279 Tories had been joined by all thirteen Liberals and eleven Scottish Nationalists as well as by eight of the ten Ulster Unionists. But she owed her triumph to Sir Alfred Broughton, a Labor MP from Yorkshire who a few days earlier had suffered a heart attack and was too ill to attend the vote. Had Broughton (who died shortly afterward) made it to the House, the result would have been a tie, in which case the deciding vote would have been cast by the speaker of the house, longtime Labor MP George Thomas, who doubtlessly would have tipped the balance in his party's favor.

Callaghan took his narrow defeat stoically, sitting quietly amid the turmoil. Mrs. Thatcher was nearly as somber, permitting herself only a small grin of satisfaction. "It was exciting," she said afterwards, looking totally unexcited. Excited or not, she was certainly looking forward to the election that must now come. The polls put the Tories anywhere from seven to eighteen points ahead of Labor. "I believe we shall win," said Mrs. Thatcher, determined not to sound overly confident. "But then every Party Leader says that. The only way to do it is to work hard at it."

The next morning Callaghan could manage only a wan smile for the small crowd of well-wishers who had gathered outside No. 10 to see him off on his short, ritual journey to Buckingham Palace. There, he formally requested the Queen to dissolve Parliament. Her Majesty, the palace announced shortly afterwards, "has been graciously pleased to signify that she will comply."

While Callaghan went through the motions required by constitutional monarchy, Mrs. Thatcher celebrated by indulging in a rare treat: she slept late and enjoyed breakfast in bed. She well knew it would be her last opportunity to relax for the next five weeks. The election was fixed for May 3, and she wouldn't be able to let up until then, even for a moment. Her party had never been kind to losers; as she observed with characteristic realism: "I'll only be given the chance to . . . lose one."

That evening Callaghan kicked off the campaign with a nationwide television broadcast in which, with no visible irony, he painted the Conservatives as the party of radical change and Labor as the party of stability. It was a measure of the curious evolution of British politics that his assessment was an accurate one.

Mrs. Thatcher's first campaign broadcast was scheduled for the next day. But a few hours before she was to go on the air, while she was paying a call on her own constituency of Finchley, word came that a bomb had gone off at the House of Commons and that someone, possibly an MP, had been killed. An hour or so later, when she arrived at the BBC studios where she was to make her televised speech, an aide brought her the news that the victim *was* an MP, and not just any MP, but her close and trusted friend, Airey Neave. An explosive planted in his car, probably by Irish terrorists, had detonated as Neave was driving out of the House of Commons's new underground parking garage. The blast ripped the car apart, sending a pall of smoke halfway up the tower of Big Ben. A doctor and two nurses pulled Neave from the wreckage and rushed him to a nearby hospital, where he died within minutes, the first MP to be assassinated within the precincts of Westminster since Prime Minister Spencer Perceval was murdered by a maniac in the Commons lobby in 1812.

Neave's death came as more than a shock to Mrs. Thatcher—it was a shattering blow. Though he was far more a tactician than a strategist, and hence never much of a statesman, she had come to trust and rely heavily on his judgement. More than any other single person, he had been responsible for her 1975 victory over Ted Heath, and in that sense she owed to him the heady opportunity that was now hers. The idea of leading the Tories into a general election without Neave was unthinkable.

Badly shaken, Mrs. Thatcher cancelled her television broadcast. Instead, she went first to the Commons where she issued a statement. Then she hurried to Neave's home to comfort his widow. The Tory campaign, she declared, would not begin in earnest until after Neave's funeral.

Nonetheless, the next day she went on television to make her postponed broadcast. She quickly set out the Conservatives' top priority: "To make it worthwhile to go out and get on in this country again, we have to cut taxes," she said, "the taxes on earnings, the taxes on savings, the taxes on talent." In a country where the tax rates on earned income started at 33 percent and ran up to 83 percent—and where "unearned" income could face levies as high as 98 percent—it was a welcome message. But having delivered it, she retreated from the stage for the next four days, until after Neave's funeral on April 6.

In effect, she had ceded Callaghan the spotlight for the first week of the campaign. As far as Tory strategists were concerned, that was just as well. The Tories were well ahead in the polls. Too much exposure could only hurt them. Certainly, the less Mrs. Thatcher appeared, the less likely she would be to make a mistake that might cost the party votes. It was for precisely this reason that Mrs. Thatcher, who had earlier expressed her eagerness to confront the prime minister on television, was persuaded to reject just such an invitation when it came shortly after the government fell. Officially, she explained that "issues and policies decide elections, not personalities. We should stick to that approach. We are not electing a President. We are choosing a Government." Privately, however, aides explained that they feared her combative approach, when contrasted with Callaghan's avuncular serenity, might alienate voters, especially men. Indeed, media adviser Gordon Reece was overheard to say that if it were possible he'd be happy to limit Mrs. Thatcher's television exposure to film clips of her getting on and off her campaign plane.

Labor had a similar sense of her weaknesses. Indeed, its main strategy in the election campaign was based on the hope—a futile one, as it turned out—that Mrs. Thatcher would crack under the pressure of her first general election campaign as Tory leader and commit a gaffe which they could exploit. (For some reason, possibly male chauvanism, no one seemed to harbor similar fears or hopes about Callaghan, who, it should be pointed out, was also participating in his first general election as party leader.)

A WATERSHED ELECTION

Callaghan insisted that he wanted to avoid a mudslinging match, especially one that turned on class lines. "If this country should by chance want a knock-down drag-out fight between various elements of our society," he said, "that's not Labor's way." As he saw it, and Mrs. Thatcher readily agreed, the nation would be voting on May 3 in a "watershed" election that would go a long way towards determining what sort of place the UK would be for the rest of the century. Callaghan and Labor unashamedly plumped for a continuation and extension of the social welfare state Britain had become over the previous three decades. The country's problem, as they saw it, wasn't too much socialism, but precisely the opposite—the greed, selfishness, and obstructionism of Britain's antisocialists, the most prominent of these being Mrs. Thatcher. They painted her as a right-wing extremist who had forsaken the traditional British middle ground, which, as Callaghan noted was "a very large territory to occupy" (meaning, presumably, that a party could be committed to socialism, as his was, and still be within its reassuring borders). Mrs. Thatcher's policies, Labor said, were divisive and reactionary; they would threaten millions of government-subsidized jobs and turn poor areas into vast "deserts of unemployment." "The question you will have to consider," Callaghan told the electorate, "is whether we risk tearing everything up by the roots." Was the nation really in favor of scrapping "programs that assist firms on which a million jobs depend, slashing spending that is needed for families and hospitals and schools, having an upheaval in industry and with the unions," he asked. "The answer must surely be no."

Mrs. Thatcher, on the other hand, took her cue from Churchill's 1951 campaign to "set the people free" from socialism. "This election," declared the Tory Manifesto (a document shaped far more by Mrs. Thatcher and her personal advisers than by the party's central office), "is about the future of Britain—a great country which seems to have lost its way." Not only did she intend to halt what she called "the slither and slide to a socialist state." She was also determined to reverse the trend and restore to Britain what she called "our unquenchable belief in freedom." The nation, she argued passionately, "must not forever take refuge behind collective decisions. Each of us must assume our own responsibilities . . . We will be free and we will be strong again so long as we have a government which serves and which does not seek to master." Yes, she readily admitted, she was tough and uncompromising. But that was hardly a mark against her. "What Britain needs," she proclaimed proudly, once again flaunting the sobriquet the Soviets had bestowed upon her, "is an Iron Lady."

Specifically, she held out the promise of substantial cuts in income taxes; strict control of the money supply; a reduction in government borrowing; wide-ranging spending cuts except for defense, which would be increased; denationalization of the state-owned aerospace, shipbuilding, and freight industries, plus a continuing reduction of other government holdings; and an end to state intervention in private-sector labor negotiations. In short, she would move the state out of the marketplace, thus encouraging a rebirth of free enterprise. "The help for ailing firms," she argued, "only comes from successful firms, and if you're going to drain away all the resources from the successful firms to help the ailing firms, what you're going to get is far too few people creating wealth, far too many consuming it." True, she conceded, that might cost Britain subsidized jobs. "Temporary help is fine, but you can't keep yesterday's jobs going forever."

She also pledged (in one of those phrases beloved by headline-writers) to erect "a barrier of steel" across "the path to social disintegration and decay" by beefing up the police. She favored restoration of the death penalty (which had been suspended in 1965), arguing that "these vicious young thugs who go out and murder people should not go out in the knowledge that their own lives cannot be forfeited."

And she committed herself and her party to major trade-union reform, including curbs on secondary picketing, limits on welfare benefits for strikers, and changes in the law covering closed shops. Though she was careful to draw a distinction between what she described as the responsible majority of unionized workers and the "few thousand wreckers . . . we have to mobilize the rest of the members against," she was determined to strip the unions of their power to create another crisis situation. ("I don't anticipate a confrontation," she said reassuringly. "I believe we shall get a great deal of cooperation. Many members of trade unions will say, 'Thank goodness, someone is prepared to tackle this in a positive way!'")

It was an impressive list, and it left no doubt as to where Mrs. Thatcher or her party stood. The trouble was that for all its length, it was not very specific. Precisely when, where, how, and to what extent a Tory government would do all these things, neither Mrs. Thatcher nor the Conservative election manifesto would say. Even the Labor party was at least willing to propose a specific target for national growth. Not only did the Tories skip that; they also declined to offer a timetable for denationalization, a particular suggested level for government borrowing, or anything approaching a detailed blueprint for tax cuts. It was the *idea* of change that counted, they seemed to be saying, not the specific methods by which it might be achieved.

In part, this deliberate vagueness was a result of simple political prudence. "Why commit ourselves to anything more than we absolutely have to," reasoned a Tory strategist. It was a lesson Mrs. Thatcher had absorbed in 1977, when she watched President Carter forced into an embarrassing retreat from his promised tax rebate. "I intend to try not to make any promises which I might not be able to deliver," she vowed at the time, and in the April 1979 campaign she proved to be as good as her word.

But her reluctance to be specific was more than a question of tactics. It ran deeper. The enormously detailed Tory election manifesto of 1970—the result of two years of intensive planning—had seemed to her to be the height of futility. Just as her own political philosophy was rooted in the experiences that had marked and shaped her life, so too she believed that government policy ought to be arrived at empirically. It was a party's duty and responsibility to spell out to the voters where it stood, what sort of society it would like to see. But how could it know just what it would take to achieve its goals until it actually began the attempt? The specificity in which Heath had indulged, and which her critics derided her manifesto for lacking, was not only imprudent; she firmly believed it was also dishonest.

Considering the high stakes, the campaign was a strangely lifeless affair. Certainly it was not the bitter, personalized battle the newspapers had been expecting. Callaghan kept his promise to avoid mudslinging, and Mrs. Thatcher responded in kind. True, the unions denounced Mrs. Thatcher and the Tories regularly, but there was something curiously perfunctory about their attacks. They seemed somehow muted and unenthusiastic. Perhaps it was because the outcome of the election was considered a foregone conclusion.

Even the party leaders themselves often seemed merely to be going through the motions. While Callaghan waited for her to do or say something foolish, Mrs. Thatcher restricted her libertarian preaching mainly to the converted. On a visit to East Anglia, for example, she avoided the troubled British Leyland automobile works and instead visited a peaceful chocolate factory. On the Tyneside, whose vast shipyards depended desperately on the government subsidies the Conservatives had pledged to cut, she restricted her tour to a tea company. And in racially mixed, overwhelmingly pro-Labor Leicester, she found a nonunion, nearly all-white family-owned firm of uniform outfitters to visit. For security reasons, her rallies were ticket-only affairs, which meant that the audiences consisted almost solely of the Tory faithful. And even under those friendly circumstances, she often felt obliged to tailor her message to fit the prejudices of the region. In the industrial northeast, she played down her opposition to industrial subsidies, while in the agricultural southwest, she played it up. "She is very good at finding appropriate ideologies," marvelled an impressed and somewhat cynical senior Tory party official.

To be sure, Mrs. Thatcher was ready and eager to argue her case vigorously with the few Labor supporters she came across in her travels. Indeed, there were a few times when her aides almost had to drag her away from impromptu debates in order to keep her tight schedule from becoming hopelessly fouled up. But such occasions were rare. For one thing, few people were willing to confront her personally. In Finchley, for example, a black man came away from a sidewalk encounter with her to tell reporters that "the Tories are worse than the National Front." Had he told *her* that? "No," he explained, "she's a lady."

Interestingly enough, though everyone speculated endlessly about the effect of Mrs. Thatcher's sex on voter attitudes, the issue of what—if anything—it might mean for Britain to have a woman prime minister rarely came up. The few times it did, she cited historical precedent, as when a housewife in Rickmansworth complained that her husband said he'd rather not vote at all than help put a woman in 10 Downing Street. "I do not think many people will think that way," Mrs. Thatcher responded. "After all, one of our great successful periods . . . was under Elizabeth I—and if your husband had been in that time, my goodness, if he had thought the same then, we might never have beaten the Spanish Armada."

In any case, her personal encounters with voters were for the most part carefully staged meetings, mainly in the course of factory tours. As a result, few were especially consequential. "You're the new elite," she told a baffled computer engineer in a plant near the "new town" of Milton Keynes. When he failed to respond to this puzzling assertion, Mrs. Thatcher turned to the man's boss and noted ruefully: "He doesn't seem very happy about it, though."

Factory visits dominated the bulk of her campaign schedule. "She loves factories," an aide explained. Indeed, she visited so many that the *Spectator,* a pro-Tory political weekly, felt obliged to complain. "She has a genuine curiosity about the industrial process," it observed, "it seems a pity she feels the need to satisfy it during a three-week campaign."

When she wasn't visiting factories, Mrs. Thatcher could be found in rural fields having her picture taken with farm animals. It was not exactly a familar setting for her. "If we're not careful, we'll have a dead calf on our hands," Denis Thatcher warned wryly as he watched his wife pose uneasily with one on an East Anglia farm. The point of these bucolic expeditions was clear, as she indicated when she ordered reporters to keep their distance while she cuddled yet another calf, this one on a farm near Ipswich. "It's not for me, it's for the photographers," she apologized. "They're the most important people on this campaign."

THE CAMPAIGN CATCHES ON

It wasn't until the final week that the campaign really began to heat up. Callaghan had been hammering away at the rather critical question of just how the Tories intended to pay for their promised "substantial" tax cuts. Their chief economic spokesman, Sir Geoffrey Howe, at first tried to get away with the unsatisfactory response that the question could not be answered until the Conservatives had a chance to study the government's books. When that ploy failed, he attempted to turn the tables by demanding that Labor spell out some of *its* vaguer proposals. But the voters didn't buy that either. They thought Callaghan's query was a good one, and they wanted to hear a straight answer. When none was forthcoming, the electorate's mood began to get a bit ugly.

Three days before the election, the pro-Tory *Daily Mail* published a poll giving Labor a tiny lead over the Tories. It was the first—and, as it turned out, the last—time anyone had given Labor an edge in the contest, and it sent shock waves roiling through the country. The stock market, which had been enjoying a sustained boom ever since Callaghan's government fell, plunged more than fourteen points the day the poll came out, while sterling slipped badly as well.

Mrs. Thatcher, too, seemed rattled. Her daily press conferences, which up to then had been relatively serene, turned edgy. She accused one reporter of "thinking like a socialist," snappishly asked the BBC's political editor where he'd been for the past fifty years and pointedly reminded the crew from Britain's independent commercial TV network that they owed their jobs to the Tories, who had created the Independent Broadcasting Authority in the first place. She got her comeuppance, however, when she turned her ire on Geoffrey Goodman, the veteran industrial editor of the pro-Labor *Daily Mirror.* "What are you afraid of?" she bristled in response to a mildly challenging question of his. "I'm not afraid of anything," he replied evenly. "I'm just asking a question."

Because she had earlier taken the precaution of consistently dismissing the polls when they were favorable, Mrs. Thatcher was able to do the same with the *Mail's* unfavorable one. Nonetheless, she began an immediate and rather obvious effort to broaden her appeal and soften her radical image. Suddenly she was insisting that a Conservative government would not "mean sudden change"—insisting that "I am not trying to bring back some nostalgic version of the past" and that "our proposals are modest."

She also stepped up her attacks on Labor, peppering her final campaign appearances with aggressive lashings of Labor's record and passionate appeals to an upbeat vision of the future. She poured scorn on Callaghan's contention that Labor knew how to get along with unions.

"Why should we believe that their so-called 'special relationship' with the unions has any meaning after last winter?" she demanded. "Never forget how near this nation came to government by picket. Never forget how workers had to beg for their right to work."

It was time, she declared, for Britain to catch up with the rest of the free world—"time we became a leader, not a straggler." "Unless we change our ways and our direction," she added in an eloquent warning, "our greatness as a nation will soon be a footnote in the history books, a distant memory of an offshore island, lost in the mists of time like Camelot, remembered kindly for its noble past."

Meanwhile, Callaghan, who had consistently run ahead of Mrs. Thatcher in the personal popularity polls, was also turning on the juice. He warned that Mrs. Thatcher's laissez-faire instincts would bring nothing less than "national catastrophe" to Britain. "A Conservative free-for-all is the road to higher prices in the shops, fewer jobs, more strikes, the weakest to the wall," he intoned. "A Conservative free-for-all will quickly end in broken dreams and shattered living standards." He summed up the theme in his final television broadcast: A Tory government, he insisted, was simply "too big a gamble for the country to take. We can't afford a Conservative Government that would sit back and just allow firms to go bankrupt and jobs to be lost in the middle of a world recession."

Election day—as always in Britain, a Thursday—dawned unseasonably cold. The nation was experiencing its worst early May weather on record. Blizzards swept the country for the second day in a row, burying the west under five inches of snow and laying down a two-inch blanket across most of the north. Bad weather, the pundits agreed, would favor the Tories, who were the better organized of the two major parties. Thus, Callaghan issued a special election-day plea. "Five minutes braving the rain and snow," he said, "is a small price to pay for avoiding five years of Tory Government."

His appeal did not fall on deaf ears. Despite the weather, an impressive 76 percent of Britain's 41 million eligible voters turned out to cast their ballots. The final polls published on election morning all gave the Conservatives the edge, by a margin of two to six points. Still, at her final press conference, Mrs. Thatcher—perhaps remembering Airey Neave's shrewdly downbeat strategy in her 1975 leadership challenge—limited herself to a highly guarded victory prediction. "We have very considerable grounds for cautious optimism," she said. "I believe there is a very good chance of a clear majority [in the House]."

A FAMILY REUNION

She spent the early part of election night at her home in Flood Street, with Denis and the children. It was a rare family reunion. Denis had traveled with her constantly on the campaign, leading the applause at rallies and helping her through the often unruly crowds that mobbed her every appearance. But Carol, who had returned for her mother's race from Australia, where she was now working as a newspaper reporter, and Mark, who still lived at home, were usually off campaigning on their own.

At about ten P.M., the family left the house and were driven in Mrs. Thatcher's official car up to Finchley, thirty minutes away, to hear the results of her own election. Party leader or not, she—like Callaghan—was still an MP, and as such her seat in the Commons depended totally on the voters of her constituency. If by some unlikely chance they decided not to reelect her she would be out of the House no matter how well the Tories did in the rest of the country.

But Finchley ran true to form. The overwhelmingly Conservative district returned Mrs. Thatcher to Parliament with a solid majority of nearly 7,900 votes.

Once the Finchley results had been announced, she drove back to London, to the Conservative Party Central Office in Smith Square, a tree-lined square ten minutes' walk from Westminster that was the home of the Tories as well as Labor's headquarters. She arrived to find one of her campaign advisers on the telephone with Australian prime minister Malcolm Fraser, a supporter of Mrs. Thatcher's who had called to see how the race was going. Obviously, the aide had given Fraser a glowing report, for when the phone was handed to Mrs. Thatcher, the Australian leader greeted her by saying: "Congratulations, you've won." Mrs. Thatcher thanked Fraser, but she felt it was too early to accept such accolades. Instead, she and her family watched the television coverage as returns slowly filtered in from Britain's 635 constituencies. Tallying the vote in Britain is a lengthy, laborious procedure. The British use paper ballots which are counted by hand, and this time the process was complicated by the fact that most constituencies were not only electing their parliamentary representative but a long list of local officials as well. By one A.M., only a quarter of the returns were in; still, it was enough for both the BBC and ITV (the idependent commercial network) to forecast a Tory victory. But computer projections don't carry the same weight in Britain that they do in the U.S., and neither Mrs. Thatcher nor Prime

Minister Callaghan, who was monitoring the results from a hotel in his Welsh constituency in Cardiff, was willing to make any assumptions just yet.

Mrs. Thatcher remained at Smith Square until nearly five A.M. By this time, it seemed clear that the Conservatives were on their way to a solid majority in the Commons. And when she and her family returned to Flood Street, they found the house surrounded by a cheering crowd that alternately sang the Tory campaign song ("Blue is the color, Maggie is the name") and chanted "We want Maggie" until the sun came up. With all the commotion outside, sleep was impossible inside; instead, the family sat round the fireplace in the magnolia-colored living room and continued to follow the count. "I feel a sense of change and an aura of calm," Mrs. Thatcher announced at dawn. Still, she was not yet ready to claim victory. The Tories needed to win at least 318 seats in the new Parliament to command a clear majority; with the count complete at that point in only about three-quarters of the nation's constituencies, the tally of Conservative victories stood at less than 300. New victories were being reported every quarter-hour or so, and it seemed clear that when all the results were in, the Tories would have well over the necessary 318. But in her cautious way, Mrs. Thatcher was determined not to count her chickens until at least 318 of them had been officially hatched.

After breakfasting on grapefruit, boiled egg, and coffee, and changing into a navy suit and a jaunty print blouse, she finally emerged from her house at 11:20 A.M. In one of those inexplicable events that always seem to attend such occasions, she was presented with a blue-and-white stuffed rabbit by a three-year-old girl who had been waiting on the lawn with her mother for several hours. Then, with a wave to the crowd, Mrs. Thatcher sped off once again to Smith Square, where a celebration had been in progress for some time. Joining in, she thanked the staff for its hard work on the Tory party's behalf, exchanging champagne toasts and digging into a huge chocolate cake that had been wheeled out in her honor. Shaped like a door to No. 10, it bore the legend "Margaret Thatcher's Success Story." But though she was willing to accept congratulations, Mrs. Thatcher herself had yet to claim her obvious triumph.

While the Tories celebrated, James Callaghan, who had returned to London early that morning, was asking aides to start moving his personal effects out of 10 Downing Street. Under the British system there is no transition period during which a lame duck prime minister and his government carry on after an electoral defeat, giving their successors time

to prepare to take over. While the transfer of power from one administration to another is not instantaneous, it seldom takes more than a few
hours. The vanquished depart quickly, leaving the center stage—and the
keys to No. 10—to the victors. Thus, once he recognized that his party
had been beaten, Callaghan wasted no time in getting out of his successor's way. Still, neither he nor Mrs. Thatcher made any formal statements about the outcome of the election until 2:45 that afternoon, when
the count of Conservative victories at last passed the 318 mark. It was
then that Mrs. Thatcher finally permitted herself a broad, triumphant
smile, acknowledging for the first time that her party had won, and that
she was about to become prime minister.

With Labor's defeat now beyond any doubt, Callaghan paid his last
visit to Buckingham Palace as prime minister to tender his resignation to
the Queen. Shortly after three P.M., it was Mrs. Thatcher's turn to request a royal audience. As leader of what had become the majority party
in the new Parliament, it was time for her to take up the reins of power.
Accompanied by her husband, she was driven to the imposing, buff-col-
ored palace where Elizabeth II awaited her. While Mr. Thatcher remained downstairs with palace aides, his wife strode up the red-carpeted
staircase to the first-floor audience chamber to "kiss hands" with the
Queen.

In fact, new prime ministers don't actually perform the medieval dem-
onstration of fealty from which the ritual gets it name. The monarch
simply asks if the victorious party leader can form a government, and,
receiving a positive reply, bids that it be done. Having received just such
an assurance from Mrs. Thatcher, and having asked her then to act upon
it, the Queen invited her new prime minister to remain for a chat. The
two women—one, Britain's head of state; the other, its new head of government—sat and talked for forty-five minutes.

From the palace, Mrs. Thatcher went straight to what would soon be
her new home, 10 Downing Street. A large crowd had gathered, and
they greeted her with a rousing chorus of "For She's a Jolly Good Fellow." While Denis beamed, Carol took snapshots and Mark told reporters how "enormously proud of her achievement" the whole family was,
Mrs. Thatcher basked in a victory that just a few years earlier even she
had believed impossible. Standing by the famous black door to No. 10,
surrounded by a shoving mob of photographers, reporters, and TV
cameramen, having won what she described as "the greatest honor that
can come to any citizen in a democracy," she found herself reflecting on
her Grantham roots and the ambitious shoemaker's son who had started

her on her long and improbable road to Downing Street. "I just owe almost everything to my own father, I really do," she told the crowd. "He
brought me up to believe all the things that I do believe and they're just
the values on which I've fought the election. It's passionately interesting
to me that the things which I learned in a small town, in a very modest
home, are just the things that I believe have won the election."

At the suggestion of Norman St. John Stevas, who on occasion could
be simultaneously a religious romantic *and* a shrewd politician, she went
on to quote St. Francis of Assisi: "Where there is discord may we bring
harmony, where there is error may we bring truth, where there is doubt
may we bring faith, and where there is despair may we bring hope."

She concluded with a call for national unity, and a tribute to a fallen
comrade. "To all the British people," she declared, "howsoever they
may have voted, may I say this: now that the election is over, may we get
together and strive to serve and strengthen the country of which we are
so proud to be a part. And, finally, one last thing: in the words of Airey
Neave, whom we had hoped to bring here with us, 'Now, there is work to
be none.' "

Meanwhile, a half-mile away at Labor party headquarters in Smith
Square, the defeated Jim Callaghan, now leader of Her Majesty's loyal
opposition, was giving a postresignation press conference. Like many of
his fellow Laborites, he refused to accept that Britain had turned to the
right and rejected socialism. "People voted against last winter," he insisted, "rather than *for* the Conservatives." But he was not about to minimize Mrs. Thatcher's unique triumph as he wished the new prime minister well. "For a woman to occupy that office," he mused, "is a
tremendous moment in our history."

8

The New
Prime Minister

*"I am not known for my objectives
or proposals being unclear."*

ACCORDING TO TIME-HONORED political lore, challengers
don't win elections, incumbents lose them. Whether or not
this was the case in the British general election of May 1979
is a matter of some debate. In the aftermath, many pundits,
including more than a few Tories, found themselves agreeing with Callaghan's downbeat assessment: just as the Tory Parliamentary Party had elected Mrs. Thatcher as its leader in 1975 mainly because
it wanted to get rid of Ted Heath, so too had the British electorate voted
Conservative four years later mainly because it was fed up with Labor.

Clearly Mrs. Thatcher had not fought a dazzling campaign. For all her
passionate intensity, the fact was that she had been something of a disappointment on the hustings. Though she had stated her positions
forthrightly, she had refused for the most part to deal with their implications. She had faltered under pressure and too often appeared willing to
retreat gratefully into the slickly wrapped media package Gordon Reece
had designed for her. Perhaps most worrisome, she had failed—whether
out of inability or lack of interest—to inspire any confidence or affection
among the unconverted. What the Tory faithful cherished in her as
deeply-held conviction often came across to the public at large as no
more than blind obstinacy. Fairly or not, Mrs. Thatcher gave the impression to many that she had (as Germain Greer put it) "no more ability to
assess her actual position or weigh opposing arguments than Joan of
Arc."

But the British people desperately wanted a change, and change was precisely what Mrs. Thatcher offered them. Thus, even though Callaghan may have come across as a far more likeable and reasonable personality, they opted for the party of the Iron Lady. "She may grate upon refined susceptibilities, but voters know what she is talking about," was how Ferdinand Mount explained it just after the election. "She dominates this Parliament ... because she has single-handedly wrenched Conservative policy, against the instincts of a consensual shadow cabinet, in the direction of an individualist and populist Toryism." Or as *The Economist* argued at the time: the nation was "ready to take a gamble on Mrs. Thatcher's personality in order to gain the benefits of her policies."

Indeed, it could be argued, as Mount did, that her performance in the campaign was irrelevant. Mrs. Thatcher was no vaguely known contender for an American-style presidency, presented to the nation as a major-party nominee just four months or so before the election. She had been Tory leader for over four years, and if, by the spring of 1979, there was anyone left in Britain still uncertain of what she stood for, the month-long campaign certainly wasn't going to make a difference. As Mrs. Thatcher herself noted with classic British understatement in her first prime ministerial appearance for Question Time in the House: "I am not known for my objectives or proposals being unclear."

SWING OF THE PENDULUM

The Thatcher camp had been hoping to win a parliamentary majority of roughly thirty seats—"enough," as one aide explained it, "to make sure we win every vote in the Commons, but not so much that we might have people building little empires in the Party." By that reckoning, they did splendidly. They exceeded their goal by a margin big enough to add to their jubilation, but at the same time sufficiently small to ensure that party discipline could be easily maintained.

When all the votes were finally counted, the Tories had won 339 seats in the new Parliament. Labor's numbers had shrunk to 269, while the minor parties wound up with a mere 27 seats (including eleven Liberals and two Scottish Nationalists). That gave the Conservatives a healthy 43-seat edge over everyone else—the first clear-cut majority since the Tories' June 1970 victory, and one big enough to assure that by-election losses notwithstanding, the Tories could plan on remaining in power for the full five-year parliamentary term.

It was the biggest swing of the political pendulum in Britain since 1945, and then the magnitude of Labor's postwar comeback was, if anything, probably exaggerated by the fact that there hadn't been an election for the previous ten years. Still, Mrs. Thatcher's triumph at the polls was in some ways an ambiguous one. Though her party had won nearly 54 percent of the seats in the House of Commons, its share of the popular vote totalled just 43.9 percent, the smallest share won by any majority party since 1922. (To be sure, that still represented a 2 million-vote edge over Labor, whose 37.7 percent share was its smallest since 1931.) The Tories' support had also proven to be heavily regional, concentrated in the suburbs and rural areas of Wales and southern England. Less than a fifth of their seats in the new Parliament came from Scotland or the industrial north of England, and only a quarter of Britain's big-city constituencies had elected Conservative MPs.

As usual, the British electorate seemed to vote mainly according to its pocketbook. For the fourth general election in a row, an election-day survey taken by the BBC and the University of Essex found that, among all the issues cited by voters as having influenced their choice, inflation was mentioned most often. Next came unemployment, followed by strikes, taxes, and crime. Strangely enough, a majority of voters said they favored Labor's approach on what seemed to be the two most important issues—prices and jobs—though only by margins of 13 and 15 percent respectively. But the Tories' policies on taxes and law and order were overwhelmingly regarded as being superior to Labor's (roughly 80 percent of those surveyed said they preferred the Conservatives' thinking on taxes, while 86 percent liked their tough line on crime). And a majority of voters, though not such a huge one, also felt the Tories would do a better job of controlling the unions.

Nor had the immigration controversy been forgotten, though the impact of Mrs. Thatcher's pronouncements on the subject may have hurt the Tories as much as it helped them. A strong shift to the Conservatives in northeast London (where the National Front had done quite well in the 1977 local elections) as well as an impressive Tory showing in the west Midlands indicated that Mrs. Thatcher had probably gained her party more than a few anti-immigration votes. At the same time, however, the two constituencies with the biggest concentration of immigrants—Bradford West and Leicester South, both of which had been relatively safe Tory seats until 1974—swung so firmly into the Labor camp this time that pundits agreed that henceforth they should be regarded as safe Labor seats.

One factor that evidently did not hurt the Tories was Mrs. Thatcher's sex. Despite Tory fears that Britain's chauvinistic men might balk at the idea of seeing a woman become prime minister, it turned out that an almost equal proportion of men and women voted Conservative in May 1979. Indeed, among former Labor voters who switched their allegiance, the men outnumbered the women by a margin of more than three to one.

Perhaps most significant, Mrs. Thatcher and her Tories had managed to inspire a massive defection of working-class voters from the ranks of the Labor party. Some thirty percent of all trade-union members voted Conservative this time—eight percent more than in October 1974. Among skilled workers, the Tory tide was even stronger: 44 percent of them voted Tory, compared with just 26 percent in the previous general election.

In short, Callaghan's Labor government had been decisively rejected. But whether Mrs. Thatcher's mandate was correspondingly impressive remained an open question that only the public's reaction to the style and substance of her government would answer.

CHOOSING A CABINET

The first major decision any new prime minister must make is to pick a cabinet, and Mrs. Thatcher wasted no time in selecting hers. "There are two ways of making a Cabinet," she had told Kenneth Harris of *The Observer* the previous February. "One way is to have in it people who represent all the different viewpoints within the Party.... The other way is to have in it only the people who want to go in the direction in which every instinct tells me we have to go." Her way, not surprisingly, would be the latter. "As Prime Minister," she explained, "I couldn't waste time having any internal arguments."

Based on that statement, many people in Britain expected her first cabinet to consist almost solely of uncompromisingly right-wing Thatcherites. In fact, it did not. When she announced it two days after the election, the nation's first impression was one of balance and moderation. Among her cabinet's twenty-two members, all of them male, were eighteen who had served as ministers in Ted Heath's 1970–74 government, including seven whom *The Economist* described as "unabashedly Heathite." (There was no place in the cabinet for Heath himself, however. Though he continued to have trouble bringing himself to mention his successor by name, the former prime minister had campaigned vigorously for a Conservative victory. Nonetheless, Mrs. Thatcher felt that imposed no obligation on her, and she certainly had no desire to invite her old adversary into her new government. Instead, she offered him a job that would have removed him from Britain entirely: the ambassadorship to Washington, a post Heath had already made clear he couldn't accept.)

In any case, the complexion of her cabinet was misleading, at least to those who thought it betokened a change of political heart by the new prime minister. For one thing, a fair number of the moderates were there more out of necessity than choice. Unlike an American president who can select anyone in the country to serve in his cabinet (provided, of course, that the Senate approves), a British prime minister is limited to members of the two Houses of Parliament. And though the Tory benches in the Commons and the Lords contained several dozen MPs considerably more committed to the Thatcher view of politics than some of the ministers she selected, there were precious few who possessed both Thatcherite conviction and the experience and ability to hold down a cabinet-level job.

Moreover, in a government whose main concern would be economic issues, all the key treasury posts were in the hands of men of impeccable monetarist credentials. Sir Geoffrey Howe, who had been Mrs. Thatcher's shadow chancellor, was now chancellor of the exchequer. And if, despite his basic fiscal conservatism, Howe was considered too easygoing to suit some of the party's more devout Thatcherites, they could take comfort in the fact that he was backed up by the uncompromising John Biffen, who as chief secretary to the treasury would be responsible for implementing the spending cuts Mrs. Thatcher had promised in the campaign. A minister's ultimate weapon in internal squabbles is the threat of resignation, and as Ferdinand Mount noted, "Mr. Biffen is the resigning type . . . if he thinks the Government is printing or spending too much money, he'll be out before you can say 'minimum lending rate.' " Nigel Lawson, the tough-minded, sometimes arrogant intellectual whom Mrs. Thatcher named as her Number Three at the treasury, was similarly hard-nosed. With a troika like that running the economy, the new prime minister would not find it easy to commit any Heath-style U-turns.

Most of the moderates in her cabinet were concentrated in the so-called "spending" ministries: agriculture, education, environment, employment, health and social security, and the home office, departments whose function it was to disburse the funds collected by the treasury. There were some weighty individuals here, most notably Willie Whitelaw, upon whom Mrs. Thatcher had increasingly come to rely since the death of Airey Neave. In addition to being named home secretary (responsible, among other things, for immigration and law and order), Whitelaw had also been designated as Mrs. Thatcher's Number Two in Cabinet, in effect, deputy prime minister. But for all of Whitelaw's relative liberalism—and it was only relative—his loyalty to Mrs. Thatcher was unquestioned. Moreover, none of the other moderate spending ministers had Mrs. Thatcher's trust—or even her ear—to the extent that Whitelaw did. And in any case, the true believers were represented in this group, too—by Keith Joseph, who had been assigned the key portfolio of minister for industry, a demanding post in which he would be responsible for dismantling the enormous program of corporate subsidies that had grown up over the previous decade.

Indeed on close inspection, the only area of the cabinet that seemed genuinely out of character with Mrs. Thatcher's inclinations was the foreign affairs and defense team. Lord Carrington, the experienced diplomat and hereditary peer she had named foreign secretary; Sir Ian Gilmour, who as lord privy seal would be Carrington's voice in the Commons; Defense Minister Francis Pym; and Lord Soames, who though he was given no specific portfolio had been included in the cabinet because of his interest and experience in European affairs—all these men were strong—in some cases, passionate—supporters of the Common Market, moderates on southern-Africa, and while suspicious of détente not nearly so outspoken about it as Mrs. Thatcher.

In any case, Mrs. Thatcher quickly made it clear that, as in opposition, she intended to run the cabinet, and not vice versa. At its first meeting, she left no doubt that what she expected most from her ministers was loyalty and discipline. "It was not quite a jolly hockey-sticks pep talk," one participant later reported, "but she wants us to work as a team. If you step out of line it's *addio*." It was not an idle threat. "Look at what happened to poor Winston," one minister noted, referring to the immediate dismissal of the young Churchill from the opposition front bench in 1978 after he had defied Mrs. Thatcher on Rhodesia.

For ministers who had not served in her shadow cabinet, Mrs. Thatcher's domineering approach came as a rude shock. "It's unbelievable," said one. "She just dictates policy and doesn't expect disagreement. And she talks on and on." An aide of hers described her attitude a bit differently, but to the same effect: "She has acquired power," he explained, "and she intends to use it."

A ROYAL WELCOME

Margaret Thatcher's effective debut as prime minister came twelve days after the election, when the Queen opened the new session of Parliament by reading a speech prepared by Mrs. Thatcher and her colleagues. As always the state opening of Parliament repeated an ancient ceremony rich in the pageantry of an imperial past. The Queen rode down the wide red-paved Mall from Buckingham Palace to Westminster, leading a grand royal procession in the horse-drawn Irish State Coach, attended by Prince Philip, Prince Charles, and Princess Anne, and accompanied by the armor-clad horsemen of the Sovereign's Escort resplendent in their red-plumed helmets. At Westminster she donned a purple and gold cloak and placed on her head the imperial state crown, studded with 300 rare jewels, among them the ruby worn by Henry V at Agincourt five and a half centuries earlier.

Once seated on the great throne in the neo-Gothic House of Lords, she nodded to the lord high chamberlain, who lifted his white wand in reply and dispatched the court official known as Black Rod to commence the ritual summoning of the members of the House of Commons. Black Rod, in everyday life a retired army general but now dressed in his ceremonial morning coat and wearing his ornate chain of office, strode across the palace of Westminster to the Commons, where, following a centuries' old tradition, the doors were slammed in his face—a reminder of that chamber's independence from the Crown. Three times he had to knock with his black rod before the doors were finally thrown open again and Mrs. Thatcher and Opposition Leader Callaghan walked out side-by-side, leading their respective troops to the Lords.

At the Lords, the new prime minister, wearing an off-white suit and a peach-colored straw hat, curtsied to the monarch and listened impassively as the Queen, still seated on the throne, and now wearing her spectacles, read the twelve-minute speech outlining the new government's legislative program. It had been handed to her just moments before by the bewigged lord chancellor—the seventy-one-year-old Lord Hailsham, who took special care not to trip over his robes as, following the strict protocol, he backed down the three steps from the throne.

In her flat but clear monotone, the Queen spelled out to her assembled Parliament her government's intentions for the coming session. In foreign affairs, it pledged to increase Britain's contribution to NATO while maintaining its own nuclear deterrent, to "play a full and constructive part" in the Common Market while seeking better terms for British membership, and to seek to "achieve a fair balance between the rights and duties of the trade-union movement," encourage tenants of public housing to purchase their homes from the state, restore local control of school systems, and tighten immigration laws. As far as the economy was concerned, the Queen read on, "by reducing the burden of direct taxation and restricting the claims of the public sector on the nation's resources, [the government] will start to restore incentives, encourage efficiency, and create a climate in which commerce and industry can flourish."

Back in the Commons after the Queen's Speech, the first debate of the Thatcher era was soon under way. After two Tory backbenchers rose to propose and second the ritual motion of thanks to the monarch for her address, Callaghan took the floor to commence what in all probability would be Labor's first five-year stint in opposition since the days of Harold Macmillan. He began by noting with mock detachment that the Tories' impregnable majority might be "a great blessing and relief" to them, but it also stripped the Conservatives of any excuse for failure since, unlike the previous Labor government, they would not be able to blame their problems on the minor parties. "Whatever they wish to do, they will be able to get a majority," he pointed out almost gleefully. "The only question is whether they have the talent."

He then launched into a scathing attack on Mrs. Thatcher's election campaign which, he declared scornfully, was based on the proposition: "What's in it for me?" With the help of what he described as "a sycophantic press," Mrs. Thatcher had promised the voters Utopia; but now, "after the election," he gibed (in a reference to a well-publicized statement of Mrs. Thatcher's that it would take at least a decade for her radical aims to be achieved), "we hear noises that Utopia is going to have to be postponed for a day or two." He scoffed at the Tories' "utterly naive" belief that their simplistic proposals would "result in a great upsurge in investment, productivity and employment, and a unified country," labeling such notions "delusions." "The country," he concluded acidly, "deserves a better analysis and more realistic remedies than this."

Both sides of the House wondered how the new prime minister would respond. A great cheer arose from the Tory benches as Mrs. Thatcher rose to speak. She looked grim. Callaghan's sarcastic style was not for her. She was the Iron Lady. The strident, didactic tone she had abandoned in the last few days of the campaign was back now, and she outlined her ambitious legislative program of seventeen major bills to be passed in the coming seventeen months in a determined, no-nonsense voice.

As the Queen had indicated, Mrs. Thatcher intended to cut income taxes, abolish price controls, reduce public spending in virtually every area except defense, reform the unions, curb immigration, restore private "pay beds" to the socialized National Health Service, and save grammar schools from Labor's plans for widespread comprehensivization. When Denis Healey, the former chancellor, interrupted her to ask if she still planned to attack the unions by introducing legislation aimed at "robbing the families of people on strike of social security benefits," she put him down neatly. "No one proposes to rob families," she snapped, as the Tory benches cheered. "We are entitled to expect union funds of those who strike to make a bigger contribution, as they do in many other countries."

THE PATH OF THE PEOPLE

Others might debate what sort of mandate she had, but Mrs. Thatcher herself had no doubts. "The Conservative party has captured and now occupies the middle ground of politics," she declared. "It was a watershed election and it was decisive . . . These are the policies we submitted to the people. The path we now take is the path the people have chosen."

Labor was not about to be cowed, either by Mrs. Thatcher or by her forty-three-seat majority. "All her policies turn out in the end to favor the haves at the expense of the have-nots," argued former Prices Minister Roy Hattersly as the debate went on. Insisting that her plans to bring back "pay beds" would allow the rich better medical care than the poor, he reminded the House of Mrs. Thatcher's speech outside No. 10 the day after the election: "She will find it difficult," he taunted, "to find a quotation from St. Francis of Assisi to justify that sort of thing."

The new prime minister shrugged off such attacks. "You had your chance," she snapped to the Labor benches, "now it's our turn."

And so it was. Margaret Thatcher's first three months in office were in many ways a frenetic time. Unlike America's Franklin Roosevelt in the early 1930s—or Britain's Harold Wilson in the mid-1960s—she had promised no activist "100 days" that would shake, if not the world, at least the nation. But she had pledged to reverse a thirty-year trend, and she was determined to waste no time in getting started. It was less than three months between the time she took office on May 4 and Parliament recessed for the summer on July 27. Yet during this relatively short period, Mrs. Thatcher radically reoriented Britain's tax system; she laid plans to limit sharply the growth of government spending; she began the state's retreat from the marketplace; and she served notice on the trade unions that as far as she was concerned the days of their hegemony were numbered. "It's one shock after another in this government," said one moderate member of her cabinet, somewhat dazed by the pace the new prime minister set. "You think you've just got over one surprise when suddenly there's another one waiting for you."

To be sure, she had to hit the ground running whether she wanted to or not. The almost instantaneous transfer of power forced her to come to grips with her new role literally overnight. No sooner had she selected her cabinet than West German Chancellor Helmut Schmidt arrived in London for an official visit. The invitation had been issued by Callaghan months before. The fact that he was no longer prime minister, and that Mrs. Thatcher had just stepped into the job a few days earlier, was no excuse for cancelling it. Indeed, it turned what would have ordinarily been merely the latest in a continuing series of routine get-togethers into a highly significant meeting. As the most powerful economy in Europe, and one that Mrs. Thatcher liked to hold up as a model to her relatively lackadaisical countrymen, West Germany was enormously important to Britain. What's more, this would not only be Mrs. Thatcher's first meeting with Schmidt, it would be her first meeting as prime minister with *any* head of a foreign government. With a summit of Common Market presidents and prime ministers scheduled for Strasbourg at the end of June, and an even higher-powered gathering of world leaders on the agenda a week later in Tokyo, Mrs. Thatcher's ability to get along and deal as an equal with her overseas counterparts was of far more than academic interest.

Schmidt would provide a stern test. For one thing, he had enjoyed a warm personal relationship with her predecessor, whom he frequently referred to as "My good friend, Jim Callaghan." For another, he had a razor-sharp intellect, and he did not suffer fools gladly. (He once reportedly referred to David Owen, Callaghan's controversial foreign secretary, as a pompous bore.)

If Mrs. Thatcher was nervous about meeting with Schmidt so early in her tenure, it didn't show. Indeed, the Conservative prime minister and the Social Democratic chancellor got on swimmingly. After their formal talks had ended, Schmidt allowed that Mrs. Thatcher was "no soft touch" and told her how impressed he was by "the spirit of decisiveness in which you want to tackle problems now facing your country and your new Government."

Though mutual backscratching is the politician's stock-in-trade, Schmidt really seemed to mean what he said. To the surprise of many, including possibly even of Schmidt himself, Mrs. Thatcher had persuaded him to endorse her hard line on détente, a particularly sensitive subject to the West Germans. "Détente is fine as long as it is a two-way street and as long as it actually happens," she said, sounding her now familiar theme. "These talks showed that our views are not incompatible. Détente should always be approached from a position of strength in defense." Schmidt did not demur. "I agree," he said. "Now, of course, the position of West Berlin makes the Germans more sensitive on this issue than some other European nations. But I agree that détente must start from a position of military balance. It must be clear to the other side that you have the ability to deter and to defend yourself."

Indeed the only disagreement between Mrs. Thatcher and Herr Schmidt was a lighthearted one which came when she tried a bit over-enthusiastically to draw parallels between her economic policies and his. "We both believe in free enterprise and incentives," she said, "and look at how [Schmidt's government] is cutting taxes . . ."—at which point a grinning Schmidt, who heads a nominally socialist party, broke in to protest. "Don't go too far," he pleaded. "You will spoil the relations between me and my party."

Mrs. Thatcher obligingly backed off, but it was one of the rare times that she did. To the astonishment of her countrymen, she quickly made it clear that she intended to run the government—and by extension, the nation—just as she had pledged she would. If the idea of a politician's taking campaign promises seriously wasn't exactly unprecedented, it certainly seemed that way to many Britons. As the American columnist George Will remarked, the shock and bewilderment with which the British reacted to Mrs. Thatcher's consistency was reminiscent of the reaction to Barry Goldwater when he won the Republican presidential nomination in 1964. Goldwater had run in the primaries on what seemed a radically right-wing platform. When he finally captured the nomination at the GOP National Convention in San Francisco, many pundits expected him to moderate his extreme position. But Goldwater had other ideas. "Extremism in the defense of liberty is no vice," he declared in his acceptance speech—at which point a reporter in the press gallery dropped his pencil and gasped, "My God, he's going to run as *Goldwater*."

By the same token, the new prime minister was going to govern as Margaret Thatcher. Nowhere was this more apparent than in her government's first budget, the heart of its economic strategy, which Chancellor of the Exchequer Sir Geoffrey Howe presented to Parliament and the nation on June 12, 1979.

BUDGETARY FIRESTORM

In the debate following the Queen's Speech a month earlier, Mrs. Thatcher had promised that Sir Geoffrey's first budget would "make a start" in cutting income taxes. But she refused to say by how much, only that such cuts would be "the highest priority." She had also promised, again without providing specifics, that the budget would shift the emphasis in taxation from direct levies on earnings to indirect levies on spending (such as the value-added-tax, or VAT); that it would clamp down on government expenditure, and that it would move the state out of the marketplace by selling off government holdings in industry and phasing out government subsidies to ailing companies. Predictably, her intentions were praised by fiscal conservatives. But few believed she would actually be able to follow through on them.

It wasn't that Mrs. Thatcher's radical proposals would be impossible to push through the Commons. In America, such massive tax reform might require years, if not decades, of intensive and frustrating negotiations with Congress. But under the parliamentary system, a majority government such as Mrs. Thatcher's could, if it chose, turn the entire tax system upside down within a matter of weeks—barring an unlikely revolt of its backbenchers. All that was necessary was to present the proposals to the Parliament, instruct its MPs to vote for them, and the deed would be done.

So the question wasn't whether Mrs. Thatcher *could* make the changes she had sketched out, but whether she *would* make them, whether she had the political gumption to risk the storm of protest that her strong budgetary medicine would inevitably provoke. And a storm there would certainly be, for the reforms she was talking about would not be painless. "The immediate effect of the promised Tory economic measures is almost bound to be unpleasant," noted Malcolm Rutherford, political editor of the conservative and highly influential *Financial Times*. "The switch to indirect taxation will push up the cost of living still further, and measures to reduce state intervention in industry will presumably cost jobs, at least in the short term."

As it turned out, Mrs. Thatcher and her chancellor had the necessary gumption—and then some. On June 12, in a seventy-five-minute speech to the Commons—a relatively short one as these things usually go—Sir Geoffrey set out one of the most radical budgets ever to be introduced by a new British government. Just as the prime minister had promised, income taxes were slashed by nearly £5 billion. At the same time, however, VAT was raised sharply, from the existing rates of 8 and 12.5 percent to a unified higher rate of 15 percent—along with duties on gasoline, alcohol, and cigarettes.

Also as promised, government spending was cut drastically for the first time in years. As part of the Tory aim to "roll back the boundaries of the public sector," Howe decreed that more than £4 billion would be lopped off appropriations for housing, energy, education, foreign aid, transport, employment, industrial subsidies, and aid to the cities. In addition, he relaxed the forty-year-old exchange controls which had severely limited the amount of money Britons could take out of the country; he announced plans to sell off about £1 billion worth of unspecified government corporate assets; and he raised the minimum lending rate—Britain's version of America's so-called "prime" rate—from twelve to fourteen percent.

To say that the budget was controversial would be a monumental understatement. The fact that tens of thousands of government-subsidized jobs would be eliminated by Howe's budget; that hundreds of thousands more might be lost as a result of the economic slowdown it would inevitably produce; that most of the income tax savings would go to the better off; that it would squeeze credit at a time when many companies were already facing liquidity problems; that the VAT increase would add at least 3.5 percent to an inflation rate that the government itself was predicting would crack 17 percent by the end of the year—all this and more provoked a full-scale political firestorm.

As Sir Geoffrey detailed his plans to the Commons, Labor MPs groaned in disbelief. One was so overcome he shouted, "Treason!" When the chancellor finished, Callaghan rose to denounce the budget as a "reckless gamble" that was unjust, inflationary, and "unfair in the distribution of rewards." Later on, Denis Healey was even more eloquently scornful. It was, he said, "a she-wolf's budget in sheep's clothing . . . a classic recipe for roaring inflation, soaring unemployment, and industrial anarchy."

And opposition politicians weren't the only ones with reservations. Even the sympathetic *Economist* conceded that "Howe's first budget deflates an economy which is already slowing down, and adds 3–4% to retail prices when inflation is already speeding up."

Most worrisome of all was the reaction of trade unionists. Up to June

12, they had been relatively quiescent, waiting, it seemed, to see just how serious Mrs. Thatcher was about her desire to roll back the socialist tide. Now they responded with an angry roar, pledging to "fight and fight and fight" against "this mean, diabolical budget" which was clearly "directed against the working class." This is a budget for people who are never ill, don't smoke or drink, are prepared to eat less, and do not intend to drive to work," stormed miners' union boss Joe Gormley. "It will ensure that the rich get richer and the poor get poorer," added Terry Duffy, head of the giant engineering workers' union. "How can they prevail on us to be moderate in our pay claims . . . when VAT is up to fifteen percent and the cost of living is soaring?" Even more menacingly, Mick McGahey, the communist leader of the Scottish miners, promised a "summer and winter of discontent" that would do to Mrs. Thatcher just what the miners had done to Ted Heath in 1974. "We will create the conditions for a general election," he vowed, "in order to ensure the defeat of the Thatcher government." McGahey was later slapped down by his national boss, Joe Gormley, who derided his call to arms as "silly and daft," adding: "We shall not, as a union, try to use our industrial strength to fight a political battle." But the message from the unions was nonetheless clear: if they couldn't prevent the Tories from implementing their budget (and short of a McGahey-style confrontation it was hard to see how they could), they certainly were not going to cooperate with the government and restrain their wage demands.

In fact, the budget had been as much of a surprise to most of Mrs. Thatcher's ministers as it was to the rest of the nation. Until a cabinet meeting held just before Howe delivered his budget speech to Parliament, only he, Mrs. Thatcher, and the other treasury ministers knew what it contained. Even Willie Whitelaw, the deputy prime minister, had been left in the dark.

Though it drew its inspiration from Mrs. Thatcher's free-enterprise, monetarist convictions, the budget was the work of Howe and his treasury colleagues. Indeed, Mrs. Thatcher had grave reservations about it. The sharp increase in VAT had shocked even her, and she was worried about the budget's inflationary potential. But Howe dug in his heels. The government was facing a deficit of more than £11 billion at a time when the economy could not afford one much over £8.5 billion. The VAT and other tax increases, plus the £1 billion sale of state-owned assets, were necessary to close the gap. Eventually, the prime minister gave in.

What she and most of her cabinet liked about the budget was that it lived up in spectacular fashion to the Tories' campaign promises. It wasn't just the pundits who had wondered whether Mrs. Thatcher's legendary resolve would desert her once she moved into No. 10. Some of her cabinet colleagues had the same doubts. When at last they heard the budget spelled out, the relief around the coffin-shaped table was palpable. "Thank God we've done what we said we would do," one minister exclaimed when Howe finished his briefing, and almost everyone in the cabinet sighed in agreement.

The cabinet was also agreed that it would be best to push the harsh measures through all at once, rather than to try to spread them out over the next year or two. The ministers all knew that the budget would be unpopular at first, and no one disputed Mrs. Thatcher's belief that they might as well bite the bullet and go through the worst as quickly as possible.

Whether Mrs. Thatcher and her cabinet were aware of just how unpopular the budget would turn out to be is not certain. What is clear is that because of it the Thatcher government had one of the all-time shortest political honeymoons ever granted a new administration. While it is customary for a new government to gain in popularity during its first few weeks in office, the Tories saw theirs decline markedly. Indeed, a nationwide poll taken in the five days after the budget was announced indicated that Labor was actually ahead, by a margin of 43.5 to 42. No government since the war had lost its popular support so quickly. Some 49 percent of those questioned in the survey felt the Conservative budget wasn't fair (vs. 40 percent who said it was). Still, Mrs. Thatcher retained a tiny edge on the question of how she was doing as prime minister: 41 percent said they were satisfied with her so far, compared with 40 percent who weren't. But an overwhelming 68 percent agreed that the Tories were carrying out their campaign promises.

SUMMIT DEBUT

Whatever the polls said about her, Mrs. Thatcher had more pressing matters to think about. She was due in Strasbourg on June 21 for the semiannual meeting of Common Market heads of government, and a week after that there was the seven-nation summit in Tokyo to attend. Though they sometimes seemed pointless, such get-togethers were more than flashy and expensive public relations exercises. Indeed, with a global recession in the making and trade relations growing increasingly edgy, multilateral summits had become an essential feature of international diplomacy.

The Strasbourg meeting presented Mrs. Thatcher with some tricky problems, not least of which was the fact that it would be her summit debut. On the one hand, Mrs. Thatcher wanted to improve Britain's rocky relationship with the rest of Europe. At the same time, however, she was commited to bettering the terms of British membership in the Common Market—something that most of its fellow members would be loath to grant. (While most of the EEC nations profit from their membership in the group, Britain actually loses money on the deal, and quite a bit of it. According to British treasury estimates, which, needless to say, are disputed by the others, the UK and Italy—the two weakest economies in the Common Market—each subsidized the rest of the nine by more than £1 billion in 1978.) The treasury calculated that on a per capita basis, Britain's contribution to the EEC budget was 25 to 30 percent larger than it should have been. Mrs. Thatcher was determined to change that. She was also determined to make a good impression.

Not surprisingly, when she started out, she was nervous. As a result she seemed at first "a bit arrogant," as one participant in the talks put it, and both Lord Carrington and Roy Jenkins (the former Labor MP and British foreign secretary who was now president of the European Commission, the Common Market's secretariat) worried that she might be overstating her case. In the end, however, she emerged as the star of the show. To be sure, she didn't precisely win her point. Though she argued long and hard for a new deal on British budget contributions, the other EEC heads of government refused even to agree that the UK had a special problem. Instead, they referred the entire matter to their finance ministers—in effect, postponing any action until the next Common Market summit six months off.

But as the only woman participant in Strasbourg, Mrs. Thatcher attracted enormous attention. Perhaps more significantly, she impressed her counterparts with her zeal, intelligence, and commitment to the European ideal.

She did similarly well in Tokyo the next week. The Japanese, who are particularly fascinated by blondes, were captivated by her. Pictures of Mrs. Thatcher went up everywhere. A perfume manufacturer even asked the British Embassy if it could use her likeness on its labels. (The embassy suggested that it wasn't a very good idea, but the firm went ahead anyway.) As once again the only woman in a group of men (except for

President Carter's wife Rosalynn, the only spouse to attend the conference), she was invariably placed in the center of the official group photographs. And at the formal banquet, her stunning white gown presented a dazzling contrast to the men's black dinner jackets.

She was equally effective in substantive areas. Of course, at this meeting she was dealing from strength. At a summit devoted mainly to coming up with ways of coping with the energy crisis, she represented a nation that would probably be self-sufficient in oil within eighteen months. Thus she was able to remain aloof from the often angry bargaining over oil-import targets and quotas that divided the Americans, French, Germans, Italians, and Japanese.

In part, this made her one of the more popular participants. So too did the fact that, as usual, she was awesomely well-briefed. Helmut Schmidt marvelled at "the knowledge of the subject, the authority and the sense of responsibility with which Mrs. Thatcher took part in the deliberations." But though she struck up a cordial relationship with the other Western leaders, it was not a familiar one. "First-name terms can lead to *artifical* familiarity," she noted. As a result, it was "Mr. President" and "Herr Chancellor," not "Jimmy" or "Helmut"—and "Madame Prime Minister," not "Margaret."

Her evident self-confidence at Tokyo had been buoyed by an unexpected achievement she enjoyed just before she got there. On her way out from Britain, Mrs. Thatcher's Royal Air Force VC-10 put down in Moscow for a brief refueling stop. It was by no means an official visit, merely a courtesy extended by the Soviets who, according to normal protocol, should have dispatched a deputy premier to greet her. Instead, to her surprise, Soviet Premier Alexi Kosygin came out to the airport himself to host a ninety-minute champagne and caviar supper over which he and Mrs. Thatcher discussed the world economy, strategic arms limitation, energy, and the plight of Vietnamese refugees (on which, as Australian Prime Minister Malcolm Fraser later put it, Mrs. Thatcher succeeded in winning nothing but a "raspberry" from the Soviet leader). It was, she noted, "a lot to get in during about one and a half hours." Nonetheless, she clearly impressed Kosygin, who pronounced it "a very good meeting" and soon afterward sent out diplomatic feelers suggesting that if Mrs. Thatcher were to indicate an interest in making an official visit, the Soviets would be happy to invite her. (It wasn't that Moscow had suddenly developed any great love for the woman it had dubbed the "Iron Lady." Rather, it had to do with the Kremlin's ruling obsession: its fear of China. Out of their long-standing belief that "the enemy of my enemy is my friend," the Chinese had been courting Mrs. Thatcher assiduously ever since her 1976 attacks on détente and Peking was now interested in buying a substantial number of Harrier jet fighters from the British. That evidently convinced the Soviets that it was now time to bury the hatchet with the new British prime minister.)

But while she performed capably in the international arena, Mrs. Thatcher was hardly an unqualified success as a diplomat. Like Jimmy Carter, she had a disconcerting habit of making off-the-cuff pronouncements on sensitive issues that occasionally threatened to undermine months of diplomatic spadework. Nowhere was this more apparent—or potentially more destructive—than in her handling of the touchy issue of Rhodesia.

Ever since the spring 1978 elections, which had replaced Ian Smith's white minority regime in Salisbury with the so-called black majority government of Bishop Abel Muzorewa, Mrs. Thatcher's personal inclination had been to end the economic sanctions (which had been imposed on Rhodesia when it made its unilateral declaration of independence in 1965) and recognize the breakaway colony as soon as possible. She was persuaded to take a more cautious stance by Lord Carrington, who argued that for the sake of its relations with black Africa—as well as with the U.S., which had been working with the Callaghan government to resolve the issue—Britain could not afford to act precipitately or on its own. Rhodesia's African neighbors had grave doubts, shared by the U.S., as to whether Muzorewa's regime, which in many ways was still controlled by whites, really represented a change from minority to majority rule. And they would not look kindly on anyone who felt that it did.

Nonetheless, on her way back from Tokyo, Mrs. Thatcher told a press conference in Canberra, Australia, that she doubted "very much" whether the British Parliament could be persuaded to renew sanctions for another year when they expired in the fall. It was a questionable judgment, not shared by many of her colleagues at Westminster, and she compounded her mistake by intimating that her government wouldn't even try to get the sanctions renewed. She quickly added that the lifting of sanctions would not necessarily be followed immediately by British recognition of the Muzorewa regime. But the implication was clear: as far as Mrs. Thatcher was concerned, Salisbury's current government was a legitimate one, and it was only a matter of time before London officially recognized it.

Unfortunately, there was quite a wide gap between her personal position and that of her government. Britain's official stance was that while the 1978 elections had made a fundamental change in the nature of what was now called Zimbabwe-Rhodesia, they had not changed things enough to warrent a lifting of sanctions or recognition of the new government just yet. Indeed, for the previous few months, British diplomats, along with their American counterparts, had been trying to persuade Muzorewa to amend his "majority rule" constitution and once and for all oust Ian Smith, who had stayed on as a minister-without-portfolio, from the government. They believed that if his regime would eliminate the veto power possessed by the Salisbury Parliament's twenty-eight white MPs—and if it would drop the clauses which virtually guaranteed that all key posts in the Rhodesian army, police, civil service, and judiciary would continue to be held by whites for at least five years—then an internationally acceptable settlement might be possible.

Muzorewa, however, was reluctant. And after Mrs. Thatcher's Australian statements, he saw no reason to act at all. If the lifting of sanctions and recognition were inevitable, as she had implied, why should he do anything but sit tight and wait? Mrs. Thatcher's impetuous gaffe had undone months of careful diplomacy.

In the end, she managed to recoup—in dazzling fashion. At the Commonwealth Conference held in Lusaka, Zambia early in August 1979, Mrs. Thatcher stunned friends and enemies alike by executing a graceful U-turn on Rhodesia that won the hearts—and support—of the previously hostile frontline Black African states and thrust Britain back into the forefront of the international effort to end the Rhodesian crisis. Under Lord Carrington's astute guidance, and following her own traditional Tory sense of foreign affairs, she bowed to the dictates of diplomatic pragmatism by calling for a cease-fire, a revised constitution, and new elections under British supervision in Zimbabwe Rhodesia. The new peace initiative—considered by many to be the last chance to avoid a brutal and bloody fight to the finish among the breakaway colony's warring factions—won immediate and lavish praise from the frontline presidents, who just a week earlier had branded the British prime minister a "racist." But Mrs. Thatcher had no illusions that peace in Rhodesia was finally just around the corner. "I'm much too cautious to be starry-eyed about it," she said. "We've got to see how we get on." Bishop Muzorewa and Ian Smith grudgingly indicated they would attend a new constitutional convention to be held under British auspices in London in September. And Presidents Julius Nyerere of Tanzania and Kenneth

Kaunda of Zambia confidently predicted that they could bring the guer-
illa leaders to the bargaining table. But it was far from certain that a document acceptable to all could be hammered out. Still, for the first time
since Rhodesia made its unilateral declaration of independence in 1965,
a settlement seemed within reach—and virtually everyone at the Lusaka
conference agreed that the lion's share of the credit belonged to Mrs.
Thatcher.

TAKING ON THE UNIONS

For all the commotion, as she moved resolutely through the heady
world of international relations, Mrs. Thatcher's thoughts never strayed
very far from Britain's domestic ailments. It would be hard to forget
them. Not only were the unions still in an uproar over the budget—
though not as big an uproar as some had expected—but the inflationary
outlook was clouded by more than the likelihood of an expensive wage-
bargaining season. One of the most disturbing discoveries made by Sir
Geoffrey Howe and his treasurey colleagues when they finally got their
long-awaited look at the government's books, was the fact that the money supply was expanding much faster than Denis Healey had indicated it
was. What made this so alarming to them was their faith in the monetarist doctrine that held that the sole source of inflation was an overly rapid
growth of the money supply. Thus they felt that if a disastrous price explosion was to be avoided, the growth of the money supply had to be
slowed—and slowed quickly.

That was far easier said than done. The problem was particularly
knotty because the British money supply was expanding due to an odd
combination of factors. One reason was that bank lending had risen
sharply as a result of a modest consumer boom. Another was that North
Sea oil and high interest rates had made sterling an attractive currency
to foreign investors. Thus, enormous amounts of overseas funds were
flowing into Britain, more than $500 million worth in June 1979 alone,
pushing the pound sky-high and swelling the money supply dangerous-
ly.

What made the problem more difficult was that the very measures that
would mitigate one factor would simultaneously exacerbate the other.
Lowering interest rates to make the pound less attractive would encourage even more borrowing. Conversely, raising interest rates to discour-

age borrowing would lure more foreign funds into the already swollen money supply.

What Mrs. Thatcher and her treasury team finally decided on was a combination of actions which they hoped would slow things down. Thus, in the budget, they raised the minimum lending rate to tighten credit. At the same time, to keep the pound from shooting out of sight, they relaxed exchange controls in the hope that enough money would begin flowing out of Britain to offset the huge inflow.

It didn't work, at least not right away. Bank lending slowed a bit, but the pound refused to come down out of orbit. By late July, it had reached $2.32—the highest rate in five years. The reason was simple: the combination of oil and interest rates. As *The Economist* noted: "A petro-economy with a 14% minimum lending rate is like a prostitute who pays her clients." Not only did this combination swell the money supply; it also created the potential for an alarming trade deficit. For an excessively strong pound meant that British exports would be more expensive, and hence, harder to sell, while imports would be cheaper than ever, and hence, would probably rise sharply. In the short run, cheap imports would tend to restrain inflation. But in the long run, the outlook was bleak: eventually, the trade gap would become so wide that the pound would crash and domestic inflation would soar.

Getting out of this bind would take some doing. Clearly what the economy didn't need was any more inflationary pressure than it already had. Thus, a top priority became the avoidance of a wage explosion. How to accomplish that? Certainly not with an incomes policy, at least not yet. Instead, it was time to try out Mrs. Thatcher's idea of reforming the unions in such a way as to limit their power to win excessive pay increases.

Originally the government had planned to wait until the fall to introduce its plans for union reform. That would give Employment Minister James Prior all summer to consult with the TUC and prepare its leaders for what was to come. On July 3, however, word leaked out that Mrs. Thatcher had changed her mind. Instead of waiting until the fall, she now intended to begin immediately her move to reform the unions. She believed that her proposals, which had been spelled out both in the campaign as well as in the Queen's Speech, were already sufficiently well known and widely supported to warrant prompt action. In addition, Mrs. Thatcher felt that the unions' anger over the budget—while real enough—was a bit more muted than might have been expected. Since that was the case, why not get all her cards on the table as soon as possible?

Six days later, on July 9, the government announced its plans for trade union reform. They contained no surprises, at least not to anyone who had been listening to Mrs. Thatcher for the previous six months. Among other things, she was seeking to outlaw secondary picketing, to encourage the use of secret ballots in strike votes and other union elections, and to make it more difficult to impose and enforce closed shops. "The changes we are proposing are limited," Prior insisted, "but they are vitally important."

Predictably, the unions were outraged. General Secretary Len Murray of the TUC called the Thatcher proposals "a major challenge to the existing rights of workers and their unions." And at the bi-annual convention of the giant Transport Workers Union, which had just gotten underway in Scarborough when the reform plans were announced, Deputy General Secretary Harry Urwin, sporting an "I Didn't Vote Tory" button, vowed that the unions would fight the government "with every means at our disposal."

But Mrs. Thatcher was not about to be crossed. "We have an absolute mandate for these proposals," she insisted angrily in the House of Commons. "They are what the people want, and the events of last winter show that they were needed . . . It is largely because of these proposals that we got more support than ever [in the election] from members of trade unions . . . I hope that union leaders will recognize that fact."

If any doubts still lingered about Mrs. Thatcher's determination to govern just as she had promised she would, they were erased over the next two weeks as she and her treasury hardliners faced down what might have become a cabinet rebellion over their plans to limit government spending. Caught up in the postelection euphoria, the cabinet had enthusiastically backed the £3 billion in spending reductions called for in the June 12 budget. But when the time came to decide just where the reductions would be made, a storm of protest erupted within the government—a storm whose fury was heightened by the fact that Mrs. Thatcher seemed determined to ax spending even more sharply than her government's first budget had indicated.

Traditionally, when cuts are called for, the treasury asks the spending ministries themselves to suggest just where their budgets might be trimmed. Mrs. Thatcher's treasury followed this practice—and Whitehall responded in equally traditional fashion. Virtually every department in the government attempted to ward off the budgetary ax by employing the time-honored strategem of proposing cuts guaranteed to provoke a maximum of public controversy. The idea was that if a ministry could come up with sufficiently outrageous proposals, the treasury might be tempted to look elsewhere to make savings rather than risk a messy and politically damaging battle. This time, however, the treasury—in the person of its hard-nosed chief secretary, John Biffen—was not about to be finessed quite so easily. Instead of reacting with horror to such injudicious proposals as the foreign office's suggestion that the BBC's famed overseas broadcast service be cut back drastically to save money, Biffen happily accepted them as part of the treasury's plans.

In short, he was calling the bluff of the cabinet's moderates—a group Mrs. Thatcher herself had disparagingly dubbed "the wets." At a stormy cabinet meeting on July 19, he made it clear that he and his treasury colleagues (and, by implication, the prime minister, too) didn't particularly care where the cuts came from as long as they were made. The cabinet also learned, to the dismay of many of its members, that the treasury was seeking to reduce the £75 billion in public spending planned by Callaghan's ousted Labor government for 1980–81, not by £3 billion, as the June 12 budget had indicated, but by £5 billion. (Government spending would still be going up, of course. What Mrs. Thatcher and her treasury men were trying to do was keep it from going up more sharply than they felt the country could afford.)

The spending ministers were outraged. Education Minister Mark Carlisle, Environment Minister Michael Heseltine, and even Mrs. Thatcher's old friend and ally, Norman St. John Stevas (who had been given several portfolios, among them responsibility for state subsidies to the arts) argued heatedly against the treasury's plans, insisting that such massive cuts would cripple public services, provoke a massive political firestorm, and thus do far more harm than good. But the prime minister was unmoved—or, to put it more accurately, she was moved only slightly. She agreed that the cuts should be as judicious as possible, and that the government should try to avoid committing political suicide. But she refused to retreat from her basic position that the British people had voted Tory in part out of a desire to limit the growth of government spending—and that such a limitation was precisely what they were entitled to get.

Five days later, the cabinet met again. At an equally stormy session lasting two hours and 22 minutes, it was presented with a revised plan by the treasury. This one eliminated some of the most politically damaging cuts and trimmed the overall level of spending reductions to just over £4 billion. Even so, it did not represent a climb-down by Mrs. Thatcher. Though the details of the government's new fiscal plans would not be announced for another three or four months, Mrs. Thatcher made it clear that her determination to reorient the government's entire economic strategy had not lessened in the slightest.

To begin with, subsidies for ailing industries, regional economic development, public housing, passenger railroad service and local government would all be slashed sharply. In addition, state-owned British Airways and British Aerospace, the aircraft manufacturing conglomerate that had been nationalized two years earlier by Callaghan's government, would at least partly be sold back to private investors, while about a third of the government's 51 percent holding in British Petroleum would be similarly hived off. The ailing British Shipbuilding company, which was also nationalized by Labor in 1977, would be given two years to wean itself away from state subsidies. If it wasn't healthy enough to be sold off by the end of 1981, it would be closed down. And the deficit-plagued British Steel Corp. would be given less than a year to get its house in order.

At the same time, the National Enterprise Board, which had been set up by Labor to rescue faltering industries and to speculate with government money by investing in new high-technology companies, would be restricted to keeping afloat a few "lame ducks" such as the perennially troubled British Leyland car-manufacturing conglomerate and the aircraft-engine division of Rolls-Royce, which had first received state aid from Ted Heath's government. Profitable NEB ventures, which included several strong electronics and engineering firms, would be sold off, while unprofitable ones would be allowed to wither and die.

On top of everything, there would be an ambitious onslaught against the size of government bureaucracy, especially the bloated administrative staff of the National Health Service. Though the extent of these cuts would not be determined until the fall, the Civil Service was asked to come up with three contingency plans for reducing the salary and administrative costs of the nation's 750,000 permanent civil servants by 10, 15 and 20 percent.

The cabinet moderates fought an angry battle against the treasury's ax. But it was a futile effort. Trade Secretary John Nott, a determined and ambitious right-wing hawk regarded by many as a likely eventual successor to Mrs. Thatcher as Tory leader, argued uncompromisingly in favor of the treasury targets. And like his No. 2, John Biffen, Chancellor Sir Geoffrey Howe refused to be budged.

To his way of thinking, Howe had good reasons for digging in his heels, and he outlined them publicly at a London business conference just hours before the crucial July 24 cabinet meeting, stating flatly, "We do not have any real choice about the need to reduce the planned scale of public spending." Domestic production had grown by only one percent in 1978, Howe noted, while consumer spending went up by five percent and imports jumped by thirteen percent. As a result, inflation was rising, and in the first half of 1979, Britain's balance of payments had slid £2 billion into the red. To make matters worse, skyrocketing oil prices had helped tip the world into a recession. "A world recession may not seem the best background against which to put our house in order," Howe conceded. "The cure may in the short term make things more uncomfortable for us. But in truth we have no choice. The treatment may seem unpalatable. But without the treatment, our condition could easily become incurable."

Howe argued that unless public spending was restrained, government borrowing requirements would become "vast and unsustainable." That, he said, would send interest rates soaring even higher than they already had gone and would set the stage for a major economic crisis. Of course, he added, the government could try to finance its spending program by raising taxes. But here the result would be an "intolerable" burden on taxpayers. "Incentives would be extinguished and we should find ourselves locked firmly into a zero-growth economy—on course for economic and social disaster," Howe insisted. "Current reductions in public spending are essential if future improvements in the quality of our public services—which we strongly desire—are ever to be possible."

Mrs. Thatcher agreed completely, and she made sure her cabinet knew it. Over the long term, she told them, she regarded the treasury's austerity program as a fundamental part of her plan to scale back the size and scope of the government in Britain. In the short term, it was necessary to enable the government to afford another income-tax cut in the spring of 1980, a cut she and her advisers figured would be essential by then to stimulate what would doubtlessly be a stagnant economy. What's more, she added, if (as seemed likely) the unions were to win big pay increases that would add substantially to the national wages bill in the coming months, there would have to be cuts somewhere to pay for it all.

In the end, the cabinet fell into line behind the determined prime minister. Even Employment Minister James Prior, a leading moderate and one of the cabinet's chief "no-men" (as well as the minister who would take the most direct heat from the unions), agreed that "cuts have to be made right across the board to get the economy on a proper balance. Otherwise, we will suffer."

The unions and the Labor opposition didn't quite see things that way.

"Public expenditure cuts such as now are being considered will bring still higher inflation, higher unemployment, more bankruptcies and a still higher public-sector borrowing requirement," warned Denis Healey. "The result," added General Secretary David Basnett of the million-member General and Municipal Workers' Union, "can only be horrendous social distress, mass unemployment, and a disastrous undermining of the level of industrial activity." What particularly irked the unions was the fact that they no longer had a say in major government decisions such as they enjoyed when Labor was in power. Though the Tories insisted that the practice of consulting with the unions over major decisions had not been discontinued, TUC General Secretary Len Murray complained that what the Thatcher government was doing wasn't so much consulting with the unions as summoning their leaders to be lectured on decisions that had already been made.

Needless to say, Mrs. Thatcher didn't feel in the least apologetic. When, in the Commons, Labor MPs denounced her government as "a curse upon the land" and charged that its "savage cuts (will) do untold harm and suffering," she responded almost gleefully to the uproar. The rough-and-tumble of parliamentary debate was what she enjoyed most about government, and she was becoming increasingly expert at it. After some initial unsteadiness in the early days of her prime ministership, she had learned to make her imperious manner and passion for detail work for her. Indeed, she had come to master the art of baiting the opposition, whose unruly backbenchers provided her with an ample supply of unwitting foils.

In the first Question Time after her fiscal program was made public, she defended herself vigorously. After arguing the familiar line that the increased freedom and incentives provided by her income-tax cuts would encourage workers to produce the wealth the nation needed to improve social services, she went on to suggest that her critics were simply afraid of liberty. "It is often said," she noted reprovingly, "that if one gives people increased responsibility, some of them fear it."

Just as she had hoped, that line prompted Callaghan to interject incautiously: "Who said it?"

"Bernard Shaw," she shot back triumphantly, and she quoted the old socialist verbatim. (Had Callaghan done his homework as thoroughly as Mrs. Thatcher did hers, he wouldn't have been caught in her rhetorical trap. She had used the same line of Shaw's—"Liberty means responsibility. That is why most men dread it"—in a television interview the previous January.)

In any case, the initial opposition to Mrs. Thatcher's spending cuts was once again surprisingly muted. In part, that was because the Labor party was consumed in one of its periodic fratricidal battles, with left-wing activists challenging the largely moderate leadership for control of the party. More to the point, however, was the fact that Mrs. Thatcher announced the outlines of her program just days before Parliament began its long summer recess, a dead time in British politics during which most politicians (to the relief of their constituents) disappear on vacation. Things would no doubt heat up in the fall, when the details of the government's plans would be released, and the TUC, along with both major parties, would hold their annual conferences.

Indeed, the preliminary agenda for the TUC convention in September included calls for massive campaigns against both Mrs. Thatcher's proposed legislation for trade union reform as well as her plans for limiting spending. Just as it had been for Ted Heath in 1974 and Jim Callaghan in 1978, the stage was now set for Margaret Thatcher to cross swords with the trade unions. But she appeared to be in a far stronger position. Unlike her predecessors, she had the advantage of a growing public antipathy towards the unions, and both she and they knew it. In addition, the union leadership she faced was a far more moderate, colorless, and uncharismatic group than that which had toppled Heath. And she was certainly not dependent in any way on trade union support as Callaghan had been. Still, the union rank and file were in no mood to be trifled with. As they had proved the previous winter, the moderation of their leaders was a poor check on their increasing militancy. With inflation already over eleven percent and unemployment heading towards the two million mark, they were not about to give up any of their bargaining leverage, at least not without a fight. Whether an eyeball-to-eyeball confrontation was thus inevitable, and who would be the one to blink if it came, only time would tell.

9

Renaissance Woman?

"There must be big changes of direction."

 EVER SINCE HER DAYS AT OXFORD, Margaret Thatcher had pursued a path traveled mainly by men, inevitably standing out (as Germain Greer has put it) as the "only treble raised in a chorus of many voices." Though it galled her, she learned to live with the fact that in the minds of most people (especially non-Britons) she was first and foremost a *woman* politician, distinguished not so much for her views and accomplishments but for her success in a field dominated by men.

She was not the first woman prime minister the world had ever seen. Long before anyone outside of Britain had ever heard of Margaret Thatcher, Indira Gandhi of India, Golda Meir of Israel, and Mrs. Bandaranaike of Sri Lanka had all risen to become the heads of their respective governments, dominating their countries and making international names for themselves. And whatever one thinks of their particular politics, it is fair to conclude that these pioneers demonstrated irrefutably (if it ever really needed demonstrating) that a woman can govern a democratic nation just as well—or as badly—as a man.

This is not to suggest that there was no significance whatsoever in the fact that Mrs. Thatcher happened to be the first woman prime minister of a major Western industrial nation. But the true importance of her accomplishment, it would seem, did not lie in the opportunity her election gave her to prove something about or for women as a group. For better or worse, that job had already been done—by Mrs. Gandhi, Mrs. Meir, and Mrs. Bandaranaike. If there was any real significance in Mrs.

Thatcher's being a woman it lay in what she had *already* demonstrated by managing to become prime minister of Britain in the first place: that the voters of a major Western industrial democracy were not so riddled with sexual prejudice as to make it impossible for a woman to climb to the top of the political heap. In this sense, once she made it to 10 Downing Street, Mrs. Thatcher's sex became irrelevant. As Oxford University political scientist Peter Pulzer has noted: "It's like John Kennedy being a Catholic—it stopped mattering the day he won the election."

SEXUAL POLITICS

But in terms of sexual politics, did Mrs. Thatcher's rise to power really prove anything? Even that is hard to say. For one thing, there is a good case to be made that the election of a woman as Tory leader in 1975 was not nearly so remarkable an occurrence as it might have seemed. As Tory historian Lord Blake has observed, "Mrs. Thatcher fits into a Party tradition of turning to extraordinary leaders in times of crisis. When the Party has had a problem on its hands it has tended to turn to unique leaders, like Disraeli [a Jew] in the late nineteenth century and then Andrew Bonar Law, [a Scots-Canadian Presbyterian] in 1911."

What's more, the same general election that swept Mrs. Thatcher into power also cut the number of women in the House of Commons by nearly a third, to 19 out of 635, the smallest number since 1951.

The fact is that Mrs. Thatcher never saw herself as some sort of feminist pioneer, nor did she appreciate being seen as such by others. Her well-known lack of sympathy for the women's movement was total and profound—as the new prime minister reminded observers during her first Question Time in the House after her election, when a somewhat unctious Tory backbencher suggested that she should abolish Britain's Equal Opportunities Commission because her "presence at the despatch box is living proof that it is unnecessary."

"Not today," she replied with a smile, "though I agree with My Honorable Friend that I did not exactly need it."

Thus, many in the women's movement in Britain regarded Mrs. Thatcher's victory as a setback for their cause. "We are quite depressed by her election," said an editor of the feminist journal *Spare Rib*. "We think it will work against feminism." Or as a group of hecklers whose chanting disrupted Mrs. Thatcher's election-night appearance in Finchley, put it: "We want a woman, not a right-wing Tory."

For all its arrogance, that bit of rhetoric put its finger quite neatly on the real import of Margaret Thatcher's rise to power. What made her truly significant and worthy of the worldwide attention she received was not the fact that she was a woman—though that certainly made her interesting—but that she was determined to succeed where both Churchill and Heath had failed. She intended to reverse the apparently inexorable process that for the previous three decades had been transforming Britain into an increasingly socialist state, to break totally with the past and bring about a libertarian renaissance that could profoundly alter the future of not her nation alone but of the entire West.

Certainly, Mrs. Thatcher herself believed this to be the single most important aspect of her electoral triumph. Why else, after all, did Britain need an Iron Lady? Because, as she told Kenneth Harris of *The Observer* when he asked her what she hoped to accomplish as prime minister, "there must be big changes of direction."

RADICAL LIBERTARIAN

Mrs. Thatcher's basic goal, as she put it, was "not the extension but the limitation of government." It was not that she was against strong government *per se*; she argued that limiting a government's powers actually strengthens them. "If you've got the role of government clearly set out, then it means very strong government *in that role*," she told Harris three months before the May 1979 election. "You weaken government if you try to spread it out over so wide a range that you're not powerful where you *should* be because you've got into areas where you *shouldn't* be." And just what were those appropriate areas? As her philosophical mentor, Sir Keith Joseph, explained: "She believes that . . . government should basically decide on taxes and enforce the law, but beyond that it is up to the people themselves."

Mrs. Thatcher's passionate commitment to *appropriate* government grew out of roots as philosophical as they were pragmatic. Not only was the sprawling welfare state that has grown up in Britain inefficient and ineffective; she felt it was morally subversive as well. It sapped the individual's sense of moral responsibility and eroded his self-worth. "The truth is," she asserted in an April 1979 speech in Cardiff, "that individually man is creative; collectively, he tends to be a spendthrift."

This radical libertarianism ran deep. Government, she was convinced, should always allow, never coerce. In January 1979, when a television interviewer asked her why, given her feelings about union power, she did not favor legislation to force employers to be tougher on strikers, she snapped back: "Why should I? We live in a free country. [The employer is] a responsible person, and should make his own choice . . . If everyone is going to come and say, 'I'm not going to make a choice myself, unless you legislate and tell me I've got to do it,' then we're well on the way to a totally different state than anything we've ever known . . ."

By the same token, she shared Churchill's belief that the government should only be a backstop of sorts, not a parent. She made the point eloquently in a 1978 sermon she preached at London's Church of St. Lawrence Jewry (whose pulpit over the years has been turned over to many a political leader): "It is one thing to say that the relief of poverty and suffering is a duty," she argued, "and quite another to say that this duty can always be most efficiently and humanely performed by the state. I am not saying, of course, that the state has no welfare functions . . . There must be a level of well-being below which a citizen must not be allowed to fall. Moreover, people cannot realize their potential without educational opportunity. But the role of the state in Christian society is to encourage virtue, not to usurp it."

In economic terms, Mrs. Thatcher's libertarian convictions translated into a profound belief in the need for incentives. "For what is the real driving force in society?" she asked. "It is the desire for the individual to do the best for himself and his family." This desire, she added, is an "elemental instinct" for which "there is no substitute." Hence, her commitment to income tax cuts, her encouragement of property owning, her attacks on the sacred cows of subsidies for housing, jobs, and industry—in short the entire retreat of the government from the marketplace. "The proper role of government," she maintained, "is to set free the natural energy of the people."

In a country where government spending had come to account for nearly sixty percent of the gross national product, and where welfare spending alone totaled twenty-five percent of the GNP—such an individualist ethic did not go down easily. Her celebration of the virtues of acquisitiveness and personal enterprise ran completely counter to the entire postwar British movement towards communal solidarity and egalitarianism. It was the old confrontation between Adam Smith and Karl Marx—or, more cynically, between the politics of greed and the politics of envy.

Which would prevail? The last prime minister to attempt such a counterrevolution was Ted Heath. He went down in flames, and as political editor Simon Jenkins of *The Economist* noted just before the May 1979 election: "The ghost of the Heath administration looms all over discussion of Mrs. Thatcher's policy and style." Indeed, she hadn't even moved into 10 Downing Street before the debate started over just where and when she would be forced to make *her* U-turn, just how long it would be before the unions would drive her from office.

But though there were many similarities between the two, Margaret Thatcher was not Ted Heath. He was a manager, an astute and possibly even brilliant one, but she was a believer. What she brought to No. 10, which Heath didn't—which Heath *couldn't* because Mrs. Thatcher learned it from his experience there—was a conviction that what was paramount in government was that the will of the leader remain firm and unswerving. Sophisticated policies, shrewd tactics and tightly-reasoned philosophies were important. But in the end, the success of a government depended on the determination of the person at its head to stand his or her ground, no matter how violent the buffetings of industrial turmoil or public outrage.

By this reckoning, what counted was not so much Mrs. Thatcher's particular politics as her personal strength. Could she stand up to the tremendous pressure that would almost certainly descend upon her? Her sense of purpose was so single-minded ("It's as if she had taken holy orders," marvelled a Tory official in Finchley) that in her first months as prime minister many worried she might crack under the strain. "Prime Ministers need things to take their minds off the job, and she doesn't have them," noted one veteran party chieftain. "She doesn't drink with the boys—or with the girls, for that matter. She doesn't tell jokes. She may relax, but I've never seen it in the fifteen years that I've known her."

Indeed, she was something of a loner, depending far more on her intensely loyal personal staff than on any of her frontbench colleagues. She had served in the House of Commons for two decades and had been the head of the party for four years, but in many ways she was still a stranger to much of the Tory leadership. "Although I served in the Cabinet with her for four years under Ted Heath," reported Lord Home, the former prime minister, "I have never been to her home." Such behavior was unsettling; her base seemed far too narrow to support the burden she now had to carry.

PUBLIC IMAGE AND PRIVATE PERSON

But such assessments told less about Mrs. Thatcher's ability to handle stress than about the degree to which she had managed to keep her private persona shielded from view. Where Heath had his music and his yacht, Wilson his nonpolitical cronies and Callaghan his beloved Sussex farm, Mrs. Thatcher had her emotional safety-valve, too—her family. "Your family are always your closest friends," she once said.

Unfortunately, the Thatcher family wasn't as close as it might have been. In part, that was the inevitable result of Mrs. Thatcher's having followed her political star so relentlessly. What's more, the children were now off on their own. Mark was still living at Flood Street, pursuing an indifferent career as an accountant in the London offices of an Australian trading company. (He had earlier embarrassed the family slightly by inaccurately describing himself as a chartered accountant, the British equivalent of an American C.P.A. In fact, Mark had never passed the necessary exams—and when the professional society of chartered accountants complained about his appropriation of the title, Mark found himself forced to issue a public apology.) Carol was back in Australia, working as a political journalist (and earning the envy and resentment of her colleagues for the top-level access she suddenly had come to enjoy). According to friends of the Thatcher family, she and her mother had never been on the best of terms—especially after Carol became involved in an affair with a Tory MP more than ten years her senior. Mrs. Thatcher disapproved strongly of the involvement, and when it finally ended, Carol moved as far away from home as she could—to Australia—returning only for the spring 1979 general election campaign.

Of course, Mrs. Thatcher still had her husband on whom to rely. Denis Thatcher and his wife agreed on virtually everything. (The only known exception—at least as far as politics were concerned—was capital punishment: she favored it, he did not.) And rely on Denis she did—for political advice ("Don't forget," noted an aide, "he has her ear every morning at breakfast"), personnel judgements, and—perhaps most important—emotional support. As she had told Kenneth Harris: "Sometimes things go wrong—let's say a really, really tough week in the House, a lot of travel, hard physical slog, and I feel I haven't done as much as I could have. Well, Denis is absolutely marvelous. He behaves, well—as a sort of shock absorber." Indeed, Mr. Thatcher was for his wife a combination cheerleader, morale-booster and sounding board, as well as a staunch and enthusiastic supporter of her politics. ("I get a good idea of what's going on," she said during the campaign, "when I hear him yelling 'Liars!' and 'That's just not true' at Labor party political broadcasts.") She might not take him along on many official visits abroad—he had a worrisome habit of being a touch too undiplomatically outspoken for that—but she counted on him to be there when she got home.

In any case, while it was quite possible, it was by no means certain that Mrs. Thatcher's nerves would be put to the test by a full-scale clash with the unions. Though like Joan of Arc, to whom she had been compared so unflatteringly by Germain Greer, the Maid of Grantham was prepared for political martyrdom, she certainly was not seeking it. As political analyst Peter Jenkins of *The Guardian* noted: "It takes two to confront and the new government is positioning itself at arm's length from the coming wages round." And while critics maintained that her proposals for trade-union reform were an open invitation to industrial anarchy, Mrs. Thatcher herself believed sincerely that the vast majority of union members agreed with her, even if their leaders did not.

Of course, if confrontation came, she would not flinch from it. "If someone is confronting our essential liberties, if someone is inflicting injury, harm and damage," she had vowed just after the 1978–79 winter of discontent, "by God, I'll confront them." But with a forty-three-seat majority in the Commons and a willingness (as Jenkins put it) "to play a long match and to lose the first couple of sets if need be," it seemed hard to see just how she would be toppled. Indeed, once through her first winter, with North Sea oil revenue swelling and the positive impact of her radical first budget finally making itself felt, her position might well be the strongest enjoyed by any prime minister since the heady days of the first Wilson government.

There was, however, another threat, the one from within her own party. She was leading from the far right of the Conservative spectrum, and though in the flush of victory most Tory MPs were content to let her have her way, they might well prove considerably less amenable to her radicalism if and when a crunch came. Her doctrinaire approach might have won her most of the policy arguments within the party, but it didn't win her all that many friends. Certainly, her domineering way with the cabinet wasn't likely to generate much personal loyalty in the hearts of the dozen or so moderates she had brought into her government. Her cause was in no way helped by brutally telling Lord Carrington to "shut up" at a meeting of ministers. Nor did she prove or accomplish anything by subjecting the youngest member of her cabinet, 43-year-old Energy Minister David Howell, to a withering stream of abuse that nearly reduced him to tears. Norman St. John Stevas once described trying to argue with her as being "like a space launching. At blast-off, she does all the talking and you just stand back. At second-stage separation, you prepare your remarks. And then, when she's in orbit, you speak."

Less jocularly, another cabinet colleague of hers noted that Mrs. Thatcher simply "talks too much. She comes into the conversation early, gives her view—Bang!—and that preempts free discussion." Her problem, he suggested, was that she was just too opinionated for her own—or her government's—good. "As you know," he pointed out, "there is no subject on which she has no view. She will have to get over that."

It wasn't impossible to persuade Mrs. Thatcher to change her mind. Lord Carrington managed to convince her that her initial instinct to recognize the Muzorewa regime in Salisbury as soon as possible was misguided. He also overcame her opposition to admitting any Vietnamese boat people to Britain, arguing successfully on both political and humanitarian grounds that Britain couldn't afford to turn its back on the refugees. And Tory backbenchers, in an unlikely alliance with Labor, forced her to grant MPs a massive and long overdue pay raise on a quicker schedule than she had intended.

Still, such occasions were the exception, not the rule. For the most part, in her early days in office, Mrs. Thatcher got what she wanted—regardless of the political cost.

VISION OF THE FUTURE

But even if she managed to survive the buffetings of her first winter and retain the support of her party, there was still the longer-term—and, in the end, far more significant—question of whether her libertarian vision of the future could be translated into reality. Much of her belief in the possibility of a free-enterprise renaissance for Britain was based on the conviction that her countrymen were—to an extent far greater than most observers would have given them credit—frustrated entrepreneurs just waiting for the shackles of high taxes and government interference to be removed. It was a generous view, to say the least. If anything, the evidence of recent years seemed to show just the opposite: that Britain was retreating from any sort of rampant individualism into what Anthony Sampson described as "a more communal, less personally ambitious society."

Even many Tories wondered whether Mrs. Thatcher wasn't possibly overestimating her fellow Britons. What if, instead of reacting to her incentives "as an opportunity for greater activity, people would seize upon them as an excuse to do even less?" worried Peregrine Worthsthorne, the influential deputy editor of the pro-Tory *Sunday Telegraph*. "What if the socialist lid is removed and very little capitalist steam bursts forth?"

Mrs. Thatcher dismissed such doubts as the cavillings of the faint at heart. Every experience of her life had taught her the same lesson: that hard work inevitably pays off. If she could guarantee them the rewards of their efforts—by God, the British would surprise even themselves. She wouldn't be reckless about it. For all her impetuosity, that wasn't really her nature. ("Her heart pulls her one way, her head the other," a longtime colleague once described her. "It's not a bad combination.") But she would see it through. She was determined that the nation would get the chance to justify her faith in it.

In this sense, hers was something of a personal crusade, one she had spent her entire life (consciously or not) preparing to lead. But its implications clearly went far beyond just one woman—or, indeed, even one nation. The question of whether free-market liberty was really the source of economic vitality was hardly a trivial one. Nor was there anything parochial about an attempt to demonstrate that free enterprise not only had a place in an overpopulated, poverty-stricken world, but that there was actually a desperate need for it. What Mrs. Thatcher had set out to do was nothing less than to disprove the central tenet of Marxist theory—that the rise and spread of socialism was a historical inevitability. If she succeeded, the beatification of the "Blessed Margaret" would be assured—and along with it, Britain's renaissance as a world power of the first rank. If she failed, history—and her fellow Britons—would not be kind. But either way, Margaret Thatcher's long and improbable journey from Grantham to 10 Downing Street would have been worth the struggle.